Endless Kiesler

Edition Angewandte

Book Series of the
University of Applied Arts Vienna
Edited by Gerald Bast, Rector

edition: ˈʌngewʌndtə

Endless
Kiesler

Editors / Herausgeber: Klaus Bollinger,
Florian Medicus and the Austrian Frederick
and Lillian Kiesler Private Foundation

Birkhäuser Basel

Endless Kiesler

Editors: Klaus Bollinger, Florian
Medicus, Institute of Architecture at
the University of Applied Arts Vienna
and the Austrian Frederick and Lillian
Kiesler Private Foundation

Editorial team: Roswitha Janowski-
Fritsch, Florian Medicus, Jill Meißner,
Gerd Zillner

Translations: Camilla R. Nielsen,
Sabine Schmidt, Sarah Fleissner

Proofreading: Word Connection
Business Translation Services,
Salzburg

Design: Atelier Dreibholz

Printing: Holzhausen Druck GmbH

Library of Congress Cataloging-in-
Publication data
A CIP catalog record for this book has
been applied for at the Library of
Congress.

Bibliographic information published
by the German National Library.
The German National Library lists this
publication in the Deutsche National-
bibliografie; detailed bibliographic
data are available on the Internet at
HYPERLINK "http://dnb.dnb.de/" \t
"_blank" http://dnb.dnb.de. This work
is subject to copyright. All rights
are reserved, whether the whole or
part of the material is concerned,
specifically the rights of translation,
reprinting, re-use of illustrations,
recitation, broadcasting, reproduction
on microfilms or in other ways, and
storage in databases. For any kind of
use, permission of the copyright
owner must be obtained.

All rights to published illustrations
and texts are with the authors.
The editors have made every reason-
able effort to obtain the necessary
permission to use the works. Errors
and omissions can be reported
to the editors and will be corrected in
subsequent editions.

© 2015 Birkhäuser Verlag GmbH,
Basel P.O. Box 44, 4009 Basel,
Switzerland Part of Walter de Gruyter
GmbH, Berlin/Boston

Printed in Austria

Printed on acid-free paper produced
from chlorine-free pulp. TCF

ISBN 978-3-0356-0624-9
ISSN 1866-248X

www.birkhauser.com

9 8 7 6 5 4 3 2 1

IO∕I INSTITUTE OF
ARCHITECTURE

edıtıon: 'ʌngewʌndtə

Contents

The More Complexity,
the More Kiesler

Foreword by Gerald Bast

Je mehr Komplexität,
desto mehr Kiesler

Frederick Kiesler was immensely formative in giving shape to his ideas. These were based on his theory of a science that he had already conceived of in the 1930s and then continued to elaborate. By eliminating the boundaries of all art genres and integrating scientific knowledge, man and environment were to be seen as a holistic system of complex interrelationships. "Function follows vision, vision follows reality," was Frederick Kiesler's principle. He became famous for his revolutionary creations in the field of architecture and design. Much of what Kiesler envisioned is more pertinent to life today than ever before.

We are becoming increasingly aware of the complexity of society and the dramatic acceleration of human life. It is thus clear that this growing complexity can soon no longer be controlled with the linear thinking traditionally associated with our science and art. Science, art, architecture and design are called upon to not just take note of the potential inter-actions as contingent collateral use but also to reveal and activate these possibilities.

If we follow the lead of Kiesler in making architecture a "socially construc-tive factor," then architecture has to be understood as an engagement with all facets of life and not just as "a series of disparate, overspecialized,

Friedrich Kiesler war ein großer Formgeber; seine Ideen bauten auf seiner schon in den 1930er Jahren und danach stetig weiter entwickelten Theorie einer Wissenschaft auf, die unter Aufhebung aller Kunstgattungen und Einbeziehung naturwissenschaftlicher Kenntnisse, Mensch und Umwelt als ganzheitliches System komplexer Wechselbeziehungen versteht. *Function follows vision, vision follows reality* war das Leitmotiv Friedrich Kieslers, der durch seine wegweisenden Entwürfe im Bereich Architektur und Design berühmt geworden ist. Vieles von dem, was Kiesler vorgedacht hat, ist heute aktueller denn je.

Die Tatsache, dass die Komplexität unserer Gesellschaften und der menschlichen Lebensbedingungen in dramatisch anwachsender Geschwin-digkeit zunimmt, wird immer deutlicher sichtbar. Und es steigt das Bewusstsein, dass diese Komplexität mit der linearen Fortsetzung dessen, was unter Wissenschaft und Kunst verstanden wird, in kurzer Zeit nicht mehr beherrschbar sein wird. Wissenschaft, Kunst, Architektur und Design sind aufgerufen, die Potenziale ihrer Wechselwirkungen nicht mehr nur als zufälligen Kollateralnutzen zur Kenntnis zu nehmen, sondern diese Potenziale frei zu legen und zu aktivieren.

Wenn man, wie Kiesler, Architektur zu einem „socially constructive factor"

and unevenly distributed products," as Kiesler wrote already in 1939 in his essay "On Correalism and Biotechnique".

In a world shaped by digitalization and robotics, social impact is not just a product of creative thinking processes, i.e., processes that in a way unthought-of or still seen as inconceivable establish connections between known and thus increasingly automatized fields of action and knowledge. When Kiesler writes that a house is "the sum of all possible movement that its inhabitants can perform," this means seeing it as more desirable and possible than the reconfiguration of space according to aesthetic and/or economic criteria. What would be the consequences if space were defined according to parameters taken from quantum physics, socio-biology and/or genetic engineering? How is architecture to respond to the redefinition of labor, leisure time, communication, social behavior and mobility that would take place against the backdrop of dramatic technological and political changes?

Kiesler's most significant legacy is not a material one. It is his commitment to the search for utopia, the unknown places, in keeping with the original meaning of the Greek word. Kiesler's conviction that visionary thinking is also realistic thinking is encouraging in times of increasing disillusionment.

machen will, dann muss man Architektur als Auseinandersetzung mit allen Bereichen des Lebens verstehen und nicht als „eine Reihe unvereinbarer, überspezialisierter und ungleich verteilter Produkte", wie Kiesler schon 1939 in seinem Essay „On Correalism and Biotechnique" schrieb.

In einer von Digitalisierung und Robotics geprägten Welt wird gesellschaftliche Wirkungskraft nur mehr durch kreative Denkprozesse herstellbar sein, also durch Prozesse, die auf bisher ungedachte oder als undenkbar gehaltene Weise Verbindungen zwischen bekannten und daher zunehmend automatisierten Handlungs- und Wissensfeldern herstellen. Wenn Kiesler schreibt, dass ein Haus „die Summe jeder möglichen Bewegung, die sein Bewohner in ihm ausführen kann" ist, dann heißt das, mehr für anstrebenswert und möglich zu halten, als die Neukonfiguration von Raum nach ästhetischen und/oder ökonomischen Kriterien. Wohin könnte es führen, wenn man Raum unter Einbeziehung von quantenphysikalischen, sozio-biologischen und/oder gentechnologischen Indikatoren definierte? Wie wird die Architektur auf die Neudefinition von Arbeit, Freizeit, Kommunikation, Sozialverhalten und Mobilität reagieren, die entlang dramatischer technologischer und politischer Umwälzungen stattfinden wird?

Kieslers bedeutendstes Vermächtnis ist nicht physischer Natur, es ist sein

What is more, Kiesler's approach is becoming ever more significant in a world determined by uncertainty and ambiguity, because the challenges we face cannot be tackled by applying algorithms but only with visionary, correlative thinking as a counterbalance to the prevailing dominance of standardization and fragmentation.

Bekenntnis zur Suche nach Utopien, den unbekannten Orten, so die ursprüngliche Bedeutung des griechischen Begriffes.

Kieslers Überzeugung, dass visionäres Denken zugleich realistisches Denken ist, macht Mut in Zeiten zunehmender Mutlosigkeit. Mehr noch: Kieslers Denkansatz wird immer wichtiger, je mehr unsere Welt von Unsicherheit und Ambiguität gekennzeichnet ist, weil diesen Herausforderungen nicht mit der Anwendung von Algorithmen begegnet werden kann sondern nur mit visionärem, korrelativem Denken, das der herrschenden Dominanz von Standardisierung und Fragmentierung kühn entgegengesetzt wird.

An Endlessness Shadow

Foreword by Hani Rashid

Der Schatten der Endlosigkeit

Frederick Kiesler, artist, architect, designer, thinker and provocateur, yearned throughout his lifetime for an inspired future completely detached from the tyranny of the past. His early experiences with the European turn of the century avant-garde, namely De Stijl, Surrealism and Dada, set him on a life-long trajectory of artistic discovery traversing tectonic installations, unorthodox and "improper" furniture designs, inverted and problematized theater designs and, above all, strange and beautiful architecture. Kiesler's work as a whole took on new meaning and a sense of urgency when he finally set foot on American soil in 1926. It was in New York City where Kiesler found himself in an unanticipated, yet exhilarating self-exile. Kiesler embraced with relentless passion his new modern existence and his reawakened search. Kiesler's ideas and projects proliferated in his mind and on paper in a time of extraordinary breakthroughs in technology and the sciences. What Kiesler set out to do now with kindred spirits such as Marcel Duchamp was to completely undo and confront any notions of confinement, restriction, finiteness or tedium and the banal. For Kiesler, it was the dismantling of the orthodoxy of the Cartesian and even geometry itself that above all else held the key for him to make new strides toward all spatial possibilities, mystical or otherwise. As Duchamp was already systematically undoing painting,

Friedrich Kiesler, Künstler, Architekt, Designer, Denker und Provokateur, sehnte sich immer nach einer Zukunft, die sich von Inspirationen nährte und von der Tyrannei der Vergangenheit loslöste. Ausgehend von seinen frühen Erfahrungen mit der europäischen Avantgarde um die Jahrhundertwende, mit Bewegungen wie De Stijl, Surrealismus und Dada, verfolgte er bis ans Ende seines Lebens einen Weg künstlerischer Entdeckung, die von tektonischen Installationen, unorthodoxen und „ungehörigen" Möbelentwürfen, unkonventionellen und nicht ganz unproblematischen Bühnendesigns zu einer Architektur von seltsamer Schönheit führte. Als er sich schließlich 1926 in Amerika, im unerwartet gewählten, aber höchst anregenden Selbst-Exil in New York City niederließ, bekam Kieslers Schaffen in seiner Gesamtheit eine neue Bedeutung und ein neues Bewusstsein der Dringlichkeit. Sein neues modernes Leben und die wiedererweckte Suche umarmte Kiesler mit unermüdlicher Leidenschaft. In einer Zeit, die von außerordentlichen Errungenschaften in der Technologie und in den Naturwissenschaften geprägt war, florierten Kieslers Ideen und Projekte im Geiste und auf dem Papier. So stellte sich Kiesler in Begleitung von Gleichgesinnten wie etwa Marcel Duchamp dem Versuch, jegliche Vorstellung von Begrenzung, Endlichkeit, Monotonie und Banalität zu durchbrechen. Für Kiesler ging es um die Dekonstruktion der

sculpture, photography, Kiesler took it upon himself to one up his friend and confidant by summarily unraveling space and spatiality. Being an architect by training afforded Kiesler the necessary tools, means and methods to take on this self-appointed monumental task in search of radical change. In this context, Kiesler set out to "perform" perhaps the most beautiful, strange and disconcerting architectural work of the past century, his *Endless House.* When designing this "house," Kiesler's search was essentially centered on revealing the tectonics and spatiality of the uncanny, the new and the yet unseen future and, put simply, manifesting in plaster and chicken wire a state of being. By first attacking interiors and shop windows in New York City, then going on to rethinking the stage, cinema and cinematic space, and then step by step dismantling form light and volume, the process ensued. With the *Endless House*, Kiesler essentially modeled an anticipated future in which architecture as a "place" would be rendered inconsequential and relegated to the service of an enigmatic and fluid endlessness. In Kiesler's shadow, that all-important search continues today with output from a number of key artists, architects and writers represented in this collection of works and essays in search of the endlessness and the next.

Orthodoxie des Cartesianismus und sogar der Geometrie selbst, die ihm den Schlüssel dafür bot, neue Schritte in allen räumlichen Möglichkeiten, seien sie von mystischer oder sonstiger Natur, zu setzen. Wie sein Freund und Vertrauter Duchamp, der schon dabei war, die Malerei, die Skulptur und die Photographie aufzulösen, ging auch Kiesler dazu über, den Raum, das Räumliche aufzulösen. Als ausgebildeter Architekt verfügte er ja über die nötigen Werkzeuge und das methodologische Instrumentarium, um sich in seinem Streben nach radikaler Veränderung dieser riesigen selbstgewählten Aufgabe zu stellen. In diesem Zusammenhang machte sich Kiesler daran, das vielleicht schönste, seltsamste und provokativste Architekturwerk des vergangenen Jahrhunderts zu „inszenieren", nämlich sein *Endless House.* Beim Entwurf dieses „Hauses" galt Kieslers Interesse vor allem der Aufdeckung der Tektonik und der Räumlichkeit des Unheimlichen, des Neuen und der noch nicht erblickten Zukunft. Einfach ausgedrückt: Er wollte einen Daseinszustand in Gips und Maschendraht wiedergeben. Er setzte den Prozess fort, indem er seinen Angriff zuerst auf die Innenräume und die Geschäftsauslagen in New York City richtete, dann dazu überging, die Bühne, den Film- und Kinoraum neuzudenken, um schließlich Schritt für Schritt Form, Licht und Volumen aufzulösen. Mit seinem *Endless House* schuf

Kiesler im Wesentlichen eine vorweggenommene Zukunft, in der sich die Architektur als „Raum" erübrigen und in den Dienst einer enigmatischen, flüssigen Endlosigkeit stellen würde. Heute setzt sich in der Nachfolge Kieslers jene überaus wichtige Suche fort, die sich in den hier versammelten Arbeiten und Aufsätzen einer Reihe von führenden Künstlern, Architekten und Autoren niederschlägt. Auch sie sind auf der Suche nach dem Endlosen und dem, was danach folgt.

Unbuildable Kiesler?!

Foreword by Klaus Bollinger

Unbaubarer Kiesler?!

Several years ago, our team at the Institute of Architecture at the University
of Applied Arts in Vienna launched a series of seminars that focus on
outstanding but unrealized designs from the history of architecture. These are
plans that were often deemed utopian and thus discarded as unbuildable.
In this seminar, we first analyze the designs in their theoretical context, then
study the feasibility of their construction both at the time they were
designed and under today's circumstances and, optionally, develop alternative
proposals for implementation.

This series has included seminars on Tatlin's *Monument of the Third Inter-national* and El Lissitzky's *Wolkenbügel*. In the former, we were able to
prove that the monument could have been built with 120 000 tons of steel.
In his *Wolkenbügel* project, El Lissitzky describes material properties
that would have been conceivable and desirable at the time. What appeared
far-sighted back then is now state-of-the-art technology.

Kiesler's *Endless House* also belongs to the series of these visionary
projects. Under the sway of classical modernism and the international style,
Kiesler with his *Endless House* developed a formally revolutionary new
language that was completely unique in technical and engineering terms, i.e.,
geometric analysis, static computation and implementation. Since antiquity,

Seit einigen Jahren beschäftigen wir uns am Institut für Architektur der Univer-sität für angewandte Kunst in Wien in einer Seminarreihe mit herausragenden
aber nicht realisierten Entwürfen der Architekturgeschichte; mit Visionen,
die oft als utopisch und damit als unbaubar abgetan wurden. Es geht in dem
Seminar zunächst darum, die Entwürfe in ihrem theoretischen Umfeld zu
analysieren, dann ihre Baubarkeit unter damaligen und heutigen Bedingungen
zu überprüfen und gegebenenfalls alternative Umsetzungsvorschläge zu
erarbeiten.

In dieser Reihe wurden unter anderen Tatlins *Monument der Dritten Inter-nationale* und El Lissitzkys *Wolkenbügel* bearbeitet. Bei ersterem wurde
nachgewiesen, dass es mit 120 000 Tonnen Stahl zu bauen gewesen wäre;
bei den *Wolkenbügeln* beschreibt El Lissitzky Materialeigenschaften, die
damals denkbar und wünschenswert waren. Was damals weitsichtig war, ist
heute Stand der Technik.

Auch das *Endless House* gehört in die Reihe dieser visionären Projekte.
Im Umfeld der klassischen Moderne und des International Style ent-wickelte Kiesler mit dem *Endless House* eine formal neue Sprache, für die es
auch technisch im Sinne von geometrischer Erfassbarkeit, statischer
Berechenbarkeit und bautechnischer Umsetzbarkeit noch keine Beispiele gab.

classical modernism continues to draw on familiar classical building elements such as vertical walls or supports and horizontal beams or slabs. With his *Endless House* design, Kiesler broke with the traditional way of thinking and designing, going on to develop a flowing approach in which there is no distinction between floor, wall and ceiling.

Kiesler did not develop form according to geometrical or mathematical rules, either. This was the approach adopted by the engineers who designed shell-constructions. The shells were supposed to be computable, which required the geometry to be defined. For Kiesler, form that evolves from intuition and function has priority over mathematical definition and static computability.

Only today, decades later, are architects and engineers once again working between the poles of intuitive geometry and the so-called authenticity of construction. And the challenge facing them here continues to be the implementation of visions and the realization of utopia.

Die klassische Moderne bediente sich im Grunde weiterhin der seit der Antike bekannten klassischen Bauteile wie vertikale Wände oder Stützen und horizontale Balken oder Platten. Kiesler aber löste sich mit dem Entwurf des *Endless House* von dieser traditionellen Denk- und Bauweise und entwickelte eine fließende Raumhülle, die nicht zwischen Boden, Wand und Decke differenziert.

Kiesler entwarf die Form auch nicht nach geometrischen oder mathematischen Regeln; das war die Vorgehensweise der Ingenieure, die den Schalenbau entwickelt hatten. Die Schalen sollten berechenbar sein und dazu brauchte es die Definition der Geometrie. Für Kiesler aber hatte die aus der Intuition und Funktion heraus entwickelte Form Vorrang vor mathematischer Definition und statischer Berechenbarkeit.

Erst heute, also Jahrzehnte später arbeiten Architekten und Ingenieure wieder in diesem Spannungsfeld zwischen intuitiver Geometrie und der sogenannten Ehrlichkeit der Konstruktion. Und weiterhin geht es um die Herausforderung der Umsetzung von Visionen, der Realisierung von Utopien.

Designing Tomorrow.
Frederick Kiesler Architect?!

Jill Meißner

Das Morgen entwerfen.
Friedrich Kiesler Architekt?!

"Frederick Kiesler—architect, artist, designer, poet, philosopher—was part Renaissance man, part space-age prophet,"[1] as Lisa Phillips wrote in the exhibition catalog for the 1989 Kiesler retrospective at the Whitney Museum of American Art. Since he worked in all artistic disciplines, it is difficult to single out one particular one—in this case, architecture. Here, however, I would still like to focus on the architect Kiesler, even though other artistic fields will inevitably be broached. How Kiesler himself assessed his productions can be gleaned from the only known self-portrait of him that appeared after his death in the magazine *Art in America* (Fig. 1). It shows him Janus-faced, as architect and sculptor, and in the statement printed here one can read: "The three aspects of my portrait are held together by the heart of the guts, and the split between the sculptor and the architect is overcome by the heart. The portrait is a psychological expression of my feeling. Somehow it is put into calligraphy; it becomes a co-realist drawing."[2]

Frederick Kiesler was born on September 22, 1890 in Czernowitz.[3] He broke off his studies in architecture at the Royal and Imperial Technical University in Vienna after only a year and he also left the Academy of Fine Arts without a diploma.[4] It can be assumed that Otto Wagner's ideas had a great influence on the young Kiesler, and in an interview years later, he called Wagner one of

„Friedrich Kiesler – Architekt, Künstler, Designer, Poet, Philosoph – war zum einen Renaissancemensch, zum anderen Prophet des Raumzeitalters",[1] schrieb Lisa Phillips im Ausstellungskatalog zur Kiesler-Retrospektive 1989 im Whitney Museum of American Art. Da er in allen künstlerischen Disziplinen tätig war, fällt es schwer, eine einzige – in diesem Fall die Architektur – herauszugreifen. An dieser Stelle soll dennoch der Versuch unternommen werden, den Architekten Kiesler hervorzukehren, wobei es sich aber nicht vermeiden lässt, auch andere künstlerische Felder zu streifen. Welche Bilanz Kiesler selbst über sein Schaffen zog, darüber gibt das einzige bekannte Selbstportrait Auskunft, das posthum in der Zeitschrift *Art in America* veröffentlicht wurde (Abb. 1). Es zeigt ihn jansuköpfig als Architekt und Bild-hauer, im abgedruckten Statement heißt es: „Die drei Aspekte meines Portraits werden zusammengehalten durch meinen Mut, und die Kluft zwischen dem Bildhauer und dem Architekten wird vom Herzen überbrückt. Das Portrait ist der psychologische Ausdruck meiner Empfindungen. Es scheint, als ob es in Kalligraphie gekleidet wurde; es wurde zu einer co-realistischen Zeichnung."[2]

Friedrich Kiesler wurde am 22. September 1890 in Czernowitz geboren.[3] Das Architekturstudium an der k. k. Wiener Technischen Hochschule brach er

Frederick Kiesler, ink drawing, 1965. Collection of Mrs. Frederick Kiesler.

Frederick Kiesler, who died in December, was an architect's architect and sculptor's sculptor; his latest triumph was the Shrine of the Book created by Kiesler-Bartos for the Dead Sea Scrolls in Jerusalem.

"Only the head is important. The rest of the body is unimportant. The three aspects of my portrait are held together by the heart of the guts, and the split between the sculptor and the architect is overcome by the heart. The portrait is a psychological expression of my feeling. Somehow it is put into calligraphy; it becomes a co-realist drawing. This is to say that nothing exists by itself. Everything coexists in ever-changing ways. Everything depends on the ever-changing human and physical environment. It is a two-way world of inhaling and exhaling. In doing my self-portrait, my craftsmanship was under the dictation of the heart and not of the mind. I was trying to catch the image of life in the trembling line."

1—Frederick Kiesler, *Self-portrait*, published in *Art in America*, 1966

the "great fathers of so-called modern architecture."[5] Wagner represented the first generation for him, followed by Adolf Loos and Josef Hoffmann in the second one. Looking back, Kiesler saw himself as the third generation in this tradition of modern Viennese architecture.[6]

After the war he was, as he himself said, without work for several years.[7] There is no evidence for a collaboration with Adolf Loos in connection with the City of Vienna's settlement movement, which Kiesler later mentioned. The first documented assignment came from Berlin in 1923—from the realm of theater, namely the stage-set design for Karel Čapek's piece *R.U.R.* (Rossum's Universal Robots) at the Theater am Kurfürstendamm.[8] Kiesler's use of film projection in particular earned him great recognition from the progressive international avant-garde scene and led to acquaintances with Theo van Doesburg, Hans Richter and László Moholy-Nagy. Even forty years later, Hans Richter sang his praises of Kiesler's set design for Berthold Viertel's staging of *The Emperor Jones* at the Berlin Lustspieltheater[9] soon thereafter: "The wanderings of nigger emperor[10] Jones through the jungle: this was made up simply of canvases without any painting, which were lowered down but placed criss-cross throughout the space, through which some erring individual would lose their way like in the jungle. Here and there a spotlight caught the

nach einem Jahr ab, und auch die Akademie der bildenden Künste verließ er ohne Abschlusszeugnis.[4] Einen großen Einfluss auf den jungen Kiesler dürften die Ideen Otto Wagners ausgeübt haben, den er viele Jahre später in einem Interview als einen der „großen Väter sogenannter moderner Architektur"[5] bezeichnete. Wagner stelle für ihn die erste Generation dar, gefolgt von Adolf Loos und Josef Hoffmann als zweiter. Kiesler selbst sah sich rückblickend als dritte Generation in dieser Tradition moderner Wiener Architektur.[6]

Nach dem Krieg war er eigenen Angaben zufolge mehrere Jahre arbeitslos.[7] Eine Zusammenarbeit mit Adolf Loos für die Siedlungstätigkeit der Stadt Wien, die Kiesler selbst später erwähnte, ist nicht erwiesen. Der erste doku-mentierte Arbeitsauftrag kam 1923 aus Berlin, und zwar aus dem Bereich des Theaters: die Bühnenbildgestaltung für Karel Čapeks Stück *W.U.R.* (Werstands Universal Robots) im Theater am Kurfürstendamm.[8] Speziell Kieslers Einsatz von Filmprojektion brachte ihm große Anerkennung seitens der fortschritts-gewandten internationalen Avantgarde ein und führte u.a. zur Bekanntschaft mit Theo van Doesburg, Hans Richter und László Moholy-Nagy. Von Kieslers Ausstattung für Berthold Viertels Inszenierung des *Kaiser Jones* im Berliner Lustspieltheater[9] kurz darauf schwärmte Hans Richter noch vierzig Jahre später: „Die Irrungen des Negerkaisers[10] Jones

'walls', the man, the path. Out of nothing an uncanny world had been created."[11]

In 1924, the *Gesellschaft zur Förderung moderner Kunst in Wien* (Society for the Promotion of Modern Art in Vienna) commissioned Kiesler with organizing an *Internationale Ausstellung neuer Theatertechnik* (International Exhibition of New Theater Techniques) as part of the City of Vienna's Music and Theater Festival.[12] This offered him the chance to invite representatives of the various European avant-garde movements—from Bauhaus and De Stijl to the Russian Constructivists and the Italian Futurists—to Vienna and to exhibit their revolutionary concepts by means of a system of spatial presentation that he had developed, the so-called *Leger- und Trägersystem* (L + T System). On the other hand, Kiesler was able, in this connection, to build the model of a stage of the future in a 1:1 scale and for it to be used for performances (Fig. 2). In his text that was published on it, he noted: "The Space Stage of the railway theater, the theater of our time, floats in space. Now it only uses the floor as a support for its open construction. The auditorium rotates in loop-like electro-motoric movements around the sphere-shaped core stage."[13] These first known projects in Berlin and Vienna already clearly show Kiesler's keen interest in the medium of space, which was to have a decisive influence on the rest of his work.

durch den Urwald: Das waren einfach heruntergelassene Soffittenleinwände ohne jede Bemalung, aber kreuz und quer gestellt, durch die der Irrende, wie im Urwald, seinen Weg verlor. Hier und da traf ein Scheinwerfer die Wände, den Mann, den Weg. Aus nichts war eine unheimliche Welt geschaffen."[11]

1924 beauftragte die *Gesellschaft zur Förderung moderner Kunst in Wien* Kiesler mit der Organisation einer *Internationalen Ausstellung neuer Theatertechnik* im Zuge des Musik- und Theaterfestes der Stadt Wien.[12] Dies bot ihm einerseits die Gelegenheit, die Vertreter der verschiedenen europäischen Avantgarde-Bewegungen – von Bauhaus und De Stijl bis zu den russischen Konstruktivisten und italienischen Futuristen – nach Wien einzuladen und ihre revolutionären Konzepte mittels eines von ihm entwickelten räumlichen Präsentationssystems, dem sogenannten *Leger- und Trägersystem*, auszustellen. Andererseits konnte Kiesler in diesem Rahmen das Modell einer Bühne der Zukunft im Maßstab 1:1 bauen und bespielen lassen (Abb. 2). In seinem dazu veröffentlichten Text heißt es: „Die Raumbühne des Railwaytheaters, des Theaters der Zeit, schwebt im Raum. Sie benützt den Boden nur mehr als Stütze für ihre offene Konstruktion. Der Zuschauerraum kreist in schleifenförmigen elektromotorischen Bewegungen um den sphärischen Bühnenkern."[13] Bereits anhand dieser ersten bekannten Projekte in Berlin und

2—Frederick Kiesler, *Space Stage, Internationale Ausstellung neuer Theatertechnik*, Vienna 1924

3—Frederick Kiesler, *City in Space, Exposition Internationale des Arts Décoratifs et Industriels Modernes*, Paris 1925

Kiesler was given an opportunity just one year later to further develop his concepts when Josef Hoffmann invited him to design the theater section at the *Exposition Internationale des Arts Décoratifs et Industriels Modernes* in Paris in 1925. Under the guise of exhibition design, Kiesler constructed a space-filling structure modeled after the Dutch neo-plasticists, the so-called *City in Space* (Fig. 3), which he then propagated as the model of a free-floating city of the future. In the avant-garde journals *De Stijl* and *G*, Kiesler published the related manifesto "Vitalbau—Raumstadt—Funktionelle Architektur" (Vital Construction—City in Space—Functional Architecture). Here he called the buildings of his time "coffins"[14] and demanded a radical new way of thinking for urban planning in particular: "And our cities? walls, walls, WALLS …

We will have NO MORE WALLS, these armories for body and soul, this whole armorized civilization; with or without ornament. We want:

1. Transformation of the surrounding area of space into cities.
2. Liberation from the ground, abolition of the static axis.
3. No walls, no foundations.
4. A system of spans (tension) in free SPACE.
5. Creation of new kinds of living, and, through them, the demands which will remold society."[15]

Wien wird Kieslers intensive Auseinandersetzung mit dem Medium Raum deutlich, die fortan sein gesamtes Schaffen prägen sollte.

Die Möglichkeit, seine Konzepte weiterzuentwickeln, erhielt Kiesler bereits im darauffolgenden Jahr, als ihn Josef Hoffmann einlud, die österreichi-sche Theatersektion auf der *Exposition Internationale des Arts Décoratifs et Industriels Modernes* 1925 in Paris zu gestalten. Unter dem Deckmantel der Ausstellungsgestaltung baute Kiesler eine raumfüllende Struktur im Stil der holländischen Neoplastizisten, die sogenannte *Raumstadt* (Abb. 3), und propagierte sie daraufhin als Modell einer frei schwebenden Stadt der Zukunft. In den Avantgarde-Zeitschriften *De Stijl* und *G* publizierte Kiesler das dazugehörige Manifest „Vitalbau – Raumstadt – Funktionelle Architektur". Darin bezeichnete er die Häuser der Zeit als „Steinsärge"[14] und forderte im Besonderen für die Stadtplanung ein drastisches Umdenken:

„Und unsere Städte?

Mauern, Mauern, Mauern.

Wir wollen keine Mauern mehr, Kasernierungen des Körpers und des Geistes, diese ganze Kasernenkultur mit oder ohne Ornamenten, wir wollen:

1. Umwandlung des sphärischen Raumes in Städte
2. Uns von der Erde loslösen, Aufgabe der statischen Achse

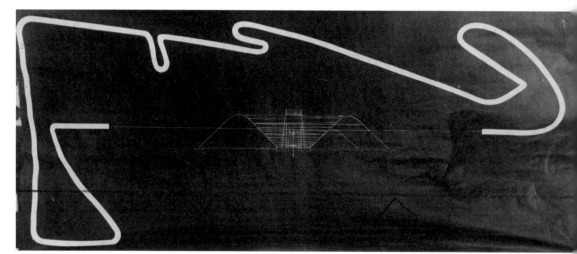

4—Frederick Kiesler, plan for redesigning Place de la Concorde, Paris 1925

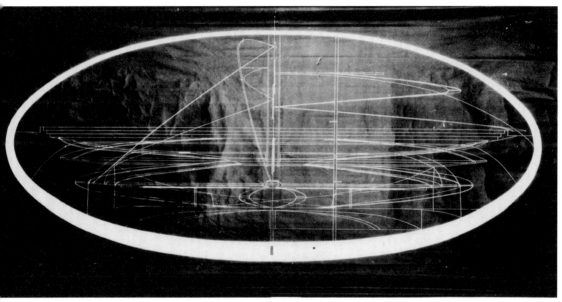

5—Frederick Kiesler, plan for *Endless Theater*, Paris 1925

During his time in Paris, Kiesler worked on further architectural projects, about which there are only fragments of information today: an automatic theater without actors *(Optophon Theater)*, horizontal skyscrapers, a spiral-shaped department store and a plan for redesigning Place de la Concorde (Fig. 4). He expanded the idea of the *Space Stage* of 1924 into a spheroid theater building, the *Endless Theater* (Fig. 5). The motive of the spiral runs through almost all his projects of this period like a guiding theme.[16]

Jane Heap, the editor of the avant-garde journal *Little Review*, invited Kiesler to help her organize a large theater exhibition in New York in the spring of 1926. On January 19, 1926 Frederick Kiesler and his wife Stefi[17] left Europe, traveling by ship to the new world. At that time, the two did not yet suspect that New York was to become the new central point of their lives. Following the modest success of the *International Theater Exposition* at the Steinway Building[18], all of the subsequent projects floundered, including the founding of an experimental theater lab that was planned together with actress Maria Carmi, and the related plan for a double theater in Brooklyn Heights (Fig. 6). For art patron Katherine Dreier, he drew plans for a museum of modern art of the *Société Anonyme* in the form of a 14-floor high-rise, furnished with the most modern lighting and ventilation. It was unrivaled in terms of approach

3.   Keine Mauern, keine Fundamente

4.   Ein System von Spannungen (tension) im freien Raume

5.   Schaffung neuer Lebensmöglichkeiten und durch sie Bedürfnisse, die die Gesellschaft umbilden."[15]

Während seiner Zeit in Paris arbeitete Kiesler an weiteren Architektur-projekten, von denen heute nur noch bruchstückhafte Informationen überliefert sind: ein automatisches Theater ohne Schauspieler *(Optophon Theater)*, horizontale Wolkenkratzer, ein Warenhaus in Spiralenform und das Konzept zur Umgestaltung des Place de la Concorde (Abb. 4). Die Idee der *Raumbühne* von 1924 weitete er zu einem sphäroidischen Theater-gebäude aus, dem *Endless Theater* (Abb. 5). Das Motiv der Spirale zieht sich wie ein roter Faden durch fast alle seiner Projekte dieser Zeit.[16]

Jane Heap, Herausgeberin der Avantgarde-Zeitschrift *Little Review*, lud Kiesler ein, mit ihr gemeinsam im Frühjahr 1926 eine große Theaterausstellung in New York zu organisieren. Am 19. Januar 1926 verließ Friedrich Kiesler mit seiner Frau Stefi[17] Europa mit dem Schiff in Richtung Neue Welt. Zu diesem Zeitpunkt ahnten die beiden noch nicht, dass New York ihr neuer Lebens-mittelpunkt werden sollte. Nach dem bescheidenen Erfolg der *International Theater Exposition* im Steinway Building[18] verliefen alle Folgeprojekte im Sande,

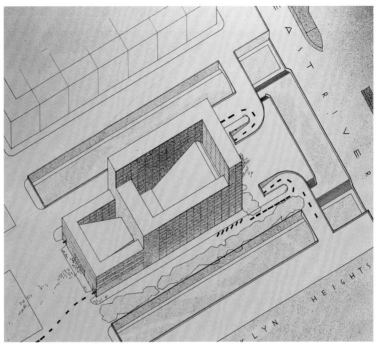

6—Frederick Kiesler, plan for a double theater in Brooklyn Heights, New York 1926/27

darunter die Gründung eines experimentellen Theaterlabors zusammen mit der Schauspielerin Maria Carmi und die damit verbundene Planung eines Doppeltheaters in Brooklyn Heights (Abb. 6). Für die Kunstmäzenin Katherine Dreier zeichnete er Entwürfe für ein geplantes Museum moderner Kunst der *Société Anonyme* in Form eines 14-stöckigen Hochhauses mit modernster Beleuchtung und Lüftung, das in seinem Konzept beispiellos war, aber aufgrund fehlender finanzieller Mittel nicht realisiert wurde (Abb. 7). Auf den vier erhaltenen Ansichtszeichnungen wirkt der Entwurf „weniger wie ein Gebäude als ein abstraktes De Stijl Design".[19] Um die Grundversorgung zu sichern, nahm Stefi Kiesler eine Vollzeitstelle in der New York Public Library an, wo sie sich rasch etablieren konnte und die Betreuung der deutsch- und französischsprachigen Sammlungen übernahm.

Kiesler erhielt 1928 den Auftrag, Schaufenster des Warenhauses Saks Fifth Avenue zu gestalten. Mit den traditionellen Präsentationsmethoden brach er, indem er konstruktivistische Formen und industriell hergestellte Materialien benutzte sowie ein ausgeklügeltes Lichtkonzept einsetzte. Die ausgestellten Waren wurden zahlenmäßig auf ein Minimum reduziert, dafür in höchstem Grade theatralisch inszeniert. Seine Theorien dazu formulierte Kiesler in dem Buch *Contemporary Art Applied to the Store and its Display*.[20] Im Jahr 1928

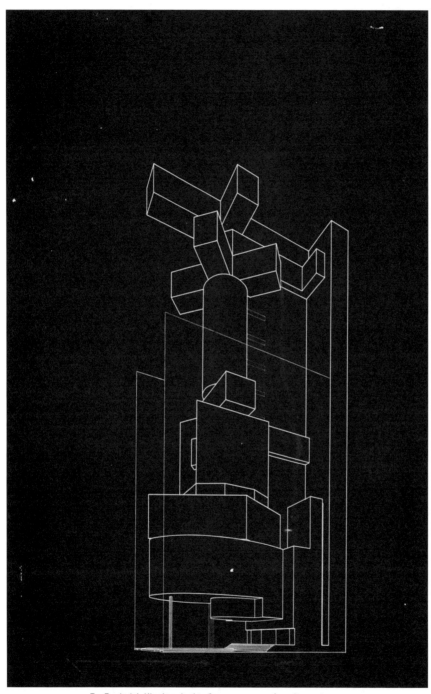

7—Frederick Kiesler, design for a museum of modern art
of the *Société Anonyme*, New York 1927

but, due to a lack of funding, it was not realized (Fig. 7). On the four surviving sketches, the design "resembles less a building than an abstract De Stijl design."[19] In order to secure their livelihood, Stefi Kiesler took on a full-time job at the New York Public Library, where she quickly established herself and was put in charge of the German and French Collections.

In 1928, Kiesler was commissioned to design the shop windows of the department store Saks Fifth Avenue. Breaking with traditional methods of presentation, he worked with constructivist forms and industrial materials and used a sophisticated lighting system. The number of goods on display was reduced to a minimum, but the way they were staged was theatrical to the utmost. Kiesler formulated his theories in his book *Contemporary Art Applied to the Store and its Display.*[20] In 1928, Kiesler also planned a novel cinema in Greenwich Village for the Film Arts Guild; in spring 1929, the *Film Guild Cinema* was opened (Fig. 8). Advertised as "The First 100 % Cinema"[21], it was to clearly stand out from classical movie theater buildings and to be specially geared to the reception demands of the young medium of film. Instead of a curtain, an iris diaphragm covering the entire wall adorned the screen *(Screen-o-scope).* The projection could be extended to the ceiling and sidewalls

plante Friedrich Kiesler außerdem für die Film Arts Guild ein neuartiges Kino im Greenwich Village, das im Frühjahr 1929 als *Film Guild Cinema* eröffnet wurde (Abb. 8). Als „The First 100 % Cinema"[21] beworben, sollte es sich deutlich von den klassischen Lichtspieltheatergebäuden abgrenzen und speziell auf die Rezeptionsbedürfnisse des jungen Mediums Film eingehen. Statt eines Vorhangs verkleidete eine wandfüllende Irisblende die Leinwand *(Screen-o-scope).* Die Projektion konnte auf die Decke und Seitenwände erweitert werden, um das Publikum atmosphärisch stärker zu involvieren, was einer Vorstufe der heutigen virtuellen Realität gleichkommt.

1930 erhielt Kiesler die offizielle Architekten-Lizenz der New York State University, vermutlich im gleichen Jahr erfolgte die Gründung seiner eigenen Designfirma *Planners Institute Inc.*, die bis 1945 existierte. Die staatliche Genehmigung, als Architekt tätig sein zu dürfen, erfolgte zu einem denkbar ungünstigen Zeitpunkt, denn die Weltwirtschaftskrise erstickte fast alle Aufträge im Keim. Zu Kieslers Projekten dieser schwierigen Jahre zählen Möbel- und Lampenentwürfe, die Planung eines Experimentaltheaters für Woodstock[22] (Abb. 9, im Wettbewerb setzte sich Kiesler gegen Konkurrenten wie Frank Lloyd Wright durch, doch infolge des Börsencrashs wurde auch dieses Projekt ad infinitum verschoben) sowie die Konzeption eines

8—Frederick Kiesler, *Film Guild Cinema*, New York 1929

in order to create an atmosphere that would draw the audience in—
a precursor of what is known as virtual reality today.

In 1930, Kiesler obtained an official license to work as an architect from
New York State University and, presumably in the same year, he founded
his own design company *Planners Institute Inc.*, which existed until 1945. He
received his license at a conceivably unfavorable moment, since the Great
Depression brought almost all commissions to naught. Kiesler's projects in
these difficult years included furniture and lamp designs, the plan for an
experimental theater in Woodstock[22] (Fig. 9, in the competition Kiesler was
able to prevail over competitors such as Frank Lloyd Wright, but as a result of
the stock market crash, this project was postponed indefinitely) as well as
the concept of a mass-produced, modular single-family house *(Nucleus House)*,
which he offered to Sears, Roebuck and Company as a "mail-order house."
Together with colleagues such as Paul T. Frankl, Donald Deskey and William
Lescaze, he was active in the *American Union of Decorative Arts and
Craftsmen* (AUDAC), the first professional organization of industrial and art
designers in the United States.

Following Theo van Doesburg's death in 1931, Kiesler left Europe and
De Stijl behind for good: "As of now, I am artistically alone,"[23] he wrote in a

massenproduzierten modularen Einfamilienhauses *(Nucleus House)*,
das er Sears, Roebuck and Company als „Versandhaus" (*Mail-order House*)
anbot. Zusammen mit Kollegen wie Paul T. Frankl, Donald Deskey und
William Lescaze engagierte er sich in der *American Union of Decorative Arts
and Craftsmen* (AUDAC), der ersten Berufsvereinigung von Industrie- und
Kunstdesignern in den Vereinigten Staaten.

Nach Theo van Doesburgs Tod 1931 kehrte Kiesler Europa und De Stijl
endgültig den Rücken. „Ich bin künstlerisch von nun an allein",[23] schrieb
er in einem Brief an Nelly van Doesburg. Sein *Space House* (Abb. 10) aus dem
Jahr 1933 weist erstmals in Kieslers Werk biomorphe Formen auf und
markiert somit eine stilistische Kehrtwende: „Die leicht gerundete Außenwand
des Hauses sollte als einzelne Oberfläche einer ,kontinuierlichen Spannung',
konstruiert sein – ähnlich der Schale eines Eis."[24] Er baute es als begehbares
Modell eines Einfamilienhauses in die Ausstellungshalle der Modernage
Furniture Company in New York. Wie bereits beim *Nucleus House* stand auch
beim *Space House* das Individuum im Zentrum von Kieslers Überlegungen:
„Indem er dem Haus die physischen Strukturen des Atoms und der biologischen
Zelle zugrunde legte, revidierte Kiesler traditionelle Formen des Einfamilien-
hauses als Nukleus familiärer Aktivitäten."[25] Einfamilienhäuser sollten nach

9—Frederick Kiesler, model of an experimental theater for Woodstock, New York 1931

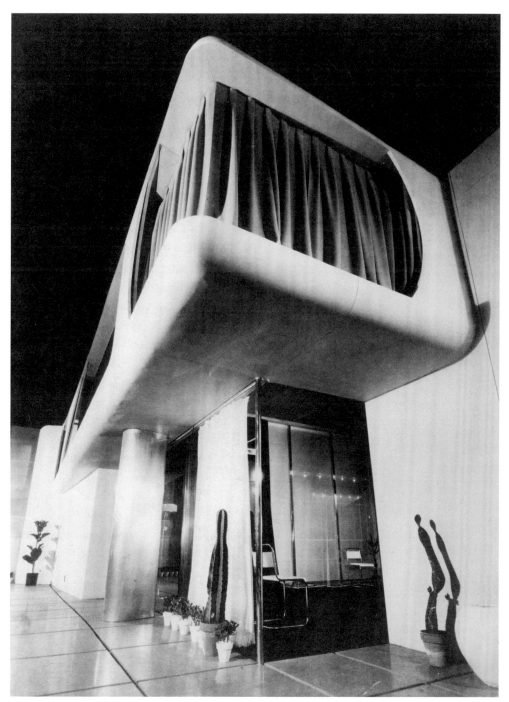

10—Frederick Kiesler, *Space House*, New York 1933

letter to Nelly van Doesburg. His *Space House* (Fig. 10) of 1933 shows biomorphous shapes for the first time in Kiesler's oeuvre, thus marking a stylistic turn: "The slightly rounded exterior of the house was to be constructed in a single surface of 'continuous tension'—much like the shell of an egg."[24] He built it into the exhibition hall of the Modernage Furniture Company in New York as a model of a single-family house that could be entered. As in the *Nucleus House*, the individual was also the central focus of Kiesler's considerations in the *Space House*: "Using the physical structures of the atom and the biological cell as the basis of the house, Kiesler revised traditional designs for the one-family shelter as a nucleus for family activities."[25] One-family houses were to be industrially produced according to the most recent technical standards, but at the same time, they also had to be adaptable to individual needs. The daily movements of the inhabitants through the space were to have an influence on the inner design which Kiesler called "Time-Space-Architecture."[26] Parallels to Buckminster Fuller's *Dymaxion House* are not coincidental, since they both knew each other and, as members of the *Structural Study Associates*, were in regular contact.[27]

From 1934, Frederick Kiesler served as a stage set designer and instructor at the Juilliard School of Music for more than two decades (Fig. 11).

neuesten technischen Standards industriell gefertigt werden und dennoch auf individuelle Bedürfnisse angepasst werden können. Die all-täglichen Bewegungen der Bewohner durch den Raum sollten Einfluss auf die Innengestaltung nehmen, dies nannte Kiesler „Time-Space-Architecture".[26] Parallelen zu Buckminster Fullers *Dymaxion House* sind wohl kein Zufall – die beiden waren miteinander bekannt und tauschten sich als Mitglieder der *Structural Study Associates* zu dieser Zeit regelmäßig aus.[27]

Ab 1934 war Friedrich Kiesler mehr als zwei Jahrzehnte lang als Bühnenbildner und Dozent an der Juilliard School of Music tätig (Abb. 11). Neben dem Vorteil eines festen Einkommens bot das Theater Kiesler die Möglichkeit einer Art Proberaum für seine Ideen. Ab 1937 lehrte Kiesler außerdem an der School of Architecture der Columbia University, wo er ein *Laboratory for Design Correlation* einrichtete und bis 1941 leitete. Ziel des Institutes war es, „die Erforschung von Lebensprozessen mit einer wissenschaftlichen Annäherung an das Design zu verbinden sowie systematische Untersuchungen elementarer Formen und ihre Anwendung in Architektur und Industrie vorzunehmen".[28] In diesem Rahmen entwickelte Kiesler seine Theorie des *Correalismus* weiter, in deren Zentrum der Mensch als „Nucleus of Forces" in ständiger Wechsel-beziehung mit den menschlichen, natürlichen und

11—*The Magic Flute* (scenic design by Frederick Kiesler), Juilliard School of Music, New York 1940

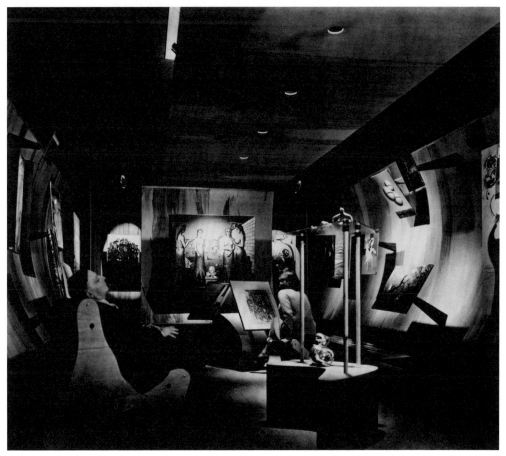

12—Frederick Kiesler, *Surrealist gallery, Art of This Century*, New York 1942

In addition to the benefit of a regular income, the theater also offered Kiesler the possibility of having a sort of rehearsal space for his ideas. From 1937, Kiesler also taught at the School of Architecture at Columbia University, where he created a *Laboratory for Design Correlation*, which he ran until 1941. The goal of the institute was "to combine the research of life processes with a scientific approach to design as well as to conduct systematic studies of elementary forms and their application in architecture and industry."[28] In this connection, Kiesler was able to further develop his theory of *Correalism*, at the center of which stood man as a nucleus of forces in constant interaction with human, natural and technological environments.[29] He also worked with students on building a flexible bookshelf *(Mobile Home Library)* as a case study and a device for visualizing the human viewing process *(Vision Machine)*.

The 1940s were mainly defined by Kiesler's pioneering exhibition designs. In 1942 Peggy Guggenheim commissioned him to redesign two former tailor workshops into gallery spaces for her art collection. The *Art of This Century* museum gallery also featured a room reserved for surrealist artworks, which had an irritating effect with its light and sound installation and where frameless artworks were extended to the viewer by means of *picture arms* (Fig. 12). The abstract objects in the adjacent room had, by contrast, been

technologischen Umwelten steht,[29] und arbeitete mit Studenten an einer flexiblen Bücherstellage *(Mobile Home Library)* als Fallstudie und einem Apparat zur Visualisierung des menschlichen Sehprozesses *(Vision Machine)*.

Die 1940er Jahre waren vor allem durch Kieslers bahnbrechende Ausstellungsgestaltungen geprägt. Peggy Guggenheim beauftragte ihn 1942 mit der Umgestaltung zweier ehemaliger Schneiderwerkstätten zu Galerieräumlichkeiten für ihre Kunstsammlung. Die *Art of This Century* Museums-Galerie beinhaltete unter anderem einen für surrealistische Kunstwerke reservierten Raum, der durch eine Licht- und Klanginstallation irritierte und in dem die rahmenlosen Kunstwerke den Besuchern von *Greifarmen* entgegengestreckt wurden (Abb. 12). Die abstrakten Objekte im Nebenraum wurden hingegen auf Bändern appliziert, die zwischen Boden und Decke gespannt waren. In seinem dazu entstandenen Text *Note on Designing the Gallery* erklärte Kiesler, dass es ihm vorrangig um die Einheit des alltäglichen Umfelds der Menschen und ihr schöpferisches Bewusstsein ginge. Daher dürften Kunstwerke nicht gerahmt an Wänden hängen und dadurch von der menschlichen Lebensrealität abgeschnitten werden. Am Textende proklamierte Kiesler: „Wir, die Erben des Chaos, müssen die Architekten einer neuen Einheit sein. Diese Galerieräumlichkeiten sind eine Demonstration einer Welt im Wandel".[30]

mounted to bands that were suspended between the floor and the ceiling.
In his text *Note on Designing the Gallery*, Kiesler declared that he was primarily interested in the unity of the daily environment and creative consciousness. Thus, artworks were not supposed to hang on walls in frames and thereby be cut off from human reality. At the end of the text, Kiesler proclaimed:
"We, the inheritors of chaos, must be the architects of a new unity. These galleries are a demonstration of a changing world."[30]

About a year after the opening of *Art of This Century*, Leo Lerman wrote the following about Kiesler in *Vogue*: "He is actually designing tomorrow—its habitations, theaters, museums, and galleries; its shop windows and public buildings; the chairs upon which it will sit, and the tables from which it will eat. He works in space. To be utterly free in a free world, man must have space, and Kiesler gives man this space."[31] In 1947, two visionary designs of Surrealist exhibitions followed: *Bloodflames 1947* at the New York Hugo Gallery[32] and the *Exposition Internationale du Surréalisme* at the Galerie Maeght in Paris.[33] Here Kiesler pursued the goal of integrating painting, sculpture and architecture, explaining this approach in his *Manifeste du Corréalisme* that was published in 1949.[34] The exhibition in Paris also marked the beginning of Kiesler's painting and sculptural activity.

Etwa ein Jahr nach der Eröffnung von *Art of This Century* schrieb Leo Lerman über Kiesler in der *Vogue*: „Er entwirft tatsächlich das Morgen – seine Behausungen, Theater, Museen und Galerien; seine Schaufenster und öffentlichen Gebäude; die Stühle, auf denen man sitzen wird, und die Tische, von denen man essen wird. Er arbeitet im Raum. Um absolut frei zu sein in einer freien Welt, muss der Mensch Raum haben, und Kiesler gibt dem Menschen diesen Raum."[31] 1947 folgten zwei visionäre Gestaltungen surrealistischer Ausstellungen: *Bloodflames 1947* in der New Yorker Hugo Gallery[32] und die *Exposition Internationale du Surréalisme* in der Galerie Maeght in Paris[33]. Kiesler verfolgte dabei das Ziel der Integration von Malerei, Skulptur und Architektur und erläuterte dieses Konzept in seinem 1949 publizierten *Manifeste du Corréalisme*.[34] Die Ausstellung in Paris markiert außerdem den Beginn von Kieslers malerischem und bildhauerischem Schaffen.

Im Jahr 1950 stellte Friedrich Kiesler sein erstes kleines Tonmodell eines *Endless House* zusammen mit einer Skulptur von David Hare im Rahmen der Ausstellung *The Muralist and the Modern Architect* in der Kootz Gallery in New York aus.[35] Die Radio- und Fernsehstation CBS ernannte ihn daraufhin zum Architekten des Jahres 1950.[36] Eine zentrale Rolle spielte für Kiesler

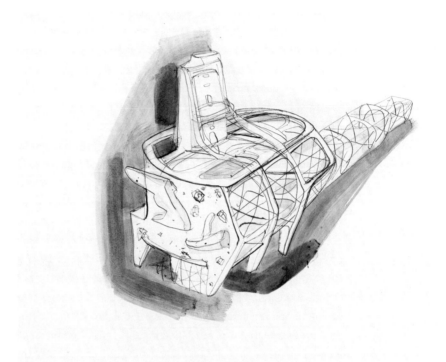

13/14—Frederick Kiesler, concept drawing for annex building for the Juilliard School of Music,
   New York 1951

In 1950, Frederick Kiesler exhibited his first small clay model of an *Endless House* together with a sculpture by David Hare in the show *The Muralist and the Modern Architect* at the Kootz Gallery in New York.[35] Subsequently, the radio and TV station CBS named him the architect of the year 1950.[36] For Kiesler, the lighting system played a central role, as he emphasized in the article *Endless House and Its Psychological Lighting*. He speaks of "an architectural form based on a lighting system designed to do more than merely give physical information."[37] The principle is based on a so-called *Color Clock*, the light filters of which would tint the inner spaces according to the time of day, so as to make the inhabitant aware of the continuity of time. The Museum of Modern Art purchased the clay model along with the related sketches and exhibited it together with a model of Buckminster Fuller's *Geodesic Dome* in the exhibition *Two Houses: New Ways to Build*.[38]

From 1951 there remain several design sketches for an almost unknown architectural project by Kiesler: an annex building for the Juilliard School of Music with workshops and rehearsal rooms.[39] A handful of axonometric views show various variants—from functional to biomorphic—of an annex building elevated from the ground through slender stilts with a steel-frame construction and generous glass façade (Figs. 13 and Fig. 14). The project did

das Beleuchtungssystem, wie er im Artikel *Endless House and Its Psychological Lighting* betont. Er spricht von „einer architektonischen Form, basierend auf einem Lichtsystem, das mehr kann, als nur physische Informationen zu geben".[37] Das Prinzip beruht auf einer sogenannten *Color Clock*, durch deren Lichtfilter die Innenräume der Tageszeit entsprechend eingefärbt werden, um dem Bewohner auf diese Weise die Kontinuität der Zeit bewusst zu machen. Das Museum of Modern Art erwarb das Tonmodell samt einiger dazugehöriger Zeichnungen und zeigte es gemeinsam mit einem Modell von Buckminster Fullers *Geodätischer Kuppel* in der Ausstellung *Two Houses: New Ways to Build*.[38]

Aus dem Jahr 1951 sind mehrere Entwurfszeichnungen zu einem nahezu unbekannten Architekturprojekt Kieslers erhalten: einem Erweiterungsbau der Juilliard School of Music mit Werkstätten und Proberäumen.[39] Eine Handvoll axonometrischer Ansichten zeigen unterschiedliche Varianten – von funktional bis biomorph – eines durch schlanke Stelzen vom Boden abgehobenen Annex-baus mit Stahlrahmenkonstruktion und großzügiger Glasfassade (Abb. 13 und Abb. 14). Über dieses erste Entwurfsstadium ist das Projekt nicht hinausge-kommen. Im Laufe der 1950er Jahre arbeitete Kiesler an weiteren Architekturprojekten, die auf den ersten Blick sehr pragmatisch

15—Frederick Kiesler, Stifel-Building, axonometric view, New York 1956

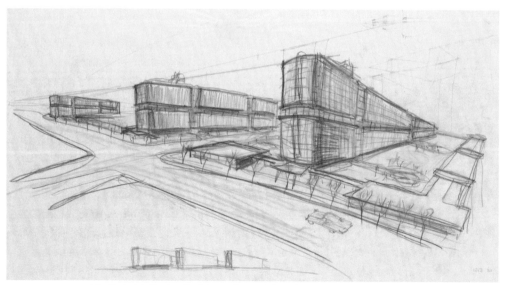

16—Frederick Kiesler, Washington Square Village Project, perspective view, New York 1956

not move beyond this first design stage. In the course of the 1950s, Kiesler
worked on further architectural projects, which at first glance appear
very pragmatic and only allow his visionary approaches to be recognized in the
details.[40] He was, for instance, supposed to rework existing plans for the
clients Arthur C. Stifel and Paul Tishman and to help give them something
special. He replaced the colonial-style façade that was planned for the *Stifel
Building* with a parabolically curved contour with glazed cladding, which
would make the building stand out self-assuredly from the neighboring brown-
stone building (Fig. 15). In the case of the *Washington Square Village
Project*, a residential building complex consisting of three apartment blocks
arranged in parallel, Kiesler saw his task as being to use his progressive
ideas to break open the prison-like appearance of the project. His proposals
included redesigning the box-shaped blocks to create continuously flowing
contours, to incorporate circling garden terraces as well as to design the
façades in a colorful way (Fig. 16). Together with Armand Bartos, with whom
he ran an architectural firm until 1962, Kiesler designed a beach house
for Karl Robbins in West Palm Beach, Florida. All three projects floundered.

What did get implemented, however, was Kiesler's and Bartos' design
of a gallery at the New York Carlyle Hotel, commissioned by entrepreneur and

wirken und nur im Detail seine visionären Ansätze erkennen lassen.[40]
So sollte er etwa für die Bauherren Arthur C. Stifel und Paul Tishman jeweils
bestehende Pläne überarbeiten und diesen dadurch zu etwas Besonderheit
verhelfen. Dem *Stifel-Building* verpasste er statt der ursprünglich im Kolonial-
stil geplanten Fassade eine parabolisch geschwungene Kontur mit gläserner
Verkleidung, wodurch sich das Gebäude selbstbewusst von den benach-
barten Sandsteinhäusern abgehoben hätte (Abb. 15). Beim *Washington Square
Village Project*, einer Wohnhausanlage bestehend aus drei parallel angeordneten Apartmentblocks, sah Kiesler seine Aufgabe darin, das gefängnis-
hafte Erscheinungsbild mit seinen progressiven Ideen aufzubrechen. Seine
Vorschläge beinhalteten unter anderem die Umformung der schachtelförmigen
Blöcke zu kontinuierlich fließenden Konturen, das Anlegen von umlaufenden
Gartenterrassen sowie eine farbenfrohe Gestaltung der Fassaden (Abb. 16).
Zusammen mit Armand Bartos, mit dem er von 1957 bis 1962 ein
gemeinsames Architekturbüro betrieb, konzipierte Kiesler ein Strandhaus für
Karl Robbins in West Palm Beach, Florida. Alle drei Projekte verliefen im Sand.

Umgesetzt wurde allerdings Kieslers und Bartos' Entwurf einer Galerie
im New Yorker Carlyle Hotel im Auftrag des Entrepreneurs und Kunstsammlers
Herbert Mayer. Die sogenannten *World House Galleries* eröffneten Anfang

art collector Herbert Mayer. The so-called *World House Galleries* opened in
early 1957 and were met with great enthusiasm from the art world: "[…]
the big show was not the paintings (a 100-year retrospective from Manet
and Monet to Picasso and Pollock), but the gallery itself."[41] In his articles
published in autumn of the same year in *Art News*[42] and in *Architectural
Forum*[43], Kiesler explained that the two floors of the gallery were united in
an ellipsis to form a continuously flowing space. "With its curvatures,
its contrasting planes, its segmented parabolas, sinuous flows, fins of sharp
crystalline columns, the illusion of *endlessness* seemed achieved."[44]
As a matter of fact, the photographs give the impression that the boundaries
between floor, walls and ceiling were done away with (Fig. 17). In a letter
to the Italian architect Bruno Zevi, Kiesler brought the *World House Galleries*
into a direct line of development of his output that was under the sway
of the idea of the *endless*, ending with the statement: "It [the gallery] is the
result of a lifetime of work."[45]

About half a year after the *World House Galleries* were opened, the
intensive planning work began for Kiesler's and Bartos' large-scale project, the
Shrine of the Book in Jerusalem. It took eight years to be completed, partly
because the location of the site was changed repeatedly. "The 'Shrine of the

1957 und wurden von der Kunstwelt begeistert aufgenommen: „[…] die große
Show waren nicht die Gemälde (eine 100-jährige Retrospektive von Manet
und Monet zu Picasso und Pollock), sondern die Galerie selbst".[41] In seinen im
Herbst desselben Jahres publizierten Artikeln in *Art News*[42] und im *Architectural Forum*[43] erklärte Kiesler, die zwei Geschoße der Galerie wären in einer
Ellipse zu einem kontinuierlich fließenden Raum vereint. „Mit ihren Krümmungen, ihren kontrastierenden Flächen, ihren segmentierten Parabolen, ge-
schwungenen Bewegungen, Lamellen von scharfkantigen kristallinen
Säulen, schien die Illusion der *Endlosigkeit* erreicht."[44] Tatsächlich erhält man
auf Fotografien den Eindruck, die Grenzen zwischen Boden, Wänden und
Decke wären aufgehoben (Abb. 17). In einem Brief an den italienischen Architekten Bruno Zevi stellte Kiesler die *World House Galleries* in eine direkte
Entwicklungslinie seines von der Idee des *Endlosen* geprägten Schaffens und
endete mit dem Satz: „Sie [die Galerie] ist das Resultat lebenslanger Arbeit."[45]

Etwa ein halbes Jahr nach der Eröffnung der *World House Galleries* be-
gannen die intensiven Planungsarbeiten an Kieslers und Bartos' Großprojekt,
dem *Shrine of the Book* in Jerusalem. Unter anderem aufgrund mehrerer
Standortwechsel vergingen acht Jahre bis zur Fertigstellung. „Der Schrein des
Heiligen Buches (*Shrine of the Book*) […] repräsentiert einen ideologisch

17—Kiesler and Bartos, World House Galleries, New York 1957

18—Kiesler and Bartos, *The Shrine of the Book*, Jerusalem 1965

19—Frederick Kiesler and Armand Bartos in front of the Isaiah Scroll on display inside *The Shrine of the Book*, Jerusalem 1965

Book' […] represents an ideologically new type of architecture and goes
far beyond being merely functional. It reflects its contents and is not
formalistic like buildings by Corbusier or à la Bauhaus,"[46] as one can read
in Kiesler's article *Eine neue Akropolis* (A New Acropolis). The building
belonging to the Israel Museum, which archives and presents a number of
Old Testament scrolls found in the caves of Qumran on the Dead Sea
between 1947 and 1956, is seen to this day as being exemplary of eloquent
architecture. The underground exhibition spaces are juxtaposed with
a dark basalt wall and a white-tiled concrete dome on the ground level
(Figs. 18 and 19). The tiles are constantly being sprinkled with water and form
a visual contrast with the volcanic basalt just like the symbolic battle
between good and evil, so that in terms of content the War Scroll is mirrored
as one of the most significant exhibits.

In 1958 Kiesler received from the Museum of Modern Art the long hoped-
for opportunity to actually implement his concept of an *Endless House*,
as a life-sized model in the museum's garden. Apart from several design
sketches and plans, he created a total of four three-dimensional studies in
various sizes during the years that followed. In the end, the 1:1 model
was never translated into reality, but Kiesler's studies were presented in the

neuen Architektur-Typ und geht weit darüber hinaus, lediglich funktionell zu
sein. Er spiegelt seinen Inhalt wider und ist nicht formalistisch, wie
Bauten von Corbusier oder à la Bauhaus",[46] heißt es in Kieslers Artikel *Eine
neue Akropolis*. Das zum Israel Museum zugehörige Bauwerk, das eine
Reihe zwischen 1947 und 1956 in den Höhlen von Qumran am Toten Meer
entdeckte alttestamentarische Schriftrollen archiviert und präsentiert,
gilt bis heute als Beispiel symbolhaft sprechender Architektur. Den unter-
irdischen Ausstellungsräumlichkeiten stehen oberirdisch eine dunkle
Basaltmauer und eine weißgekachelte Betonkuppel gegenüber (Abb. 18 und
19). Die Kacheln werden ständig mit Wasser besprengt und stehen im
optischen Widerstreit mit dem vulkanischen Basalt wie der symbolische Kampf
von Gut gegen Böse, wodurch inhaltlich die Kriegsrolle als eines der bedeut-
samsten Ausstellungsstücke reflektiert wird.

Vom Museum of Modern Art erhielt Kiesler 1958 die langersehnte
Gelegenheit, sein Konzept eines *Endless House* praktisch umzusetzen, und
zwar als lebensgroßes Modell im Garten des Museums. Neben einigen
Entwurfszeichnungen und Plänen entstanden in den darauffolgenden Jahren
insgesamt vier dreidimensionale Studien unterschiedlicher Größe. Das
1:1-Modell wurde letztlich nicht realisiert, Kieslers Studien wurden dafür

Visionary Architecture[47] exhibition. Before that, illustrations of Kiesler with his largest *Endless House* model were already featured in the fashion magazines *Vogue* and *Harper's Bazaar*. A text accompanying the latter reads as follows: "According to Kiesler, man must live, not in a box, but in free, exuberant space which seems alternately to contract and to expand to fit his changing moods as he moves within it. [...] 'Endless House' [...] is the triumph of individuality. It cannot be industry-built. It must be handmade."[48]

In the final years of his life, Kiesler focused more on sculpture. He called the works he created *Galaxies*, *Shell Sculptures* and *Environmental Sculptures*. Several of the in part room-filling sculptures were staged theatrically with light and sound installations. The Ford Foundation awarded him a grant for designing an ideal theater, for which he took up his earlier idea of a double theater and developed it further. *The Universal*, in which Kiesler was finally able to bring together all his ideas and demands from earlier decades, thus stands in one line of development with the *Endless Theater* of 1925 and the experimental theater for Woodstock of 1931. It was supposed to offer a maximum of flexibility and to be complemented by a 10-story high-rise with offices, radio stations and galleries. Kiesler's plans and aluminum model (Fig. 20) were presented between January 1962 and January 1964—alongside

in der Ausstellung *Visionary Architecture*[47] präsentiert. Zuvor fanden sich jedoch bereits Abbildungen von Kiesler mit seinem größten *Endless House*-Modell in den Modemagazinen *Vogue* und *Harper's Bazaar*. Im Begleittext des letzteren heißt es: „Kiesler zufolge muss der Mensch nicht in einer Kiste, sondern im freien, überschwänglichen Raum leben, der sich abwechselnd zusammen-zuziehen und zu entfalten scheint, um sich den wechselnden Gemütslagen anzupassen, während er sich darin bewegt. [...] Das endlose Haus [...] ist der Triumph der Individualität. Es kann nicht industriegefertigt werden. Es muss von Hand gefertigt werden."[48]

In seinen letzten Lebensjahren widmete sich Kiesler verstärkt der Bildhauerei. Die dabei entstandenen Werke nannte er *Galaxies*, *Shell Sculptures* und *Environmental Sculptures*. Einige der zum Teil raumfüllenden Skulpturen waren mit Licht- und Klanginstallationen theatral inszeniert. Von der Ford Foundation erhielt er ein Stipendium für die Gestaltung eines Ideal-Theaters, wofür er seine frühere Idee eines Doppeltheaters aufgriff und weiterent-wickelte. *The Universal*, in dem Kiesler schließlich all seine Konzepte und Forderungen der vorherigen Jahrzehnte zusammenfassen konnte, steht folglich in einer Entwicklungslinie mit dem *Endless Theatre* von 1925 und dem Experimentaltheater für Woodstock von 1931. Es sollte maximale

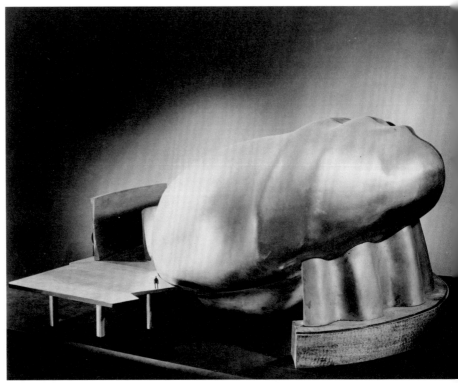

20—Frederick Kiesler, aluminium model for *The Universal*, New York 1961

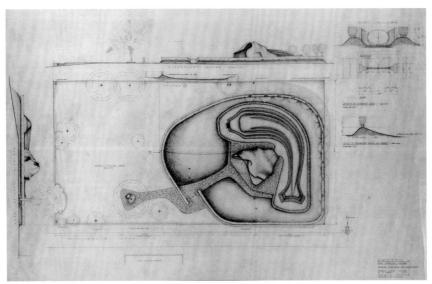

21—Frederick Kiesler, plan for a *Grotto for Meditation*, New York 1963

seven further concepts—in the traveling exhibition *The Ideal Theater: Eight Concepts* organized by the American Federation of Arts.[49]

The last architectural project planned by Kiesler (but never realized) was a *Grotto for Meditation* for Jane Blaffer Owen and the New Harmony Community in Indiana (Fig. 21). As in the *Endless House*, it was a shell construction in continuous tension[50], made of reinforced concrete. The symbolically laden building was to help people create a connection with the cosmic world, and in Kiesler's eyes it represented the opposite of a no longer topical functional architecture.[51] In April 1965, the *Shrine of the Book* was officially opened in Jerusalem, yielding an award for both Kiesler and Bartos, namely the *Gold Medal of Honor in Design and Craftmanship* of the Architectural League of New York. Frederick Kiesler died in New York on December 27, 1965.

As an architect, Kiesler had to wait until his 75th birthday for a work that he had planned to be built, his one and only realized and still existing building: the *Shrine of the Book*. Philip Johnson's remark about Kiesler as the "greatest non-building architect of our time" became famous.[52] Yet, as the quote continues, it is often forgotten: "[…] but his ideas are profound, his influence enormous. His conception of the 'Endless House' […] is one of the few original conceptions of our day."[53] Asked by a newspaper to respond to this in

Flexibilität bieten und durch ein zehnstöckiges Hochhaus mit Büros, Rundfunkstationen und Galerien ergänzt werden. Kieslers Pläne und Aluminium-Modell (Abb. 20) wurden zwischen Januar 1962 und Januar 1964 neben sieben weiteren Konzepten in der von der American Federation of Arts organisierten Wander-ausstellung *The Ideal Theatre: Eight Concepts* präsentiert.[49]

Das letzte von Kiesler geplante (und nicht realisierte) Architekturprojekt war eine *Grotto for Meditation* für Jane Blaffer Owen und die New Harmony Community in Indiana (Abb. 21). Wie beim *Endless House* handelte es sich um eine Schalenkonstruktion in durchgängiger Spannung[50] aus Stahlbeton; das symbolhafte Gebäude sollte Menschen unterstützen, die Verbindung zur kosmischen Welt herzustellen, und stellte für Kiesler den Gegensatz zur seiner Meinung nach nicht mehr zeitgemäßen funktionalen Architektur dar.[51] Im April 1965 wurde der *Shrine of the Book* in Jerusalem feierlich eröffnet und brachte Kiesler und Bartos eine Auszeichnung mit der Goldmedaille für *Design and Craftmanship* der *Architectural League of New York* ein. Am 27. Dezember 1965 verstarb Friedrich Kiesler in New York.

Als Architekt musste Kiesler bis zu seinem 75. Lebensjahr auf die Ausführung eines von ihm geplanten Werkes warten, seines einzigen realisierten und heute noch existierenden Gebäudes: dem *Shrine of The Book*.

22—Frederick Kiesler working on a plan drawing, New York early 1960s

writing, Kiesler explained: "It is true that I have continuously rejected purely commercial orders. I still feel that it is better to concentrate on a few honest possibilities to build and otherwise wait, unconcerned at being named 'the greatest non-building architect of our time,' than to be, as is sometimes the case, a most building non-architect."[54] Thus, he went down in the history of architecture as an uncompromising visionary (Fig. 22).

1   Lisa Phillips, "Architect of Endless Innovation", in *Frederick Kiesler*, ed. Lisa Phillips (New York: Whitney Museum of American Art/W.W. Norton & Company, 1989), 13.
2   *Art in America* 2 (1966), 53.
3   For a chronology on Kiesler's life and work cf. Dieter Bogner and Matthias Boeckl, "Friedrich Kiesler 1890–1965", in *Friedrich Kiesler. Architekt Maler Bildhauer 1890–1965*, ed. Dieter Bogner (Vienna: Löcker, 1988), 8–191. A detailed reconstruction of his first three decades can be found in Barbara Lesák, *Die Kulisse explodiert. Friedrich Kieslers Theaterexperimente und Architekturprojekte 1923–1925* (Vienna: Löcker, 1988), 7–31.
4   According to information from the University Archives of the Vienna Academy of Fine Arts, Kiesler already took the entrance exam in 1908/09 but was rejected. He then enrolled at the Royal and Imperial Technical University in the winter semester of 1908/09, where he studied for one year. In 1910, he took the entrance exam again at the academy and was successful this time. Kiesler completed six semesters, two of them at the Allgemeine Malerschule (General Painters' School) and four at a special school of Ferdinand Schmutzer (etching).
5   Thomas H. Creighton, "Kiesler's Pursuit of an Idea", in *Progressive Architecture* 7 (1961), 105.
6   Cf. Creighton, "Kiesler's Pursuit of an Idea", 105.
7   See above, 106.
8   "R.U.R." theater piece by Karl Čapek, staged by John Gottowt, Theater am Kurfürstendamm, Berlin (German first performance); ran from March 29 to May 31, 1923.

Berühmtheit erlangte Philip Johnsons Kommentar zu Kiesler als „größtem nicht-bauenden Architekten unserer Zeit".[52] Doch wie das Zitat weitergeht, wird oft vergessen: „[…] aber seine Ideen sind tiefgreifend, sein Einfluss enorm. Sein Konzept des *Endless House* […] ist eines der wenigen originellen Konzepte unserer Zeit."[53] Von einer Zeitung um eine schriftliche Reaktion gebeten, erklärte Kiesler: „Es ist wahr, dass ich wiederholt rein kommerzielle Aufträge abgelehnt habe. Ich bin noch immer der Ansicht, dass es besser ist, sich auf ein paar ehrliche Möglichkeiten des Bauens zu konzentrieren und ansonsten zu warten, gleichgültig ob man ‚der größte nicht-bauende Architekt unserer Zeit', genannt wird, als, wie es manchmal der Fall ist, ein meist-bauender Nicht-Architekt zu sein."[54] Als kompromissloser Visionär ging er in die Architekturgeschichte ein (Abb. 22).

9 "The Emperor Jones", theater piece by Eugene O'Neill, staged by Berthold Viertel, Lustspieltheater, Berlin; ran from Jan. 8 to 18, 1924.

10 In the language usage at the time, the word "nigger" did not have a discriminating connotation. It was indeed the word commonly used to refer to a dark-skinned person.

11 Hans Richter, *Köpfe und Hinterköpfe* (Zürich: Die Arche, 1967), 77. (Translated from German)

12 "Internationale Ausstellung neuer Theatertechnik" (International Exhibition of New Theater Techniques), exhibition at the Wiener Konzerthaus as part of the Music and Theater Festival of the City of Vienna, ran from Sept. 24 – Oct. 12, 1924.

13 Friedrich Kiesler, "Das Railway-Theater", in *Internationale Ausstellung neuer Theatertechnik* (exhibition catalog), ed. Friedrich Kiesler (Vienna, 1924), no page(s) indicated. (Translated from German)

14 Frederick Kiesler, *Contemporary Art Applied in the Store and its Display* (New York: Brentano's, 1930), 48.

15 See above.

16 Frederick J. Kiesler, "Art and Architecture. Notes on the Spiral-Theme in Recent Architecture", in *Partisan Review* 1 (1946), 98–104.

17 Stefi Kiesler, née Stephanie Frischer, was born in Skotschau in 1897. In Vienna she met Frederick Kiesler, whom she wed at the Vienna synagogue on Seitenstettengasse in 1920.

18 "International Theater Exposition", exhibition at the Steinway Building, New York; ran from Feb. 27 to March 21, 1926.

19 Don Quaintance, "Erecting the Temple of Non-Objectivity: The Architectural Infancy of the Guggenheim Museum", in *The Museum of Non-Objective Painting. Hilla Rebay and the Origins of the Solomon R. Guggenheim Museum*, ed. Karole Vail (New York: Guggenheim Museum Publications, 2009), 184.

20 Cf. Kiesler, *Contemporary Art Applied*, 1930.

21 Frederick Kiesler in front of the opening poster of the "Film Guild Cinema." ÖFLKS, PHO 27977/1.

22 Cf. Frederick Kiesler, "A Festival Shelter. The Space Theater for Woodstock, N.Y.", in *Shelter* 4 (1932), 42–47.

23 Letter from Frederick and Stefi Kiesler to Nelly van Doesburg. ÖFLKS, LET 1018/0_N3. (Translated from German)

24 Laura McGuire, "Space House", in Space House, ed. Monika Pessler (Vienna: Austrian Frederick and Lillian Kiesler Private Foundation, 2012), n. pag. (19).

25 Op. cit., n. pag. (15).

26 Cf. Frederick J. Kiesler, "Notes on Architecture. The Space-House", in *Hound & Horn* 6 (1934), 293–297.

1 Lisa Phillips, „Architect of Endless Innovation", in *Frederick Kiesler*, hg. v. Lisa Phillips (New York: Whitney Museum of American Art/W.W. Norton & Company, 1989), 13. (Übersetzt aus dem Englischen)

2 *Art in America* 2 (1966): 53. (Übersetzt aus dem Englischen)

3 Für eine Chronologie zu Kieslers Leben und Werk vgl. Dieter Bogner und Matthias Boeckl, „Friedrich Kiesler 1890–1965", in *Friedrich Kiesler. Architekt Maler Bildhauer 1890–1965*, hg. v. Dieter Bogner (Wien: Löcker, 1988), 8–191. Eine detaillierte Rekonstruktion seiner ersten drei Lebensjahrzehnte findet sich in Barbara Lesák, *Die Kulisse explodiert. „Friedrich Kieslers Theaterexperimente und Architekturprojekte 1923–1925"* (Wien: Löcker, 1988), 7–31.

4 Laut Auskunft des Universitätsarchivs der Akademie der bildenden Künste Wien hat Kiesler dort bereits 1908 die Aufnahmeprüfung abgelegt, wurde allerdings abgelehnt. Daraufhin inskribierte er im Wintersemester 1908/09 an der k. k. Technischen Hochschule, wo er ein Jahr lang studierte. Der erneute Antritt bei der Aufnahmeprüfung an der Akademie im Jahr 1910 war erfolgreich. Insgesamt sechs Semester absolvierte Kiesler dort, zwei davon in der Allgemeinen Malerschule und vier in der Spezialschule von Ferdinand Schmutzer (Kupferstecherei).

5 Thomas H. Creighton, „Kiesler's Pursuit of an Idea", in *Progressive Architecture* 7 (1961): 105. (Übersetzt aus dem Englischen)

6 Vgl. Creighton, „Kiesler's Pursuit of an Idea", 105.

7 Vgl. Creighton, „Kiesler's Pursuit of an Idea", 106.

8 *W.U.R.*, Theaterstück von Karel Čapek, Inszenierung von John Gottowt, Theater am Kurfürstendamm, Berlin (deutschsprachige Erstaufführung); Laufzeit: 29. März bis 31. Mai 1923.

9 „Kaiser Jones", Theaterstück von Eugene O'Neill, Inszenierung von Berthold Viertel, Lustspieltheater, Berlin; Laufzeit: 8. bis 18. Januar 1924.

10 Im damaligen Sprachgebrauch war das Wort „Neger" nicht diskriminierend konnotiert, sondern die gängige Bezeichnung für einen dunkelhäutigen Menschen.

11 Hans Richter, Köpfe und Hinterköpfe", (Zürich: Die Arche, 1967), 77.

12 *Internationale Ausstellung neuer Theatertechnik*, Ausstellung im Wiener Konzerthaus im Rahmen des Musik- und Theaterfestes der Stadt Wien; Laufzeit: 24. September – 12. Oktober 1924.

13 Friedrich Kiesler, „Das Railway-Theater", in *Internationale Ausstellung neuer Theatertechnik* (Ausstellungskatalog), hg. v. Friedrich Kiesler (Wien, 1924), o.S.

14 Friedrich Kiesler, „Vitalbau – Raumstadt – Funktionelle

27 Cf. Laura McGuire, "Space Within—Frederick Kiesler and the Architecture of an Idea" (PhD diss., The University of Texas at Austin, 2014), 220. On the "Structural Study Associates" cf. Joachim Krausse, *Unsichtbare Architektur. Knud Lönberg-Holm und die Structural Study Associates* (Nürnberg: AdBK, 2011).

28 Bogner and Boeckl, "Friedrich Kiesler 1890–1965", 91.

29 Cf. Frederick J. Kiesler, "On Correalism and Biotechnique. Definition and Test of a New Approach to Building Design", in *Architectural Record* 3 (1939), 60–75.

30 Frederick Kiesler, "Brief Note on Designing the Gallery", (typescript), ÖFLKS, TXT 188/0_N2.

31 Leo Lerman, "Before Band Wagons", in *Vogue*, Oct. 1, 1943, 141.

32 "Bloodflames 1947", exhibition at the Hugo Gallery, New York, opening on March 3, 1947.

33 "Exposition Internationale du Surréalisme", exhibition at the Galerie Maeght, Paris, ran from July 7 to Sept. 30, 1947.

34 Cf. Frederick Kiesler, "Manifeste du Corréalisme", in *L'Architecture d'Aujourd'hui* 2 (1949), 79–105.

35 "The Muralist and the Modern Architect", exhibition at the Kootz Gallery, New York; opening on Oct. 3, 1950. The exhibition ran until Oct. 23, 1950. The participating architects were: The Architects Collaborative, Marcel Breuer, Philip Johnson, Frederick Kiesler and Town Planning Associates; participating painters and sculptors: William Baziotes, Adolph Gottlieb, David Hare, Hans Hofmann and Robert Motherwell.

36 Bogner and Boeckl, "Friedrich Kiesler 1890–1965", 141.

37 Frederick Kiesler, "Frederick J. Kiesler's Endless House and Its Psychological Lighting", in *Interiors* 4 (1950), 122–129.

38 "Two Houses: New Ways to Build", exhibition at the Museum of Modern Art, New York; ran from Aug. 27 – Oct. 13, 1952.

39 Regarding the cited design sketches, there are two different opinions: Barbara Lesák attributed them to a planned new building of the Juillard School of Music in the late 1950s and Gerd Zillner saw them as being an addition in 1951 which was commissioned but never realized. The author of this text agrees with the second view. On the discussion cf. Barbara Lesák und Thomas Trabitsch, ed., *Frederick Kiesler. Theatervisionär – Architekt – Künstler* (Vienna: Brandstätter, 2012), 235.

40 Cf. Gerd Zillner, "Unknown & Unbuilt? Kiesler's Architectural Projects from the 1950s", in *Unknown & Unbuilt? Kiesler's Architectural Projects from the 1950s*, ed. Peter Bogner (Vienna: Austrian Frederick and Lillian Kiesler Private Foundation, 2014), 16–23.

Architektur ", in *De Stijl* 10&11 (1925), 144.

15 Kiesler, „Vitalbau – Raumstadt – Funktionelle Architektur ", 144.

16 Frederick J. Kiesler, „Art and Architecture. Notes on the Spiral-Theme in Recent Architecture ", in *Partisan Review* 1 (1946): 98–104.

17 Stefi Kiesler, geboren Stephanie Frischer, wurde 1897 in Skotschau geboren. In Wien lernte sie Friedrich Kiesler kennen, den sie 1920 in der Wiener Synagoge in der Seitenstettengasse heiratete.

18 *International Theatre Exposition*, Ausstellung im Steinway Building, New York; Laufzeit: 27. Februar bis 21. März 1926.

19 Don Quaintance, „Erecting the Temple of Non-Objectivity: The Architectural Infancy of the Guggenheim Museum ", in *The Museum of Non-Objective Painting. Hilla Rebay and the Origins of the Solomon R. Guggenheim Museum*, hg. v. Karole Vail (New York: Guggenheim Museum Publications, 2009), 184. (Übersetzt aus dem Englischen)

20 Vgl. Frederick Kiesler, „Contemporary Art Applied to the Store and its Display" (New York: Brentano's, 1930).

21 Friedrich Kiesler vor dem Eröffnungsplakat des „Film Guild Cinema". ÖFLKS, PHO 27977/1.

22 Vgl. dazu Frederick Kiesler, „A Festival Shelter. The Space Theatre for Woodstock, N.Y. ", in *Shelter* 4 (1932): 42–47.

23 Brief von Friedrich und Stefi Kiesler an Nelly van Doesburg. ÖFLKS, LET 1018/0_N3.

24 Laura McGuire, „Space House ", in *Space House*, hg. v. Monika Pessler (Wien: Österreichische Friedrich und Lillian Kiesler-Privatstiftung, 2012), o.S. [10]

25 McGuire, „Space House ", o.S. [5]

26 Vgl. Frederick J. Kiesler, „Notes on Architecture. The Space-House ", in *Hound & Horn* 6 (1934): 293–297.

27 Vgl. Laura McGuire, „Space Within —Frederick Kiesler and the Architecture of an Idea" (PhD diss., The University of Texas at Austin, 2014), 220. Zu den „Structural Study Assoicates" vgl. Joachim Krausse, *Unsichtbare Architektur. Knud Lönberg-Holm und die Structural Study Associates* (Nürnberg: AdBK, 2011).

28 Bogner und Boeckl, „Friedrich Kiesler 1890–1965", 91.

29 Vgl. Frederick J. Kiesler, „On Correalism and Biotechnique. Definition and Test of a New Approach to Building Design ", in *Architectural Record* 3 (1939), 60–75.

30 Frederick Kiesler, „Brief Note on Designing the Gallery ", (Typoskript), ÖFLKS, TXT 188/0_N2. (Übersetzt aus dem Englischen)

31 Leo Lerman, „Before Band Wagons ", in *Vogue*, 1. Oktober 1943, 141. (Übersetzt aus dem Englischen)

32 *Bloodflames 1947*, Ausstellung in der Hugo Gallery, New York; Eröffnung: 3. März 1947.

41 "Flowing Gallery", *TIME Magazine*, Feb. 4, 1957, 60.

42 Frederick J. Kiesler, "The art of architecture for art", in *Art News* 6 (1957), 38–43, 50, 52, 54.

43 Frederick J. Kiesler, "Design in continuity: The World House Gallery", in *Architectural Forum* 4 (1957), 126–131.

44 Kiesler, "The art of architecture for art", 52.

45 Letter from Frederick J. Kiesler to Bruno Zevi from Jan. 16, 1958. ÖFLKS, LET 2185/0_N2v.

46 Frederick J. Kiesler, "Eine neue Akropolis", in *Aufbau*, 28 May 1965, 16. (Translated from German)

47 "Visionary Architecture", exhibition at the Museum of Modern Art, New York, ran from Sept. 29 to Dec. 4, 1960.

48 "New concepts of architecture", in *Harper's Bazaar* 2975 (1959), 183.

49 Cf. Frederick Kiesler, "The Universal", in *The Ideal*

Theater: Eight Concepts (exhibition catalog) (New York: American Federation of Arts, 1964), 93–104.

50 Frederick Kiesler, untitled, (typescript), ÖFLKS, TXT 2971/0_N2.

51 Cf. Frederick Kiesler, "The Grotto for Meditation", in *Craft Horizons* 4 (1966), 22–27.

52 Philip Johnson, "Three Architects", in *Art in America* 1 (1960), 70.

53 Ibid.

54 Frederick J. Kiesler, "Building Architect. To the Art Editor", in *New York Sunday Times*, April 17, 1960.

33 *Exposition Internationale du Surréalisme*, Ausstellung in der Galerie Maeght, Paris; Laufzeit: 7. Juli bis 30. September 1947.

34 Vgl. Frederick Kiesler, „Manifeste du Corréalisme", in *L'Architecture d'Aujourd'hui* 2 (1949): 79–105.

35 *The Muralist and the Modern Architect*, Ausstellung in der Kootz Gallery, New York; Eröffnung am 03.10.1950. Die Ausstellung lief bis 23. Oktober 1950. Die beteiligten Architekten waren: The Architects Collaborative, Marcel Breuer, Philip Johnson, Friedrich Kiesler und Town Planning Associates; beteiligte Maler und Bildhauer: William Baziotes, Adolph Gottlieb, David Hare, Hans Hofmann und Robert Motherwell.

36 Bogner und Boeckl, „Friedrich Kiesler 1890–1965", 141.

37 Frederick Kiesler, „Frederick J. Kiesler's Endless House and Its Psychological Lighting", in *Interiors* 4 (1950): 122–129. (Übersetzt aus dem Englischen)

38 „Two Houses: New Ways to Build", Ausstellung im Museum of Modern Art, New York; Ausstellungsdauer: 27. August bis 13. Oktober 1952.

39 Zu den genannten Entwurfszeichnungen gibt es zwei unterschiedliche Auffassungen: Barbara Lesák ordnet sie einem geplanten Neubau der Juilliard School of Music in den späten 1950er Jahren zu, Gerd Zillner einem in Auftrag gegebenen, jedoch nicht ausgeführten Erweiterungsbau 1951. Die Autorin des vorliegenden Textes schließt sich der zweiten Meinung an. Zur Diskussion vgl. hg. v. Barbara Lesák und Thomas Trabitsch, Frederick Kiesler. Theatervisionär – Architekt – Künstler (Wien: Brandstätter, 2012), 235.

40 Vgl. Gerd Zillner, „Unbekannt & ungebaut? Kieslers Architekturprojekte der 1950er Jahre", in *Unbekannt & ungebaut? Kieslers Architekturprojekte der 1950er Jahre*, hg. v. Peter Bogner (Wien:

Österreichische Friedrich und Lillian Kiesler-Privatstiftung, 2014), 5–15.

41 „Flowing Gallery", *TIME*, 4. Feb. 1957, 60. (Übersetzt aus dem Englischen)

42 Frederick J. Kiesler, „The art of architecture for art", in *Art News* 6 (1957): 38–43, 50, 52, 54.

43 Frederick J. Kiesler, „Design in continuity: The World House Gallery", in *Architectural Forum* 4 (1957): 126–131.

44 Kiesler, „The art of architecture for art", 52. (Übersetzt aus dem Englischen)

45 Brief von Frederick J. Kiesler an Bruno Zevi vom 16.01.1958. ÖFLKS, LET 2185/0_N2v. (Übersetzt aus dem Englischen)

46 Frederick J. Kiesler, „Eine neue Akropolis", in *Aufbau*, 28. Mai 1965, 16.

47 *Visionary Architecture*, Ausstellung im Museum of Modern Art, New York; Laufzeit: 29. September bis 4. Dezember 1960.

48 „New concepts of architecture",
in *Harper's Bazaar* 2975 (1959):
183. (Übersetzt aus dem
Englischen)

49 Vgl. Frederick Kiesler, „The
Universal", in *The Ideal Theatre:
Eight Concepts*
(Ausstellungskatalog) (New York:
American Federation of Arts,
1964), 93–104.

50 Frederick Kiesler, o.T.,
(Typoskript), ÖFLKS, TXT 2971/0_
N2. (Übersetzt aus dem
Englischen)

51 Vgl. Frederick Kiesler, „The Grotto
for Meditation", in *Craft Horizons*
4 (1966): 22–27. (Übersetzt aus
dem Englischen)

52 Philip Johnson, „Three Architects",
in *Art in America* 1 (1960): 70.
(Übersetzt aus dem Englischen)

53 Johnson, „Three Architects", 70.
(Übersetzt aus dem Englischen)

54 Frederick J. Kiesler, „Building
Architect. To the Art Editor", in
New York Sunday Times, 17. April
1960. (Übersetzt aus dem
Englischen)

Energy, Correalism, and the *Endless House*

Laura M. McGuire

Energie, Correalismus und das *Endless House*

> "The house must become a cosmos in itself, a transformer of
> life-forces, which develop naturally in this man-made environment to
> incredible dimensions of space and seclusion. The house must
> no longer vegetate as leprosy and warts on the earth's surface, but
> must take its place in the world of creations like a crystal, a planet,
> a fruit, an eye and muscle, an atom. It must become a creature,
> an aggregate of forces that add up to a new body."
> —Frederick Kiesler, untitled and undated manuscript.[1]

For Frederick Kiesler, architecture was the crystallization of environmental
energies, harnessed and directed into forms by a scientist-architect.
The *Endless House* was the culmination of this architectural philosophy developed over the long course of his professional life. He conceptualized the
house around a peculiar theory that energy exchanges between people and
the natural environment comprised all human material culture, a concept
that would lead him to develop his idea of *Correalism* in the late 1930s.
Correalism was a broad philosophical outlook that considered the intrinsic
interconnections between phenomena in the natural world and in human
culture and life—it was anthropological (and ostensibly scientific) as much

> „Das Haus muss endlich ein Kosmos in sich selbst werden, ein
> Transformator von Lebenskräften, die sich natürlich in dieser
> künstlichen Umgebung zu unglaublichen Dimensionen der Weite und
> Zurückgezogenheit entwickeln. Das Wohnhaus muss nicht mehr
> als Aussatz und Warze der Erdoberfläche vegetieren, sondern einem
> Kristall, einem Planeten, einer Frucht, einem Auge und Muskel,
> einem Atom gleich, seinen Platz in der Welt der Kreationen einnehmen.
> Es muss Kreatur werden, ein Aggregat von Kräften, die sich zu
> einem neuen Körper verbinden."
> —Friedrich Kiesler, ohne Titel, undatiertes Manuskript.[1]

Für Friedrich Kiesler war Architektur die Kristallisation von Umweltenergien,
die durch einen forschenden Architekten dirigiert und nutzbar gemacht wurden.
Das *Endless House* bildete den Höhepunkt dieser im Laufe seines langen
Berufslebens entwickelten Architekturphilosophie. Seine Konzeption des
Hauses beruht auf einer ganz besonderen Theorie, wonach der Energieaus-
tausch zwischen den Menschen und ihrer natürlichen Umgebung die gesamte
materielle Kultur beinhaltet. Diese Vorstellung mündete in den späten
1930er Jahren in die Entwicklung seines Konzepts des *Correalismus*. Diese

as it was architectural (Fig. 1). To grasp the purpose of the *Endless House's*
ceaseless curvatures, we must understand the house not as a formal
organization of floors, walls, and ceilings, but as Kiesler's vision of an enclosure that transcended discrete structural elements and operated
as a vessel to concentrate and enhance human life energies.

Because he completed few built works, Kiesler's status as a theorist may
be stronger than his reputation as an architect. He labored on the *Endless
House* for almost twenty years between 1944 and 1965, executing numerous
drawings and multiple models. A lack of sufficient technology for its construction, not to mention a suitable client, relegated the *Endless House* to the
pages of architecture magazines and fodder for museum exhibitions. The
house also foundered in Kiesler's continuous redesigning toward increasingly
unrealizable plastic and biomorphic forms. In 1960, Philip Johnson called
Kiesler the "greatest non-building architect of our time."[2] Johnson opined that
Kiesler's inability to complete his projects was because he "could not bear
endings" at a personal level.[3] Yet there was also a methodological basis in
Kiesler's disposition toward *endlessness*. Endings were fundamentally
antithetical to his overarching philosophy of design. If objects and buildings
were to be developed in a Correalistic universe—an ever-changing web of

umfassende philosophische Anschauung, die die wesenhaften Zusammenhänge zwischen den Phänomenen der natürlichen Welt einerseits und
der Kultur des Menschen sowie des Lebens andererseits betrachtete, war
ebensosehr anthropologisch (und angeblich wissenschaftlich) als auch
architektonisch geprägt (Abb. 1). Damit sich der Zweck der kontinuierlichen
Krümmungen des *Endless House* erschließt, ist das Haus nicht als formale Anordnung von Böden, Wänden und Decken zu verstehen, sondern
Kieslers Vorstellung entsprechend als ein Gehäuse, das einzelne
Strukturelemente transzendiert und als Behälter für die Konzentration und
die Verstärkung menschlicher Lebensenergien dient.

Da Kiesler wenige Bauwerke fertigstellte, genießt er wohl einen höheren
Status als Theoretiker im Vergleich zu seiner Reputation als Architekt.
Zwischen 1944 und 1965 – über einen Zeitraum von beinahe zwanzig Jahren –
arbeitete er unermüdlich an dem *Endless House*, wobei er zahlreiche Skizzen
sowie eine Vielzahl an Modellen anfertigte. Der Mangel an ausreichenden
Technologien für die bauliche Umsetzung, von einem geeigneten Auftraggeber
ganz zu schweigen, verbannte das *Endless House* auf die Seiten von
Architekturzeitschriften und den Ausstellungsraum in Museen. Was ebenso
zum Scheitern des Hauses führte waren Kieslers ständige Überarbeitungen

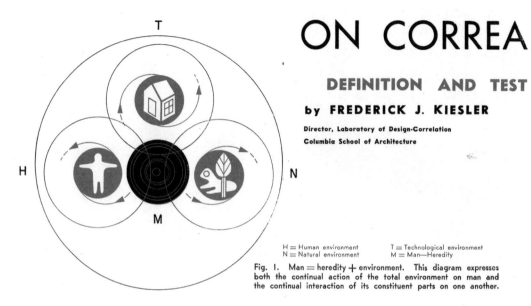

ON CORREA

DEFINITION AND TEST

by FREDERICK J. KIESLER

Director, Laboratory of Design-Correlation
Columbia School of Architecture

H = Human environment   T = Technological environment
N = Natural environment   M = Man—Heredity

Fig. I. Man = heredity + environment. This diagram expresses both the continual action of the total environment on man and the continual interaction of its constituent parts on one another.

1—Frederick Kiesler, *Man = heredity + environment*, diagram published
in *Architectural Record*, 1939

in Richtung immer weniger realisierbarer plastischer und biomorpher Formen. Im Jahr 1960 bezeichnete Philip Johnson Kiesler als den „größten nicht bauenden Architekten unserer Zeit".[2] Johnson zufolge war Kieslers Unvermögen, seine Projekte zu verwirklichen, darauf zurückzuführen, dass er auf persönlicher Ebene „keine Endpunkte ertragen konnte".[3] Dennoch hatte Kieslers Neigung zum *Endlosen* auch eine methodologische Grundlage. Endpunkte bildeten einen klaren Gegensatz zu seiner übergeordneten Design-Philosophie. Wenn Objekte und Gebäude in einem *correalistischen* Universum – einem sich ständig verändernden Geflecht aus Umweltkräften und Tätigkeiten des menschlichen Lebens – entstehen sollten, dann stellte eine iterative und intrinsisch unvollendete Design-Methode die einzig authentische Lösung des Problems der menschlichen Behausung dar. Ähnlich dem formalen Thema der Endlosigkeit der Böden des Hauses, die in Wänden und Decken übergingen und sich dann wieder zurückbildeten, war Kieslers Design-Prozess daher ebenso von kontinuierlichen Zyklen bestimmt.

Energie-Architektur
Kiesler artikulierte seine Ideen, die sowohl die Grundlage seiner Theorie des *Correalismus* und seines Entwurfs des *Endless House* bilden würden,

2—Frederick Kiesler, *Space House*, New York 1933

environmental forces and human life activities—an iterative and intrinsically
unfinished design method was the only authentic solution to the problem
of human habitation. Thus akin to the formal theme of endlessness in the
house's floors, which became walls and ceilings and back again, continuous
cycles also governed Kiesler's design process.

Energy Architecture

Kiesler first articulated the ideas that would form the basis of both his theory
of Correalism and his design for the *Endless House* in his *Space House* project
of 1933 (Fig. 2). The *Space House* was to be a die-cast shell of thin metal
whose interior would be coated with rubber in order to deaden ambient noise,
resembling the shell of an egg.[4] Automatic doorways, lighting controls, and
climate control would regulate the environment.[5] In published and unpublished
notes, he explained that he had conceptualized the *Space House* as a
"generator for the individual," in which the sensory environments created
by temperature, color, and material combinations worked together to enhance
life activities (Fig. 3).[6] More enigmatically, he believed that a house with
continuous shell construction and mobile interior partitions (Fig. 4) could
charge a resident like a battery cell. Through enclosure in a sleeping area or

erstmals im 1933 entstandenen Projekt des *Space House* (Abb. 2). Dieses war
konzipiert als eine aus Dünnblech gefertigte Druckgussschale und ähnelte
einer Eierschale. Das Innere war zur Dämpfung von Umgebungsgeräuschen mit
Gummi beschichtet.[4] Automatische Türöffnungen, Lichtsteuerungs- und
Klimasysteme sollten der Regulierung der Umwelt dienen.[5] In sowohl veröffentlichten als auch unveröffentlichten Notizen erläuterte er, das *Space House*
als „Generator für das Individuum" konzipiert zu haben, in dem durch das Zusammenwirken der aus Temperatur, Farbe und Materialkombinationen
erzeugten sensorischen Umgebungen die Lebensaktivitäten verbessert wurden
(Abb. 3).[6] Hintergründiger war wohl seine Auffassung, wonach ein Haus mit
kontinuierlicher Schalenkonstruktion und beweglichen Innenraumtrennwänden
(Abb. 4) einen Bewohner wie eine Batteriezelle aufladen konnte. Durch
die Abschirmung in einem Schlafbereich oder einem Arbeitszimmer sollte sich
eine Rückgewinnung und Sammlung der körperlichen Energien vollziehen.
Die nachfolgende Entfernung der Trennwände (bzw. deren Versetzung in einen
anderen Teil des Hauses ermöglichte die Verteilung dieser Energien in der
lokalen Umgebung – Kiesler verstand die materiellen Werke der menschlichen
Schöpfung als „Energie-Zentren und Kraftansammlungen".[7] Kieslers
Formulierungen zur Beschreibung der Funktion des Hauses stammen direkt

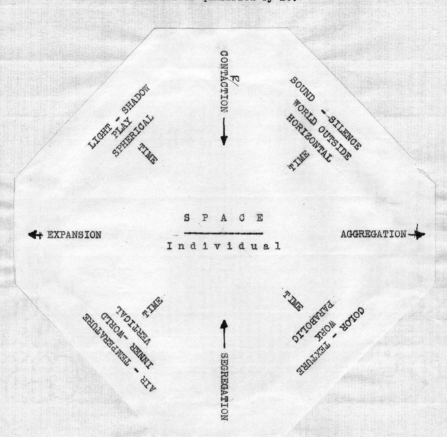

- 12 -

METABOLISM CHART OF THE HOUSE

Illustrating the operation of the Two-Way-Principle
regarding sensory properties, mobile space enclosures,
and the individual as qualified by it.

FOOTNOTE
x) Metabolism: The individual passing through time as
subjected to two forces; Anabolism: building up;
Catabolism: breaking down.

3—Frederick Kiesler, *Metabolism Chart of the House*, New York 1933

4—Frederick Kiesler, *Space House*, rubber curtain for room partition, New York 1933

study, the body would recuperate and gather its energy. The subsequent removal of partitions (or movement to another part of the house) allowed this energy to be dispersed into the local environment—Kiesler believed physical works of human creation were centers of "energy" and "accumulation[s] of power."[7] He borrowed directly from biology to articulate the function of the house, describing it as enabling a process of anabolism (the metabolic phase in which simple molecules are synthesized into more complex ones storing energy) and catabolism (the phase during which complex molecules break down into simpler ones and release energy).[8] The *Space House* would regulate the "spiritual metabolism of individuals," with the ultimate goal of facilitating more productive lives.[9]

Kiesler probably derived his pseudo-scientific ideas about architecture's effect on human energy metabolism from diverse Central European theories of psychology and physiology, as well as from thermodynamics.[10] It is also likely he drew on William James's *On Vital Reserves* (1911), which elucidated the effects of the environment on physical and mental energy.[11] In this popular work, James suggested that energy could be physically transferred from an environment to a person, affecting psychological and physiological structures in accordance with surroundings. He also emphasized the physical and mental

aus der Biologie. Diese bestehe in der Aktivierung eines anabolen Prozesses, d. h. der metabolischen Phase, in der einfache Moleküle zu komplexeren synthetisiert werden, wo Energie gespeichert wird, und eines katabolen Prozesses, d. h. der Phase, in der komplexe Moleküle in einfachere aufgespalten werden, die Energie freisetzen.[8] Das *Space House* sollte den „spirituellen Metabolismus von Individuen" regulieren, wobei das Ziel letztendlich in der Unterstützung eines produktiveren Lebens bestand.[9]

Vermutlich lassen sich Kieslers pseudowissenschaftliche Vorstellungen von den Auswirkungen der Architektur auf den menschlichen Energiemetabolismus auf verschiedene in Mitteleuropa verbreitete psychologische und physiologische Theorien sowie die Thermodynamik zurückführen.[10] Möglicherweise berief er sich ebenso auf das von William James verfasste Werk *On Vital Reserves* (1911), in dem die Wirkungen der Umwelt auf die physische und mentale Energie untersucht wurden.[11] In dieser berühmten Schrift postulierte der Autor die Möglichkeit einer physischen Übertragung von Energie aus der Umwelt auf einen Menschen, was dem Milieu entsprechend mit einer Beeinflussung psychischer und physiologischer Strukturen einherging. Ebenso betonte James das körperliche und geistige Bedürfnis nach Entspannung und Introspektion – Kiesler markierte relevante Passagen in James' Werk mit

need for relaxation and introspection—Kiesler marked relevant passages in James's book in pencil.[12] In the midst of a world of restless impressions, periodic isolation from surrounding stimuli was critical not only to the maintenance of one's self, but also to the execution and attainment of meaningful life activities and goals.[13] By suggesting that houses should facilitate the conservation and renewal of human energy, Kiesler may have conceptualized an architectural response to James's ideas: A house was like a beaker in which chemical processes sustained life, broke down to release energies, and generated new complexities.

He emphasized the metabolic and biological aspects of the *Space House* with his use of terms like "morphology," "Bio-Architecture," and "bio-technical" to describe his design.[14] With its ovoid, exterior metal membrane and mutable interior of free-moving enclosures, objects, and inhabitants, there is a profound sense in which the *Space House* was the architectural embodiment of an organic cell, or an atom circumnavigated by its swirling electrons. Referring to the latter metaphor, Kiesler in his notes explicitly defined architecture as "polarization," alluding to the balancing positive and negative charges of atomic structures.[15]

einem Bleistift.[12] In einer Welt ständig einstürmender Eindrücke war eine regelmäßige Absonderung von den Umgebungsreizen nicht nur für die Erhaltung des Selbst entscheidend, sondern auch für die Ausübung sinnvoller Lebensaktivitäten und die Erreichung von Zielen.[13] Mit seinem Vorschlag, dass Häuser die Erhaltung und Erneuerung menschlicher Energien begünstigen sollten, konzipierte Kiesler wohl eine architektonische Antwort auf James' Ideen: Ein Haus war gleichsam ein Reagenzglas, in dem chemische Prozesse lebenserhaltend wirkten, durch Zerlegung Energien freisetzten und neue komplexe Gebilde hervorbrachten.

Die auf den Stoffwechsel bezogenen und biologischen Aspekte des *Space House* hob er durch die Verwendung von Begriffen wie „Morphologie", „Bio-Architektur" und „bio-technisch" für die Beschreibung seines Designs hervor.[14] Mit seiner ovoiden Außenmembran aus Metall und dem wandelbaren Innenraum mit frei beweglichen Unterteilungen, Objekten und Bewohnern vermittelt das *Space House* den starken Eindruck der architektonischen Verkörperung einer organischen Zelle oder eines Atoms, um dessen Kern Elektronen wirbeln. In Bezug auf die zuletzt angeführte Metapher definierte Kiesler Architektur in seinen Aufzeichnungen explizit als „Polarisierung" in Anspielung auf den Ausgleich zwischen positiven und negativen Ladungen von Atomstrukturen.[15]

Correalism

Through the late 1930s and 1940s, Kiesler would continue to research
the relationship between energy and design, eventually developing a theory he
called *Correalism*. The term derived in part from his use of *correlation* in
his earlier projects and essays. In the early 1930s, he planned to establish a
design firm, CORRELATION INC., and publish a journal of the same name
that would cover diverse topics such as science, architecture, music and
dance.[16] His use of the term no doubt arose in conjunction with his affiliation
with the group Structural Study Associates; Buckminster Fuller and SSA
subtitled their magazine, *Shelter, a correlating medium for the forces of architecture.* Fuller's May 1932 editorial entitled *Correlation* outlined how
various designers had coordinated to form a unified program for *Shelter* and
SSA.[17] Kiesler would reuse the term several years later in the series of
Design Correlation essays he published in *Architectural Record* throughout
1937. The eclectic collection dealt with diverse topics including the design of
humane, curvilinear enclosures for zoo animals and the scientific evolution of photography and cinema in relation to human vision.[18] For Kiesler, correlation embodied the physically and psychologically interactive aspects of
design and the extent

Correalismus

Kiesler setzte seine Erforschung der Beziehungen zwischen Energie und
Design bis in die späten 1930er und 1940er fort und entwickelte letztendlich
jene Theorie, die er als *Correalismus* bezeichnete. Der Terminus leitete
sich zum Teil von dem in seinen früheren Projekten und Essays verwendeten
Begriff der *Korrelation* ab. Anfang der 1930er Jahre beabsichtigte er die
Gründung des Designunternehmens CORRELATION INC und die Veröffentli-
chung einer gleichnamigen Zeitschrift zu unterschiedlichen Themen wie
Wissenschaft, Architektur, Musik und Tanz.[16] Zweifellos kam sein Gebrauch
des Begriffs in Zusammenhang mit seiner Zugehörigkeit zur Gruppe Structural Study Associates auf; Buckminster Fuller und die SSA versahen ihre Zeitschrift *Shelter* mit dem Untertitel *ein Medium zur Korrelation der architektonischen Kräfte.* In seinem im Mai 1932 erschienenen Leitartikel *Correlation* skizzierte Fuller, wie sich verschiedene Designer zur Schaffung eines
einheitlichen Programms für *Shelter* und SSA zusammengetan haben.[17]
Mehrere Jahre später griff Kiesler den Begriff in der Serie der *Design Correlation*-Essays erneut auf, welche er im Laufe des gesamten Jahres 1937 im
Architectural Record publizierte. Die eklektische Sammlung widmete sich
verschiedenen Themen einschließlich des Designs humaner, kurvenförmiger

to which products and environments could be developed to respond to a "common denominator" of human health.[19]

That same year, he founded the Laboratory for Design Correlation at Columbia University's School of Architecture. The objective of the laboratory was to study methods of product design in relation to contemporary culture. Work at the laboratory would be both theoretical and practical in nature: Research would be undertaken to examine design as an evolutionary process and to "correlate design to the physical and psychological needs of the human being," in order to "develop new standards" for manufacturing.[20] The central objective of the laboratory was to teach students to identify pertinent physiological and environmental factors that should guide contemporary design methodologies (Fig. 5). Inspired partly by Harvard University's Fatigue Laboratory (which employed a staff of physiologists, chemists, biologists, and psychologists who studied exercise physiology, the effects of aging, and climate stress, as well as researched clothing and foodstuffs for military personnel), Kiesler's students studied human physiology and undertook time-motion and fatigue studies of manufacturing workers.[21] Kiesler's growing interest in fatigue science aligned closely with his earlier efforts to design an energy-enhancing house: In a lecture to his students, he

Gehäuse für Zootiere und der wissenschaftlichen Entwicklung der Fotografie und des Kinos im Verhältnis zum menschlichen Sehvermögen.[18] Kiesler zufolge verkörperte die Korrelation die physisch und psychologisch interaktiven Aspekte des Designs und zeigte das Ausmaß der Entwicklungsmöglichkeit von Produkten und Umgebungen als Antwort auf einen „gemeinsamen Nenner" menschlicher Gesundheit auf.[19]

Im gleichen Jahr gründete er an der School of Architecture der Columbia University das Laboratory for Design Correlation mit dem Ziel der Erforschung von Methoden der Produktgestaltung im Verhältnis zur zeitgenössischen Kultur. Die Arbeit am Laboratory war sowohl theoretisch als auch praktisch ausgerichtet. Die Forschungstätigkeit widmete sich dem Thema Design als evolutionärem Prozess, um „das Design mit den physischen und psychischen Bedürfnissen des Menschen zu korrelieren" mit dem Ziel der „Entwicklung neuer Standards" für die Fertigungsindustrie.[20] Das zentrale Anliegen des Laboratory bestand in der Vermittlung der Fähigkeit zur Identifizierung der relevanten physiologischen und umweltbedingten Faktoren, die als Grundlage für zeitgenössische Design-Methodologien dienen sollten (Abb. 5). Zum Teil angeregt durch das Fatigue Laboratory an der Harvard University (an dem ein Stab von Physiologen, Chemiker, Biologen und Psychologen sich

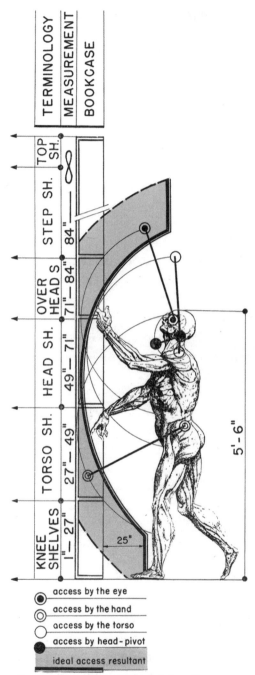

TERMINOLOGY / MEASUREMENT / BOOKCASE

TOP SH. — ∞

STEP SH. — 84"

OVER HEADS — 71"—84"

HEAD SH. — 49"—71"

TORSO SH. — 27"—49"

KNEE SHELVES — 1"—27"

5'-6"

25"

◉ access by the eye
◎ access by the hand
○ access by the torso
● access by head-pivot
▬ ideal access resultant

Fig. 12. Correlation-chart of book-storing. New measurements and terms.

5—Frederick Kiesler, Correalism-chart of book-storing, published in "Architectural Record", 1939

pronounced that architecture was primarily a regulator of fatigue and "regeneration" for the human body, and he described the practice of design as the production of "polarized and crystallized energy form[s]."[22]

From 1937—1938, Kiesler conceptualized a book that would promote his design ideas to the wider public. The planned title was *Correalism Biotechnic Architecture: From Architecture to Life.* In a prospectus, he promised that it would lay out a method of architectural practice based entirely on science, broadly defined. He explained that this new paradigm was necessary because science had shown that "everything influences everything," and designed objects and structures therefore had to respond to the "constant exchange of influences" if they were going to be properly adapted to serve human health. A Correalist architect was analogous to a physician who, through scientific research and treatments, fostered the effective performance of activity in people's daily lives and incorporated (or ameliorated) new events in a "continuous flow of … correlation."[23]

Although the book was never published, *Architectural Record* published Kiesler's essay, "Correalism and Biotechnique: A Definition and Test of a New Approach to Building Design", in 1939.[24] In this piece, Kiesler detailed a theory of interactive design based on his Correalist science of energetic

mit Fragen der Leistungsphysiologie, Auswirkungen des Alterungsprozesses und Klimabelastungen auseinandersetzten und auch Forschungsarbeiten zur Kleidung und zur Lebensmittelversorgung für das militärische Personal durchführten) widmeten sich Kieslers Studenten dem Studium der Humanphysiologie sowie Zeit-Bewegungs- und Ermüdungsuntersuchungen an Menschen, die in den verarbeitenden Industrien tätig waren.[21] Kieslers wachsendes Interesse an der Ermüdungswissenschaft stand in engem Zusammenhang mit seinen früheren Versuchen, ein energieverstärkendes Haus zu entwerfen: So erklärte er seinen Studenten im Rahmen einer Vorlesung, dass Architektur vor allem ein Regler der Ermüdung und der *Regeneration* des menschlichen Körpers sei und beschrieb die Gestaltungspraxis als die Produktion „polarisierter und kristallisierter Form[en] von Energie".[22]

Von 1937 bis 1938 entwarf Kiesler ein Buch, das seine Gestaltungsideen einer breiteren Öffentlichkeit zugänglich machte. Der vorgesehene Titel des Werks lautete *Correalism Biotechnic Architecture: From Architecture to Life.* In einem Prospekt stellte Kiesler in Aussicht, dass darin eine rein auf Wissenschaft im weitesten Sinne des Wortes beruhende Methode der Architekturpraxis beschrieben werden sollte. Wie Kiesler erläuterte, ergab sich die Notwendigkeit dieses neuen Paradigmas aus dem Umstand,

relationships. He painted a vision of a trembling world, flowing with energetic forces that comprised both humankind and its environment.

> The interrelation of organic and inorganic matter is a mutual bombardment of energies which have two characteristics: those of integration and those of disintegration. By means of gravitation, electricity generates energy into solids of visible matter. This is integration. By magnetism and radiation, electricity degenerates energy into tenuous, invisible matter. This is disintegration. If this general principle of anabolic and catabolic energies were the sole principle of existence, we would have a static, unchanging world. But these two forces (positive and negative) interchange through physico-chemical reactions, one force striving always for a preponderance over the other. In this way, variations are constantly created; and in this process of creation, new nuclear concepts and new environments are in continual formation…What we call *forms*, whether they are natural or artificial, are only the visible trading posts of integrating and disintegrating forces mutating at low rates of speed.[25]

Designed forms were a physical manifestation of environmental energies

dass die Wissenschaft gezeigt habe, dass „alles von allem beeinflusst" werde. Demzufolge mussten entworfene Objekte und Strukturen der „ständigen wechselseitigen Beeinflussung" Rechnung tragen, um in geeigneter Weise auf die menschliche Gesundheit ausgerichtet werden zu können. Ein correalistischer Architekt verhielt sich analog zu einem Mediziner, der über die wissenschaftliche Forschung und Behandlungen eine Förderung der effektiven Leistung der Alltagsaktivitäten der Menschen bewirkte und neue Ereignisse in einen „ständigen Fluss der … Korrelation" inkorporierte (oder verbesserte).[23]

Obwohl das Buch unveröffentlicht blieb, publizierte Architectural Record Kieslers Essay „Correalism and Biotechnique: A Definition and Test of a New Approach to Building Design" im Jahre 1939.[24] In diesem Werk bot Kiesler detaillierte Ausführungen zu einer Theorie der interaktiven Gestaltung, deren Grundlage seine Wissenschaft des Correalismus der Energieverhältnisse bildete. Er schilderte die Vision einer bebenden Welt, die von energetischen Kräften durchflossen wurde, welche sowohl die Menschheit als auch deren Umgebung miteinbezog:

> Die Wechselbeziehung zwischen organischer und anorganischer Substanz gestaltet sich als gegenseitiger Beschuss mit Energien,

which were constantly in flux. If the architect was to advance human health and society in a positive way, it was necessary to develop a science of architecture in relationship to the forces it sought to control and direct. Drawings from the *Laboratory for Design Correlation* pinpointed design activity as the "field of plastic creation" between human cognitive and sensory structures, the environment, and the inanimate object. "Biotechnique" was Kiesler's proposed design method to direct unregulated forces of energy into objects. One of the first natural results of applying biotechnique to architecture, for example, would be the standardization of "continuous construction" shells for building, eliminating fussy perpendicular joints that inhibited flows of energy. Biotechnique also recognized that continuously shifting forces in human environments rendered "functionality" a mutable thing.[26] Good architectural form could therefore only develop using an interactive, iterative approach to design.[27]

Ten years later, in the 1949 essay "Pseudo-Functionalism in Modern Architecture", published in the journal *Partisan Review*, he reiterated his earlier calls for interactive design methodology and sharply criticized so-called functionalism as an oversimplification of human needs in favor of reductionist asceticism.[28] Were design to be truly functional, Kiesler contended,

> die durch zwei Merkmale gekennzeichnet sind: die Integration und die Desintegration. Aufgrund der Gravitation wird in Festkörpern aus sichtbarer Materie durch Elektrizität Energie generiert. Darin besteht die Integration. Durch Magnetismus und Strahlung wird Energie durch Elektrizität in wenig schwere, unsichtbare Materie degeneriert. In diesem Fall liegt Desintegration vor. Wäre jenes der anabolen und katabolen Prozessen unterliegenden Energien das alleinige Prinzip der Existenz, so würden wir in einer statischen, sich nicht verändernden Welt leben. Es vollzieht sich jedoch ein Austausch dieser beiden (positiven und negativen) Kräfte durch chemisch-physikalische Reaktionen, wobei eine Kraft stets nach einem Überhang gegenüber der anderen strebt. Auf diese Weise entstehen ständig Variationen; im Rahmen dieses Entstehungsprozesses findet eine kontinuierliche Bildung neuer Nuklearkonzepte und neuer Umgebungen statt ... Was wir als *Formen* bezeichnen – seien sie natürlich oder künstlich – sind nur die sichtbaren Handelsstationen der sich langsam verändernden integrierenden und desintegrierenden Kräfte.[25]

Gestaltete Formen waren eine physische Manifestation ständig im Fluss befindlicher Umweltenergien. Eine positive Verstärkung der Gesundheit des

progressive iteration had to form its basis. Since he believed that architecture and objects existed in fields of continuous energy exchange, advantageous design would manifest at the points of interaction between consciousness, intention, and the environment. A "law of creative transmutation" was the only authentic approach for a "true functionialist," and he illustrated this with a diagram that represented the design process as "creation-mutation," in which "existing facts" would flow into a "new objective" resulting in a "new object." Over time, the ideal process would repeat itself infinitely (Fig. 6).[29]

The same year, Kiesler's "Manifeste du Corréalisme" was published in *L'Architecture d'Aujourd'hui*.[30] He reiterated his conclusion that architects had to study the energy transfers between people, environmental forces, and the inanimate. Understanding these relationships would allow architects to generate an authentically human-centered architecture through which people could finally "back up" and "re-enter ourselves." Moreover, he vividly described architectural space as having an atomic structure and behaving like a "cellular nucleus," with building elements such as surface, colors, and lights comprising architectonic "electrons, neutrons, protons, mesons and positrons." (Fig. 7) He claimed that he had discovered an "enigmatic language" in his designs that could be gradually translated into "weights and measures"

Menschen und der Gesellschaft durch die Architektur erforderte die Entwicklung einer Wissenschaft der Architektur im Verhältnis zu den Kräften, nach deren Steuerung und Lenkung sie trachtete. Die Entwürfe des *Laboratory for Design Correlation* identifizierten die Designtätigkeit als das zwischen den menschlichen kognitiven und sensorischen Strukturen, der Umwelt und dem unbelebten Objekt abgesteckte „Feld der plastischen Gestaltung". Die „Biotechnik" war die von Kiesler vorgeschlagene Design- methode zur Lenkung ungeregelter energetischer Kräfte in Objekte. Eines der ersten natürlichen Resultate der Anwendung der Biotechnik auf die Architektur war beispielsweise die Standardisierung der „kontinuierlichen" Schalen-„Konstruktion" für Bauwerke, welche die den Energiefluss behindern- den überfrachteten Stoßfugen beseitigten. Ebenso nahm die Biotechnik den Umstand zur Kenntnis, dass „Funktionalität" durch die ständige Verschie- bung der Kräfte im menschlichen Umfeld veränderlich wurde.[26] Daher konnte nur ein interaktiver, iterativer Designansatz zur Entwicklung guter archi- tektonischer Formen führen.[27]

Zehn Jahre später wiederholte er in dem in der Zeitschrift *Partisan Review* erschienenen Essay „Pseudo-Functionalism in Modern Architecture" von 1949 seine früheren Forderungen nach einer interaktiven Designmethodologie

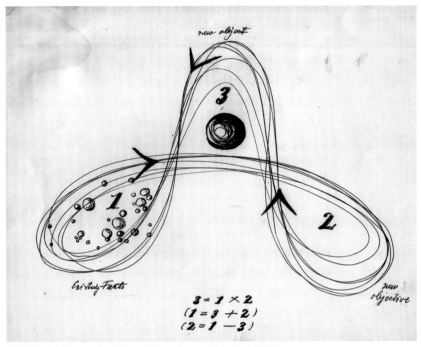

6—Frederick Kiesler, *Creation-mutation diagram*, New York 1947

und übte scharfe Kritik am so genannten Funktionalismus, den er als zu starke Vereinfachung der menschlichen Bedürfnisse zugunsten eines reduktionistischen Asketismus bezeichnete.[28] Kiesler erhob den Einwand, dass progressive Iteration als Grundlage verwendet werden musste, wenn Design tatsächlich funktional sein sollte. Da die Architektur und die Objekte nach seiner Überzeugung in Feldern kontinuierlichen Energieaustausches existierten, würde sich vorteilhaftes Design an den Interaktionspunkten zwischen dem Bewusstsein, der Intention und der Umwelt manifestieren. Für einen „wahren Funktionalisten" war ein *Gesetz* „kreativer Umwandlung" der einzige authentische Ansatz. Dies veranschaulichte Kiesler anhand eines Diagramms, in dem der Designprozess als „Kreation-Mutation" dargestellt wurde. Innerhalb dieses Prozesses flossen „vorhandene Sachverhalte" einer neuen Zielsetzung zu, wodurch ein *neues Objekt* entstand. Im Laufe der Zeit würde sich der ideale Prozess unendlich wiederholen (Abb. 6).[29]

Im gleichen Jahr wurde Kieslers „Manifeste du Corréalisme" in der französischen Architekturzeitschrift *L'Architecture d'Aujourd'hui* veröffentlicht.[30] Darin bekräftigte er zum wiederholten Male sein Fazit, dass Architekten die Energieübertragung zwischen Menschen, Umweltkräften und dem Unbelebten untersuchen mussten. Das Verständnis dieser Beziehungen

to develop a system to coordinate the transfers and transformations of energy between an artist/architect, object, and spectator, which would be "born then in atomic space." He likened the revelation of this language to "the signs of the zodiac in celestial space."[31] Kiesler was perhaps more open in his esotericism than he had admitted in earlier writings, but he still primarily considered Correalism in terms of nervous processes and energy exchanges, even if his conception of them bordered on the metaphysical.

The *Endless House*

At the same time he worked on the manifesto, he refined its formal embodiment in the *Endless House*.[32] With construction elements again reduced to a basic, spheroid shell, it would be "a living organism… the epiderm of the human body."[33] The biomorphic design, which he developed from the mid-1940s until his death in 1965, became Kiesler's best known project. In November 1950, articles on the *Endless House* appeared in two journals, *Interiors* and *Architectural Forum*.[34] The house consisted of a basic concrete (or plastic) shell with a central utility tree.[35] The main floor would consist of bedrooms, a workshop and children's playroom, a sound-proofed study, and a group living area which flowed into kitchen and dining spaces (Figs. 8 and 9).

würde den Architekten die Schaffung einer authentischen auf den Menschen ausgerichteten Architektur ermöglichen, mit Hilfe derer sich die Menschen endlich „regenerieren" und „wieder in sich selbst zurückkehren" konnten. Ferner lieferte er eine bildhafte Beschreibung des architektonischen Raumes, der eine Atomstruktur aufwies und sich wie ein „Zellkern" verhielt, wobei die Konstruktionselemente wie Oberflächen, Farben und Lichter architektonische „Elektronen, Neutronen, Protonen, Mesonen und Positronen" enthielten (Abb. 7). Kiesler erhob den Anspruch, in seinen Entwürfen eine „rätselhafte Sprache" entdeckt zu haben. Diese könne allmählich in „Gewichte und Maße" übertragen werden, um ein System zur Koordinierung der Übertragungen und Transformationen von Energie zwischen einem Künstler/Architekten, Objekt und Betrachter zu schaffen, das „dann im atomaren Raum entstehen" würde. Er verglich die Offenbarung dieser Sprache mit den „Tierkreiszeichen im Himmelsraum".[31] Möglicherweise zeigte hier Kiesler seinen Esoterismus offener als er dies in früheren Werken getan hatte; allerdings betrachtete er den Correalismus nach wie vor im Sinne der Prozesse im Nervensystem und des Energieaustausches, wenngleich seine diesbezügliche Auffassung an das Metaphysische grenzte.

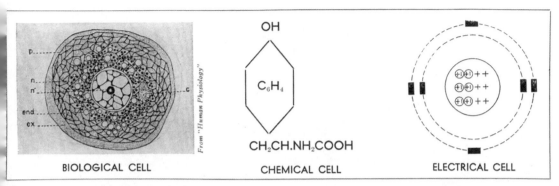

BIOLOGICAL CELL   CHEMICAL CELL   ELECTRICAL CELL

Fig. 2—The nuclear concept of production as expressed in three of the sciences. Note that though the forces involved are expressed in different terms, their basic organization is similar. Technological design must also be seen in the light of a nuclear concept.

7—Frederick Kiesler, *Nuclear concept of production*, published in *Architectural Record*, 1939

Das *Endless House*

Während er sich der Arbeit an dem Manifest widmete, verfeinerte er dessen formale Verkörperung im *Endless House*.[32] Da die Bauelemente erneut auf eine grundlegende sphäroidische Schalenkonstruktion reduziert waren, sollte ein „lebender Organismus ... die Oberhaut des menschlichen Körpers" entstehen.[33] Sein bekanntestes Projekt wurde die von ihm ab Mitte der 1940er Jahre bis zu seinem Tod im Jahre 1965 entwickelte biomorphe Formgebung. Im November 1950 erschienen in den beiden Zeitschriften *Interiors* und *Architectural Forum* Artikel zum *Endless House*.[34] Das Gebäude bestand aus einer Grundschale aus Beton (oder Plastik) mit einem im Zentrum angeordneten Versorgungsbaum.[35] Das Hauptgeschoss enthielt Schlafräume, eine Werkstätte, ein Kinderspielzimmer, ein schalldichtes Studierzimmer und einen in Küchen- und Essräume übergehenden Gruppenwohnbereich (Abb. 8, 9). Ein oberhalb gelegenes Mezzanin sollte ein Atelier und eine Galerie beherbergen; darüber sollte ein Rückzugsraum mit Balkon Platz finden. Im Wohnbereich stellte ein einzelnes „Sichtfenster" den visuellen Kontakt zur Außenwelt her, während mehrere kleine Öffnungen für die Tageslichtbeleuchtung der Schlafzimmer, des Spielzimmers und des Ateliers sorgten. In dem Gebäude waren keine geraden Wände zu finden – als

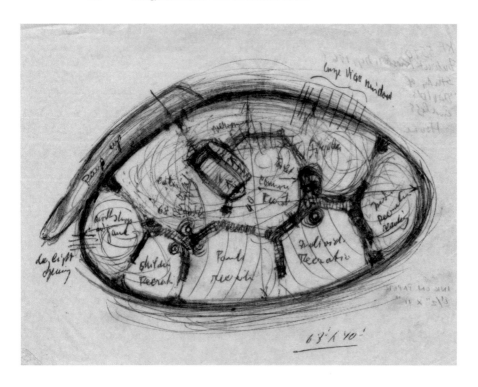

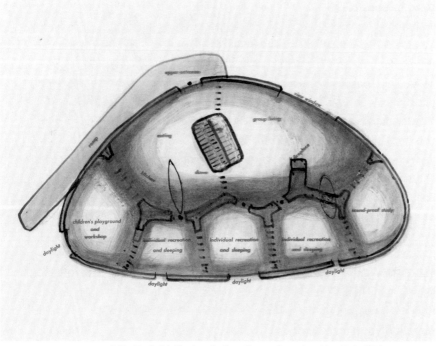

8/9—Frederick Kiesler, *Endless House*, floor plan, New York 1950

On a mezzanine above would be a studio and gallery, and above that, a
seclusion chamber with a balcony. A single *view window* would provide visual
contact with the outside in the living area, while several small openings
admitted daylight to the bedrooms, playroom, and studio. There were no
straight walls in the house—partitions were irregular bands, governed entirely
by the desired morphology of the rooms. The plan resembled a cellular
formation or the cross-section of a heart—with venal openings, valves, atria,
and ventricles. Kiesler's first model of the house looked like smoothly
weathered rock set on a natural stone outcropping (Fig. 10).

The penetration of the external environment into the house was carefully
supervised. Several small openings for daylight punctured the skin, but
primary illumination would be controlled through a system of automatic lighting, which would respond to human bodies as they moved through the
house. It would also be lit with a *Color Clock*, a large, prismatic crystal and
mirror device integrated into the upper surface of the house shell. This clock
would refract daylight into the house over the course of the day, producing
predictable daily sequences of colored light that would sooth or stimulate the
inhabitants.[36]

Although its name, *Endless*, implicitly referred to Kiesler's theory of

Trennwände dienten unregelmäßige Bänder, die zur Gänze entsprechend der
gewünschten Gestalt der Räume ausgerichtet wurden. Der Entwurf hatte
Ähnlichkeit mit einer zellulären Bildung oder den im Querschnitt durch das
Herz erkennbaren Venenöffnungen, Klappen, Vorhöfen und Kammern. Kieslers
erstes Modell des Hauses wirkte wie eine sanft verwitterte Felsgruppe auf
heraustretendem Naturstein (Abb. 10).

Das Eindringen der äußeren Umwelt in das Gebäudeinnere wurde sorgfältig
überwacht. Die Haut war von mehreren kleinen Tageslichtöffnungen
durchstochen, für die Steuerung der Grundbeleuchtung war jedoch ein automatisches Beleuchtungssystem vorgesehen, das auf die Bewegung
der menschlichen Körper durch das Haus reagierte. Zur Beleuchtung diente
ebenso eine *Farbuhr*, ein großer, in die Oberseite der Gebäudeschale
integrierter Apparat mit einem prismatischen Kristall und Spiegelausführung.
Diese Uhr sollte das im Laufe des Tages in das Haus einfallende Tages-
licht brechen und vorhersehbare tägliche Sequenzen farbigen Lichtes erzeugen,
das die Bewohner beruhigen oder anregen sollte.[36]

Trotz des impliziten Verweises der Bezeichnung *Endless* auf Kieslers
Theorie der wechselseitigen „Kreation-Mutation" und die Interaktivität
zwischen den Menschen und deren Objekten vermittelte das *Endless House*

10—Frederick Kiesler, *Endless House*, model, New York 1950

das Gefühl praktisch absoluten Eingeschlossenseins. Wie Kieslers Skizzen, in denen er beharrlich auf eine kohärente Fassadengestaltung verzichtete, zum Ausdruck brachten, hatte das Innen grundsätzlich Vorrang gegenüber dem Außen. Es stellte einen eigenen vollständigen inneren Kosmos dar, in dem die sensorielle und energetische Einbindung das Potenzial zukünftiger Formen erwarten ließ. Letzten Endes existierte das Haus im Grunde in seinen irrwitzig von Hand gezeichneten Skizzen und seinen fortwährenden Konstruktionen aus Draht und Modellierton. Es war nicht nur ein Gebäude. Es war ein Organismus, der dem anhaltenden evolutionären Druck von Kieslers eigenem kreativen Bewusstsein ausgesetzt war.

Kieslers Betonung der Innerlichkeit war nicht nur in Bezug auf die energetische und psychische Kontinuität zwischen dem einzelnen Bewohner und dessen Behausung entscheidend. Sie hatte umfassendere Auswirkungen auf die Architektur. Häuser boten einen Zufluchtsort vor den hektischen Energien der modernen Welt außerhalb. Das Zuhause war jener Ort, an den sich ein Mensch begeben konnte, um sich wieder mit dem eigenen Selbstsein zu vereinen. Mit der Hervorhebung der Bedeutung einer inneren Schutzhülle erstellte Kiesler gleichzeitig eine Absage an die zu einer Beherrschung der architektonischen Moderne ansetzenden glatten Glas- und Stahlformen

reciprocal *creation-mutation* and interactivity between people and their objects and spaces, the sense of enclosure in the *Endless House* was virtually absolute. As expressed in his renderings, which persistently eschewed a coherent design for the façade, inside fundamentally took precedence over outside. It represented its own complete interior cosmos, and yet one in which sensory and energetic involvement promised the potential of future forms. The house, after all, existed fundamentally in his madly penciled drawings and in his ongoing constructions of wire and modeling clay. It was not just a building, it was an organism undergoing the persistent evolutionary pressures of Kiesler's own creative consciousness.

Kiesler's emphasis on interiority was not only critical in terms of the individual inhabitant's energetic and psychic continuity with his or her home, it also had broader implications for architecture. Houses offered a place of refuge from the frenetic energies of the modern world outside. Home was the place that a person could come to reconnect with his or her essential selfhood. By emphasizing the importance of a protective interior envelope, he rejected the slick rectilinear glass and steel forms that were coming to dominate architectural modernism, and searched for something more fundamental—a need for total shelter that went to the core of the animalistic

und begab sich auf die Suche nach etwas Grundlegenderem – einem Bedürfnis nach vollkommenem Rückzug, das zum Kern der animalischen Natur vordrang. In einem Interview aus dem Jahr 1961 erläuterte er diesen Aspekt folgendermaßen: „Tatsächlich wollen wir unser unbedeutendes Leben, unsere unbedeutende emotionale Befriedigung schützen und in emotionalem Frieden, einem Zustand psychischer Ausgeglichenheit leben". „Tiere wissen recht genau, wie sie sich in Momenten der Gefahr zu verhalten haben; sie rennen um ihr Leben, verstecken sich oder rollen sich zusammen und stellen sich tot … Emotionen hüllen uns ein wie die Turbulenzen des Weltraumes und bringen ihr Gegenteil hervor – den inneren Frieden."[37] Kieslers Aussage könnte als autobiographisches Sinnbild für seine eigene innere Unruhe verstanden werden und das *Endless House* dürfte er zur Lösung persönlicher emotionaler Ungleichgewichte und der im Laufe seines Lebens erlebten äußeren Gefahren herangezogen haben: Wie der Historiker Anthony Vidler zudem betonte, wies das Haus eine nahezu uterusähnliche Struktur auf.[38] Während das Haus jedoch gewissermaßen eine Rückkehr zu den Anfängen der Architektur repräsentierte – zumal die Gebärmutter jener Ort ist, in dessen organische Architektur ursprünglich alles Leben hineingeboren wird, repräsentierte es für Kiesler auch ein Mittel zu energetischem Wachstum und Entwicklung.

nature: "We really want to save our small lives, our small emotional satisfactions, and live in an emotional peace, in a balanced psychic state," he explained in a 1961 interview. "Animals know pretty well what to do in moments of danger; they run for their lives, hide, or curl up and play dead…Emotion engulfs us like the turbulence of outer space and creates its counterpart—the peace within."[37] Kiesler's statement could be read as an autobiographical allegory of his own inner turbulence, and the *Endless House* may have been his solution to personal emotional imbalances and the outside perils he had experienced over the course of his life: and as historian Anthony Vidler has noted, its structure was almost womb-like.[38] Yet while in one sense the house represented a return to the origins of architecture—for the womb is the original organic architecture into which we are all born—for Kiesler it also represented a means to grow and to evolve energetically.

1   Kiesler, Friedrich, undatiertes Manuskript, TXT_6454/0, Österreichische Friedrich und Lillian Kiesler Privatstiftung (nachstehend ÖFLKS).

2   Englisches Originalzitat: „greatest non-building architect of our time." in Johnson, Philip: „Three Architects". In *Art in America* 48, Nr. 1. Frühjahr 1960, 70.

3   Englisches Originalzitat: „could not bear endings". Philip Johnson zugeschrieben, in Borsik, Helen: „Fame is Endless". Rezension zu *Inside the Endless House*, nicht identifizierter Zeitungsausschnitt, zitiert in Colomina, Beatriz: „Space House: The Psyche of Building", in Borden, Ian / Rendell, Jane (Hrsg.): *Intersections: Architectural Histories and Critical Theories*. (New York: Routledge) 2000. 66, 69.

4   Englisches Originalzitat in Kieslers Aufzeichnungen: „the separation into floor, columns and roof is done away with: the floor continues into the wall, the wall continues into the roof and so on, and comes back to its start. This might be called: conversion of compression into continuous tension…The egg-shell is a continuous construction. It is the most exquisite sample, that we know, of utmost resistance to outer and inner stress with a minimum of strength." in Kiesler, Frederick: „Structural Problem", TXT_6450/0, ÖFLKS. Vgl. auch Kiesler, Frederick: „Notes on Architecture: The Space-House" in *Hound & Horn* 7, Nr. 2, Januar – Februar 1934; Stellungnahme gegenüber der Presse in „New Space House is Built Along Eggshell Lines", *Brooklyn Times Union*, 19. Oktober 1933; „Space House: Streamlined Home".

5   Vgl. Kiesler, Frederick: „New Space House is Built Along Eggshell Lines".

6   Vgl. Kiesler, Frederick: „Notes on Architecture", 294; Kiesler, Frederick: „The Metabolism Chart of the House" in TXT 3584/0; TXT 3856/0; zwei nicht inventarisierte Schriftstücke: box_spf_03, ÖFLKS

7   Englische Originalzitate: „energy", „accumulation[s] of power". Quelle: Kiesler, Frederick: „Architectural Solution" in TXT 6456/0, ÖFLKS; Kiesler, Frederick: „The Space House and the Future of Painting", TXT 6463, ÖFLKS.

8   Vgl. Kiesler, Frederick: „Metabolism Chart of the House".

9   Kiesler, Frederick: „The Space House", TXT 6461/2, ÖFLKS; Frederick Kiesler: „The Space House and the Future of Painting". (Übersetzt aus dem Englischen)

10 Kieslers Ausrichtung seiner Auseinandersetzung mit der Kunst- und Architekturtätigkeit am menschlichen Körper in Bezug auf Metabolismus und Energie zeigte den Einfluss der im 19. Jahrhundert im deutschsprachigen Raum erzielten Fortschritte in den Bereichen Physik, Physiologie und Psychologie. Vgl. McGuire, Laura, „Space Within – Frederick Kiesler and the Architecture of an

1 Frederick Kiesler, undated manuscript, TXT_6454/0, Austrian Frederick and Lillian Kiesler Private Foundation (hereafter ÖFLKS). (Translated from German)

2 Philip Johnson, "Three Architects", *Art in America* 48, no. 1 (Spring 1960), 70.

3 Quote attributed to Philip Johnson in Helen Borsik, "Fame is Endless", review of *Inside the Endless House*, unidentified newspaper clipping, cited in Beatriz Colomina, "Space House: The Psyche of Building", in *Intersections: Architectural Histories and Critical Theories*, ed. Iain Borden and Jane Rendell (New York: Routledge, 2000), 66, 69.

4 In his notes, Kiesler wrote that "the separation into floor, columns and roof is done away with: the floor continues into the wall, the wall continues into the roof and so on, and comes back to its start. This might be called: conversion of compression into continuous tension ... The eggshell is a continuous construction. It is the most exquisite sample, that we know, of utmost resistance to outer and inner stress with a minimum of strength." Kiesler, "Structural Problem", TXT_6450/0, ÖFLKS. See also Frederick Kiesler, "Notes on Architecture: The Space-House", *Hound & Horn* 7, no. 2 (Jan.–Feb. 1934); and his statements to the press in "New Space House is Built Along Eggshell Lines", *Brooklyn Times Union*, Oct. 19, 1933; "Space House: Streamlined Home".

5 "New Space House is Built Along Eggshell Lines."

6 Kiesler, "Notes on Architecture", 294; Frederick Kiesler, "The Metabolism Chart of the House", TXT 3584/0; TXT 3856/0; and two uninventorized sheets, box_spf_03, ÖFLKS.

7 Kiesler, "Architectural Solution", TXT 6456/0, ÖFLKS; Kiesler, "The Space House and the Future of Painting", TXT 6463, ÖFLKS.

8 Kiesler, "Metabolism Chart of the House."

9 Kiesler, "The Space House", TXT 6461/2, ÖFLKS; Frederick Kiesler, "The Space House and the Future of Painting."

10 By framing his discussion of the activity of architecture and art on the human body in terms of metabolism and energy, Kiesler revealed the influence of nineteenth century advancements in physics, physiology, and psychology in German-speaking regions. See Laura McGuire, "Space Within—Frederick Kiesler and the Architecture of an Idea" (PhD diss., University of Texas at Austin, 2014), 226–229.

11 The Kieslers owned at least six volumes of James' work in psychology and philosophy in their library. William James, *The Principles of Psychology* (New York: Henry Holt and Company, 1890); William James, *On Vital Reserves: The Energies of Men and the*

Idea". (Dissertation: The University of Texas at Austin, 2014) 226–229.

11 Im Besitz der Kieslers standen zumindest sechs in ihrer Bibliothek untergebrachte Bände von James' psychologischem und philosophischem Oeuvre. James, William: *The Principles of Psychology* (New York: Henry Holt and Company, 1890); James, Williams: *On Vital Reserves: The Energies of Men and the Gospel of Relaxation* (New York: Henry Holt and Co., 1899 (1911)); James, William: *Pragmatism and Four Essays from the Meaning of Truth* (New York: Meridian Books, 1907); James, William: *The Philosophy of William James* (New York: The Modern Library, 1925); James, William: *The Energies of Men* (New York: Moffat, Yard and Company, 1911); James, William: *The Letters of William James* (Boston: The Atlantic Monthly Press, 1920).

12 James, William: *On Vital Reserves: The Energies of Men and the Gospel of Relaxation*. New York: Henry Holt and Co., 1899 (1911), 15.

13 James, William: *On Vital Reserves*. 53, 56–59.

14 Englische Originalzitate: „morphology", „Bio-Architecture", „bio-technical". Quelle: Kiesler, Frederick: „Naturally, no concept" ... in TXT 6457/0; Kiesler, Frederick: „The Space-House at Modernage..." in TXT 6460/0; Kiesler, Frederick: „A functional design..." in TXT 6458/0, box_sfp_03, ÖFLKS. Darüber hinaus bezeichnete er seine morphologische Architekturgraphik auf einer in seinen Aufzeichnungen enthaltenen Seite als „Tracing Architecture conception (biological & historically)." Quelle: Kiesler, Frederick: „Time-Space-Architecture..." in TXT 6447/0, box_sfp_03, ÖFLKS.

15 Englisches Originalzitat: „polarization". Am Ende eines Manuskriptes schrieb Kiesler: „Architecture is polarization." Quelle: Kiesler, Frederick: „The Space-House at Modernage..." in TXT 6460/0, box_sfp_03, ÖFLKS.

16 Frederick Kiesler gegenüber Badovici, Jean, in 8/3/1933, LET 609/0, ÖFLKS. Die Bezeichnung „Correlation" ging möglicherweise aus Kieslers Zusammenarbeit mit Buckminster Fuller und der Structural Study Associates hervor; vgl. Kapitel 9.

17 Englisches Originalzitat: „a correlating medium for the forces of architecture". Quelle: Fuller, Buckminster. Editorial, Correlation, in *Shelter* 2, Nr. 4, Mai 1932, 1.

18 Die Artikel erschienen von Februar bis Juni 1937. Quelle: Kiesler, Frederick: „The Architect in Search of ... Design Correlation. A Column on Exhibits, the Theater and the Cinema" in *Architectural Record* 81, Nr. 2. Februar 1937. 7–15; Kiesler, Frederick: „Design-Correlation. Animals and Architecture" in

Gospel of Relaxation (New York: Henry Holt and Co., 1899 (1911)); William James, *Pragmatism and Four Essays from the Meaning of Truth* (New York: Meridian Books, 1907); William James, *The Philosophy of William James* (New York: The Modern Library, 1925); William James, *The Energies of Men* (New York: Moffat, Yard and Company, 1911); and William James, *The Letters of William James* (Boston: The Atlantic Monthly Press, 1920).

12 William James, *On Vital Reserves: The Energies of Men and the Gospel of Relaxation* (New York: Henry Holt and Co., 1899(1911)), 15.

13 James *On Vital Reserves* 53, 56–59.

14 Kiesler, "Naturally, no concept…" TXT 6457/0; Kiesler, "The Space-House at Modernage…" TXT 6460/0; and Kiesler, "A functional design…" TXT 6458/0, box_sfp_03, ÖFLKS. In one page of notes, he also referred to his morphological chart for

architecture as "Tracing Architecture conception (biological & historically)" Kiesler, "Time-Space-Architecture …" TXT 6447/0, box_sfp_03, ÖFLKS.

15 At the end of a manuscript, Kiesler writes: "Architecture is polarization." Kiesler, "The Space-House at Modernage…" TXT 6460/0, box_sfp_03, ÖFLKS.

16 Frederick Kiesler to Jean Badovici, 8/3/1933, LET 609/0, ÖFLKS. The name "Correlation" may have come through Kiesler's collaboration with Buckminster Fuller and Structural Study Associates; see Chapter 9.

17 Buckminster Fuller, "Editorial, Correlation", *Shelter* 2, no. 4 (May 1932), 1.

18 The articles appeared from February through June 1937: Frederick Kiesler, "The Architect in Search of … Design Correlation. A Column on Exhibits, the Theater and the Cinema", *Architectural Record* 81, no. 2 (Feb. 1937), 7–15; Frederick Kiesler, "Design-

Correlation. Animals and Architecture", *Architectural Record* 81, no. 4 (April 1937), 87–92; Frederick Kiesler, "Design-Correlation", *Architectural Record* 81, no. 5 (May 1937), 53–59; Frederick Kiesler, "Design-Correlation. Towards a Prefabrication of Folk Festival", *Architectural Record* 81, no. 6 (June 1937), 93–96. Frederick Kiesler, "Design-Correlation. Certain Data Pertaining to the Genesis of Design by Light. Part I", *Architectural Record* 82, no. 7 (July 1937), 89–92; Frederick Kiesler, "Design-Correlation. Certain Data Pertaining to the Genesis of Design by Light. Part II", *Architectural Record* 82, no. 8 (Aug. 1937), 79–84.

19 In his *Space House* notes, Kiesler had emphasized that the impetus of "design-correlation" was health: "no more frames that separate, no more walls that are barriers, no more isolation as a principle, it means: design-correlation with

barriers, no more isolation as a principle, it means: design-correlation with a specific purpose. It means: the will of the inhabitant and the will of the design-builder must be merged on a common denominator. This common denominator is: health." Quelle: Kiesler, Frederick: "The Space House and the Future of Painting".

20 Englische Originalzitate: "correlate design to the physical and psychological needs of the human being", "develop new standards". Quelle: "Columbia Plans New Departure in Architecture" in *Washington Post*. 6. Juni 1937.

21 Undatierter Entwurf eines Briefs an Bruce Dill vom Fatigue Laboratory an der Harvard University mit der Bitte um Anregungen für "appropriate methods for measuring fatigue and regeneration" in Verbindung mit der Bibliothekswissenschaft. Box_rec_09, ÖFLKS. Ausführliche Notizen

Architectural Record 81, Nr. 4, April 1937. 87–92; Kiesler, Frederick: „Design-Correlation" in *Architectural Record* 81, Nr. 5, Mai 1937. 53–59; Kiesler, Frederick: „Design-Correlation. Towards a Prefabrication of Folk Festival" in *Architectural Record* 81, Nr. 6, Juni 1937. 93–96; Kiesler, Frederick: „Design-Correlation. Certain Data Pertaining to the Genesis of Design by Light. Part I" in *Architectural Record* 82, Nr. 7, Juli 1937. 89–92; Kiesler, Frederick: „Design-Correlation. Certain Data Pertaining to the Genesis of Design by Light. Part II" in *Architectural Record* 82, Nr. 8, August 1937. 79–84.

19 Englisches Originalzitat: „common denominator". In seinen Anmerkungen zum Space House hatte Kiesler die Gesundheit folgendermaßen als impulsgebend für „Design-Correlation" hervorgehoben: „no more frames that separate, no more walls that are

von Studenten zu Ermüdungsmessverfahren, Zeit-Bewegungs-Untersuchungen und Kontaktzyklus-Studien sowie allgemeine Aufzeichnungen zur menschlichen Physiologie sind durchwegs verteilt auf mehrere Boxen mit Material aus dem Laboratory for Design Correlation. Vgl. insbesondere die Notizen von Alden Thompson und Henry Belinsky in box_rec_07; box_rec_08, box_rec_09, and box_rec_10, ÖFLKS.

22 Englische Originalzitate: „regeneration", „polarized and crystallized energy form[s]". Quelle: Kiesler, Frederick: Vortrag von Ende 1930, Ordner Vortrag an Laboratory, in TXT 5274/0, box_rec_09, ÖFLKS.

23 Englische Originalzitate: „everything influences everything", „continuous flow of … correlation". Quelle: Kiesler, Frederick: „Perspektive und Aufzeichnungen zu CORREALISM BIOTECHNIQUE ARCHITECTURE", ÖFLKS.

a specific purpose. It means: the will of the inhabitant and the will of the design-builder must be merged on a common denominator. This common denominator is: health." Frederick Kiesler, "The Space House and the Future of Painting."

20 "Columbia Plans New Departure in Architecture", *Washington Post*, June 6, 1937.

21 Undated draft of letter to Bruce Dill of the Fatigue Laboratory at Harvard University, requesting suggestions for "appropriate methods for measuring fatigue and regeneration" in connection with the study of libraries. Box_rec_09, ÖFLKS; Students' extensive notes on fatigue measurement, time-motion studies, and contact cycle studies, as well as general notes on human physiology are scattered throughout several boxes retaining materials from the Laboratory for Design Correlation. See especially notes by Alden Thompson and Henry

Belinsky, located in box_rec_07; box_rec_08, box_rec_09, and box_rec_10, ÖFLKS.

22 Frederick Kiesler, Lecture, late 1930s, folder "Vortrag an Laboratory", TXT 5274/0, box_rec_09, ÖFLKS.

23 Frederick Kiesler, prospectus and notes for *CORREALISM BIOTECHNIQUE ARCHITECTURE*, ÖFLKS.

24 Kiesler was also able to deliver a synopsis of the book in a lecture "Biotechnique Versus Architecture", at a symposium on the need for science to guide social reform at the Massachusetts Institute of Technology on June 6, 1938.

25 Frederick Kiesler, "On Correalism and Biotechnique: A Definition and Test of a New Approach to Building Design", *Architectural Record* 86, no. 3 (Sept. 1939), 60–61.

26 Ibid., 67.

27 Ibid., 69.

28 Frederick Kiesler, "Pseudo-Functionalism in Modern Architecture",

Partisan Review 7 (July 1949):, 735.

29 Ibid., 736–737.

30 Frederick Kiesler, "Manifeste du Corréalisme", *L'Architecture d'Aujourd'hui* 2 (June 1949, 79–105.

31 Frederick Kiesler, "Manifesto of Correalism", TXT_6409/0/engl, ÖFLKS.

32 A photomontage entitled "Endless House" was first published in 1944. Frederick Kiesler, "Endless House", *VVV*, Feb. 1944, 60–61.

33 Kiesler, "Manifesto of Correalism", TXT_6409/0/engl, ÖFLKS.

34 Frederick Kiesler, "The Endless House", *Architectural Forum* (Nov. 1950), 124–126; Frederick Kiesler, "The Endless House and its Psychological Lighting", *Interiors* 60, no. 4 (Nov. 1950), 122–129.

35 Kiesler explained that the *Endless House* could either be constructed of concrete cast and sprayed, or "reinforced plastics (including

24 Eine Gesamtschau des Werkes gelang Kiesler in dem Vortrag Biotechnique Versus Architecture im Rahmen des am 6. Juni 1938 am Massachusetts Institute of Technology abgehaltenen Symposiums zur Notwendigkeit der Wissenschaft für die Leitung sozialer Reformen.

25 Englisches Originalzitat: „forms". Quelle: Kiesler, Frederick: „On Correalism and Biotechnique: A Definition and Test of a New Approach to Building Design" in *Architectural Record* 86, Nr. 3, Sept. 1939. 60–61.

26 Englisches Originalzitat: „functionality". Ebd. 67.

27 Ebd. 69.

28 Kiesler, Frederick: „Pseudo-Functionalism in Modern Architecture" in *Partisan Review* 7, Juli 1949. 735.

29 Ebd. 736–737.

30 Kiesler, Frederick: „Manifeste du Corréalisme" in *L'Architecture d'Aujourd'hui* 2, Juni 1949. 79–105.

31 Englische Originalzitate: „back up", „re-enter ourselves", „cellular nucleus", „electrons, neutrons, protons, mesons and positrons", „enigmatic language", „weights and measures", „born then in atomic space", „the signs of the zodiac in celestial space". Quelle: Kiesler, Frederick: „Manifesto of Correalism" in TXT_6409/0/engl, ÖFLKS.

32 Eine Fotomontage mit dem Titel „Endless House" wurde erstmals im Jahre 1944 veröffentlicht. Quelle: Kiesler, Frederick: „Endless House" in *VVV*, Feb. 1944. S. 60–61.

33 Englisches Originalzitat: „a living organism...the epiderm of the human body". Quelle: Kiesler, Frederick: „Manifesto of Correalism" in TXT_6409/0/engl, ÖFLKS.

34 Kiesler, Frederick: „The Endless House" in *Architectural Forum*. November 1950. 124–126; Kiesler, Frederick: „The Endless House and its Psychological Lighting" in *Interiors* 60, Nr. 4, November 1950. 122–129.

35 Kiesler erläuterte, dass für den Bau des Endless House entweder Betonmodelle und ein Sprühverfahren oder „reinforced plastics (including glass)" [glasfaserverstärkter Kunststoff] zum Einsatz kommen konnten. Quelle: Kiesler, Frederick: „The Endless House" in *Architectural Forum*. 126.

36 Englische Originalzitate: „view window", „color clock". Quelle: Kiesler, Frederick: „The Endless House" in *Interiors*, 126–127. Während der gesamten ersten Hälfte des 20. Jahrhunderts war Forschungstätigkeit im Bereich der Farbpsychologie verbreitet. Zwischen 1900 und 1950 erschienen hunderte von Büchern und Artikel zu dem Thema; das namhafteste ist wohl Faber Birrens einflussreiches Werk zu den psychologischen Auswirkungen der Farben aus dem Jahr 1950: *Color Psychology and Color Therapy; A Factual Study of the Influence of Color on Human Life*

glass.)" Kiesler, "The Endless
House", *Architectural Forum*, 126.

36 Kiesler, "The Endless House",
Interiors, 126–127. Research in
color psychology was common
throughout the first half of the
twentieth century; hundreds of
books and articles were
published on the subject between
1900 and 1950; perhaps most
notably Faber Birren's influential
1950 book on the psychological
effects of color: *Color Psychology
and Color Therapy; A Factual
Study of the Influence of Color on
Human Life* (New York: McGraw-
Hill, 1950). Kiesler included
some of Birren's work on color in
his bibliographic lists for the
Laboratory for Design Correlation.

37 Thomas Creighton, "Kiesler's
Pursuit of an Idea", *Progressive
Architecture* 42, no. 7 (July 1961),
115.

38 Anthony Vidler, *The Architectural
Uncanny: Essays in the Modern
Unhomely* (Cambridge, MA: MIT
Press, 1994), 153.

(New York: McGraw-Hill, 1950).
Kiesler nahm einige der von
Birren verfassten Arbeiten über
die Farben in sein für das
Laboratory for Design Correlation
erstelltes Literaturverzeichnis auf.

37 Englische Originalzitate:
„We really want to save our small
lives, our small emotional
satisfactions, and live in an emotional peace, in a balanced
psychic state"; „Animals know
pretty well what to do in
moments of danger; they run for
their lives, hide, or curl up and
play dead… Emotion engulfs
us like the turbulence of outer
space and creates its counterpart—the peace within." Quelle:
Creighton, Thomas: „Kiesler's
Pursuit of an Idea" in *Progressive
Architecture* 42, Nr. 7, Juli 1961.
115.

38 Vidler, Anthony: *The Architectural
Uncanny: Essays in the Modern
Unhomely* (Cambridge, MA: MIT
Press, 1994) 153.

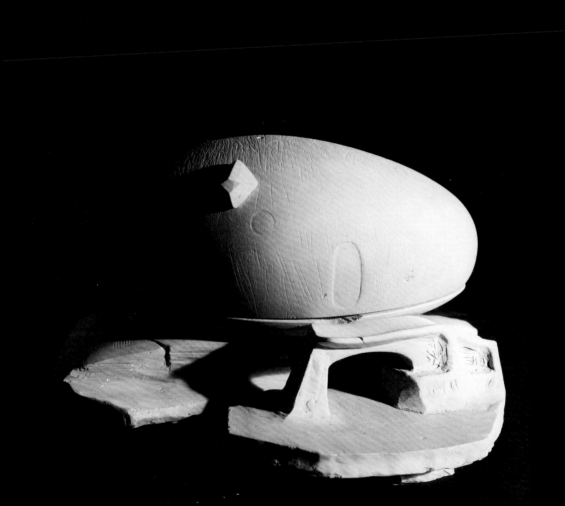

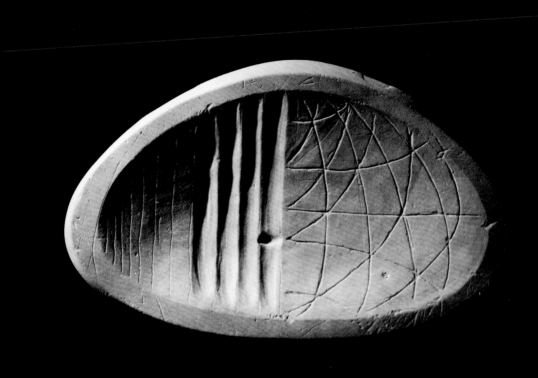
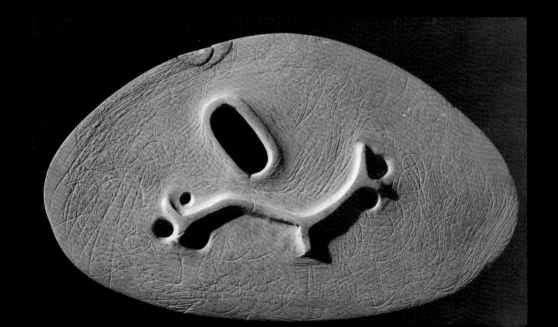

Frederick Kiesler's *Endless House.* An Attempt to Retrace an Endless Story

Gerd Zillner

Friedrich Kieslers *Endless House.* Versuch, eine endlose Geschichte nachzuzeichnen

> "I believe that everybody has only one basic creative idea and no
> matter how he is driven off, you will find that he will always come back
> to it until he has a chance to prove it in purity, or die with the idea
> unrealized."[1]
> —Frederick Kiesler

Frederick Kiesler's own basic idea was certainly that of endlessly flowing
space. It was manifested as space stage and space theater, city in space and
space sculpture, in exhibition spaces or as space-time architecture. It
runs through his entire oeuvre, culminating in the *Endless House* as an endless life project. How can the story of an endless project be told—without
a beginning and without an ending? How can we approach it? Since Kiesler's
Endless House was never actually built, it cannot be entered, walked
through or even inhabited. There is also the question as to the sources that
can be used to reconstruct the history of the project. Instead of built
architecture, we must rely on manifestos, texts, articles from the daily press
and professional magazines, several hundred sketches and photographs,
studies, drawings, plans and several models as well as autobiographical notes,
interviews and poetic texts. Precisely these sources are to be assembled

> „Ich glaube, jedermann hat nur eine schöpferische Grundidee, und
> egal wie sehr man von ihr abkommt, Sie werden feststellen, daß man
> immer wieder zu ihr zurückkehrt, bis man eine Chance hat, sie in
> Reinheit zu beweisen, oder man stirbt, ohne diese Idee realisiert zu
> haben."[1]
> —Friedrich Kiesler

Friedrich Kieslers eigene Grundidee war wohl der endlos fließende Raum. Sie
manifestiert sich als Raumbühne und Raumtheater, als Raumstadt und
Raumskulptur, in Ausstellungsräumen oder als Raum-Zeit-Architektur. Sie zieht
sich durch sein gesamtes Schaffen und kulminiert im *Endless House* als
endlosem Lebensprojekt. Wie lässt sich nun die Geschichte eines endlosen
Projektes erzählen – ohne Anfang und ohne Ende? Wie kann man sich ihr
annähern? Da Kieslers *Endless House* nie realisiert wurde, kann man es nicht
betreten, nicht durchschreiten oder gar bewohnen. Es stellt sich zusätzlich
die Frage nach den Quellen, die herangezogen werden können, um die Geschichte dieses Projektes nachzuzeichnen. Anstelle der gebauten Architektur
müssen Manifeste, Texte, Artikel in der Tagespresse und in Fachmagazinen,
mehrere hundert Zeichnungen und Fotografien, Studien, Skizzen, Pläne und

1—Ladislaus Tuszynsky, *The Space Stage*, caricature published in *Der Götz von Berlichingen*, Oct. 3, 1924

here in the following just like the various pieces of a puzzle to create a whole picture.[2]

Vienna—Paris—New York

Asked about when he conceived his *Endless House* for the first time, Kiesler always made reference to his first years of work in Vienna. "I originally conceived my *Endless House* for the theater and music festival of the City of Vienna." What at first sight may appear to be simply an attempt to date the idea of his *Endless House* as early as possible, gains relevance and credibility when one accepts Kiesler's dictum of "a basic creative idea" and joins him on a journey to the early stops of his *Endless* in Vienna and Paris. According to Kiesler, the *Space Stage* at the Vienna Konzerthaus (Fig. 1) was to become the central component of his *Endless Theater* buildings (Fig. 2). He used the plans that he put together, most likely in 1925 in Paris, as illustrations for this passage of the interview. "The total plan of the Endless (House) was intended for a capacity of ten thousand people, all in a double shell of pressed glass. This double shell was to contain both heating and air conditioning and an endless stage extending through the entire space. It was to consist of an interplay of ramp, platform and elevators. This theater and music center was

einige Modelle sowie autobiographische Notizen, Interviews und poetische Texte herangezogen werden. Genau diese Quellen sollen im Folgenden wie einzelne Puzzlesteine zu einem großen Ganzen zusammengesetzt werden.[2]

Wien – Paris – New York

Mit der Frage konfrontiert, wann er denn sein *Endless House* zum ersten Mal konzipiert hätte, wird Kiesler nicht müde auf seine ersten Schaffensjahre in Wien zu verweisen. „Mein Endloses Haus [deutsch im Originaltext] konzipierte ich ursprünglich für die Theater- und Musikfestwochen der Stadt Wien." Was auf den ersten Blick als plumper Versuch erscheinen mag, die Idee seines *Endlosen Hauses* möglichst früh anzusetzen, gewinnt jedoch an Relevanz und Glaubwürdigkeit, wenn man sich auf Kieslers Diktum der „einen schöpferischen Grundidee" einlässt und sich mit ihm auf die Reise zu den frühen Stationen seines *Endless* nach Wien und Paris begibt. Die *Raumbühne* im Wiener Konzerthaus (Abb. 1.), so Kiesler, sollte der zentrale Bestandteil seiner *Endless Theater*-Gebäude werden (Abb. 2). Die Pläne, die er wohl 1925 in Paris anfertigt, dienen ihm als Illustrationen für diese Interviewpassage. „Die Gesamtplanung des Endlosen [Hauses] sah eine Kapazität von zehntausend Menschen vor, alle in einer doppelten Schale aus Pressglas.

also to include hotels, parking spaces and gardens—all in this shell.
[…] The principle of continuous tension was applied here throughout—there
was no column in the entire structure."[3] Kiesler's plans for the *Endless*
contain no measurements. Their concentric circles and spiral-shaped arrangements as well as their high degree of abstraction are difficult to read
as architectural plans and, thus, again and again unleashed speculations of
Marcel Duchamp having possibly been the one who designed it.[4]

Kiesler took them to New York in 1926 to exhibit at the *International
Theater Exposition* and also presented a first model of his *Endless* alongside
his plans. Several photographs of the exhibition document the almost
two-meter-wide and approximately one-meter-high spheroid object (Fig. 3).[5]

A further step in Kiesler's development of the *Endless House* is his *Space
House*.[6] He built it in 1933 as a display for the premises of the Modernage
Furniture Company. It can be employed as an ideal illustration of his
approach. Just as in Vienna and Paris, Kiesler used the design of an exhibition
space to present his architectural concepts by means of a kind of model.
The streamlined, rounded corners of the façade of the second floor as well
as the elasticity of the freely floating space on the inside anticipate, in
their radicalness, the later *Endless House*. It was not without reason that the

Diese doppelte Schale würde sowohl Heizung als auch Kühlung beinhalten und
als ein endloser Schauplatz durch den gesamten Raum aus einem Zusammenspiel von Rampe, Plattform und Aufzügen bestehen. Dieses Theater- und
Musikzentrum würde auch Hotels, Parkplätze und Gärten – alles in dieser
Schale – inkludieren. […] Das Prinzip der kontinuierlichen Spannung wurde
hier total angewandt – in der ganzen Struktur gab es keine Säule."[3] Kieslers
Pläne für das *Endless* weisen keine Maßangaben auf. Ihre konzentrischen
Kreise und spiralförmigen Anordnungen sowie ihr hoher Grad an Abstraktion
lassen sich nur schwer als Architekturpläne lesen und erwecken immer
wieder Spekulationen über die mögliche Urheberschaft Marcel Duchamps.[4]

Als Exponate der *International Theater Exposition* nimmt Kiesler sie 1926
mit nach New York und stellt auch ein erstes Modell seines *Endless* neben den
Plänen aus. Auf mehreren Fotos der Ausstellung ist das annähernd zwei Meter
breite und ca. einen Meter hohe sphäroide Objekt dokumentiert (Abb. 3).[5]

Ein weiterer Schritt in Kieslers Entwicklung des *Endless House* ist
sein *Space House*.[6] Er errichtet es 1933 als Display für das Geschäftslokal
der Modernage Furniture Company, und es kann als ideales Fallbeispiel
zur Erläuterung seiner Arbeitsweise herangezogen werden. Wie schon in Wien
und Paris, nutzt Kiesler die Gestaltung eines Ausstellungsraumes, um

2—Frederick Kiesler, *Endless Theater*, plan, Paris 1925

3—Stefi Kiesler in front of *Endless Theater* model, *International Theater Exposition*, New York 1926

Endless Space House appears on the cover sheet of a bundle of drawings by Kiesler.[7] The radical nature applies in particular to the texts that Kiesler wrote to accompany this project with theoretical backup. The *Space House* represented for him two crucial principles of modern architecture: "besides its solution as One-Family-Shelter: (a) the Time-Space Concept of architecture; (b) the Shell-Construction in continuous tension."[8] Kiesler himself also visually documented this direct line of development. He reworked the photographs of the *Space House* by means of montage, spattered paint and thick coats of opaque white lines (Fig. 4), so that the streamlined, rounded façade, still recognizable here as a rectangle, was increasingly adapted to the spheroid shape of the *Endless House*.[9]

Kiesler used the term *Endless House* for the first time in 1944 in a text for the *VVV* magazine. He designed a double page with a photomontage (Fig. 5) by mounting the above-mentioned reworked *Space House* onto the model of the *Endless Theater* and bringing it into direct connection with the hand-written notes. As he noted: "*Endless House* / Paris 1924 / 1934 New York / *Space House* / both of these projects were designed by Kiesler, 'Structures in continuous tension' to facilitate both the pre- and fabrication in molds for plastics, as well as to shelter those 'continuous mutations' of the life-force which seem

modellhaft seine Architekturkonzepte zu präsentieren. Die stromlinienförmig abgerundeten Ecken der Fassade des Obergeschoßes sowie die Elastizität des frei fließenden Raumes im Inneren weisen in ihrer Radikalität auf das spätere *Endless House* voraus. Kiesler dürfte nicht ohne Grund ein Deckblatt für ein Zeichnungskonvolut als *Endless Space House* bezeichnet haben.[7] Die Radikalität gilt insbesondere auch für die Texte, die Kiesler als theoretische Begleitung für dieses Projekt verfasst. So repräsentiere für ihn das *Space House* zwei wesentliche Prinzipien moderner Architektur, „[n]eben der Lösung als Einfamilien-Behausung: (a) das Zeit-Raum-Konzept der Architektur; (b) die Schalen-Konstruktion in kontinuierlicher Spannung."[8] Kiesler selbst hält diese direkte Entwicklungslinie auch visuell fest. Er überarbeitet Fotografien des *Space House* durch Montage, Spritzgitter und dick aufgetragene Deckweißstriche dergestalt (Abb. 4), dass die zwar stromlinienförmig abgerundete, aber noch als Querrechteck erkennbare Fassade immer mehr an die sphäroide Form des *Endless House* angeglichen wird.[9]

Den Begriff *Endless House* verwendet Kiesler zum ersten Mal 1944 in einem Beitrag für das *VVV*-Magazin. Kiesler gestaltet eine Doppelseite mit einer Fotomontage (Abb. 5), indem er auf das Modell des *Endless Theater* die zuvor erwähnte Überarbeitung des *Space House* montiert und mit

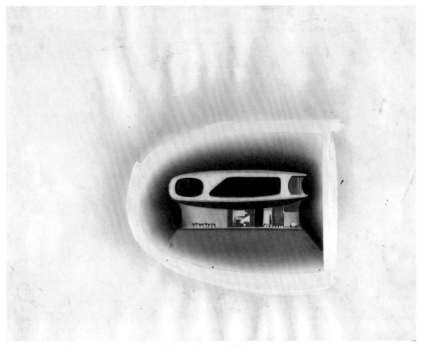

4—Frederick Kiesler, *Space House*, collage, New York 1944

handschriftlichen Anmerkungen in einen direkten Zusammenhang stellt.
Er vermerkt „*Endless House* / Paris 1924 / 1934 New York / *Space-House*".
Diese beiden Projekte wurden von Kiesler entworfen, ‚Strukturen in
kontinulierlicher Spannung erleichtern sowohl die Vor- und Fabrikation von
Gussformen für Kunststoff, als auch die Unterbringung jener ‚kontinuier-
lichen Veränderungen' der Lebensenergie, welche ein Teil des ‚Praktischen'
und des Magischen ist."[10] Die Montage hinterlegt Kiesler weiters mit einem
Zitat Leonardo da Vincis.[11] In leicht abgewandelter Form verwendet er die
Fotomontage auch für die Titelseite seines „Manifeste du Corréalisme".[12]

Kieslers Ei, das *Paris Endless* und das *Tooth House*
1947 laden André Breton und Marcel Duchamp Kiesler ein, für die *Exposition
Internationale du Surréalisme* in der Pariser Galerie Maeght einen Ausstellungsraum, den *Salle de Superstition* (Abb. 6), zu gestalten.[13] „Architektonisch war der Raum aus zwei offenen Ellipsen (in Bandform) konstruiert,
die eine vertikal, die andere horizontal. Das Atmen des Raumes durch die
Kiemen dieser Ringe war so indiziert, die Enge des Erstickens und die Weite
der Befreiung."[14] Kieslers *Salle de Superstition* ist wohl jene räumliche
Umsetzung, die dem Innenraum seines *Endless House* am nächsten kommt.

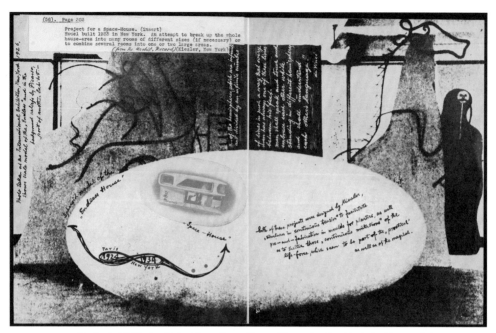

5—Frederick Kiesler, Project for a *Space House*, illustration for "Magic Architecture", 1945–47

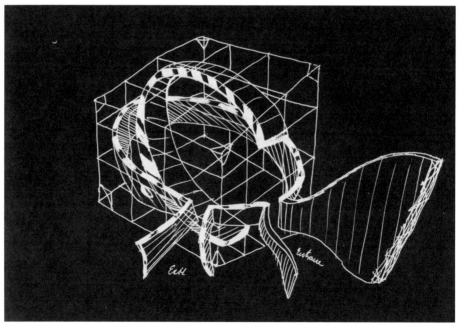

6—Frederick Kiesler, *Salle de Superstition*, axonometric fair drawing, 1947

to be part of the 'practical' as well as of the magical."[10] Kiesler depicted the montage against the background of a handwritten quote from Leonardo da Vinci.[11] In a slightly modified form, he also used the photomontage (Fig. 5) for the title page of his "Manifeste du Corréalisme."[12]

Kiesler's Egg, the *Paris Endless* and the *Tooth House*

In 1947, André Breton and Marcel Duchamp invited Kiesler to design an exhibition space, the *Salle de Superstition* (Fig. 6) for the *Exposition Internationale du Surréalisme* at the Galerie Maeght in Paris.[13] "Architecturally, the room was constructed out of two open ellipses (ribbon-shaped), one vertical and the other horizontal. The breathing of the space through the gills of these rings was thus induced, the tightness of suffocating and the breadth of liberation."[14] Kiesler's *Salle de Superstition* was the implementation of space that resembled the interior of his *Endless House* the most. Hans Arp dedicated an article to this spatial creation in which, proceeding from the exhibition space, he referred to Frederick Kiesler's "egg-shaped" architecture.[15]

In the summer months of 1947, which Kiesler spent designing the Surrealists' exhibition in Paris,[16] he created a series of architectural studies,

Hans Arp widmet dieser Raumschöpfung einen Artikel, in dem er ausgehend vom Ausstellungsraum auf die „eiförmige" Architektur Friedrich Kieslers verweist.[15]

In den Sommermonaten des Jahres 1947, die Kiesler zur Gestaltung der Surrealisten-Ausstellung in Paris verbringt,[16] entsteht eine Serie von Architekturstudien, die er unter anderem als *Paris Endless* bezeichnet.[17] Bei der Betrachtung dieser Werkgruppe kann man prinzipiell zwei unterschiedliche Komplexe herausarbeiten: Der Erste umfasst Aquarelle, die an *Écriture Automatique* erinnern. Kiesler setzt geometrische Formen auf das Blatt. Daraufhin werden diese mit Aquarellfarbe oder einfach nur mit Tusche ausgefüllt (Abb. 7, 8, 9, 10 und 11). Da er zuvor das Blatt angefeuchtet hat, laufen nun die Farben oder die Tusche auseinander und brechen dabei die geometrischen Formen auf. Die neu entstandenen Farbverläufe fängt Kiesler wiederum mit Konturen ein und versieht die neu entstandenen Gebilde etwa mit Schraffuren oder mit weiteren Details, wodurch sie räumliche Tiefe und einen architektonischen Charakter bekommen. Dass Kiesler mit der *Écriture Automatique* und ihrer Abwandlung für die bildende Kunst vertraut war, kann man mehrfach belegen. Interessanterweise verfasst Kiesler selbst einen Aufsatz, in dem er anhand der Zeichnungen für das *Endless House* die

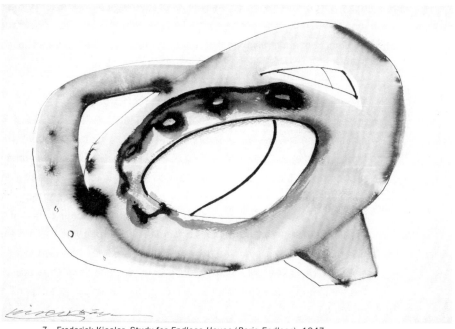

7—Frederick Kiesler, Study for *Endless House* (*Paris Endless*), 1947

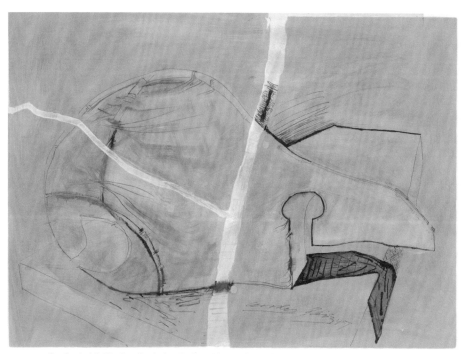

8—Frederick Kiesler, Study for *Endless House* (*Paris Endless*), 1947

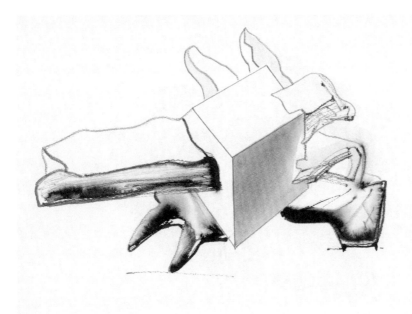

9—Frederick Kiesler, Study for *Endless House* (*Paris Endless*), 1947

Automatismen seiner Zeichenpraxis erklärt. „Entwerfen bedeutet, eine Vision aufs Papier zu übertragen, mit Bleistift, Tinte oder – oder. Mit verbundenen Augen zu gleiten statt zu entwerfen […]. Zeichnung, Bildhauerei oder Malerei nach dem Zufallsprinzip heißt, loslassen zu können, ganz Werkzeug zu sein statt das Werkzeug zu führen. Es bedeutet, mit ganzem Körper und Geist zu entwerfen und dabei an keinen der beiden zu denken."[18] Gemeinsam ist den Arbeiten die Durchdringung von geometrischen und organischen Strukturen. Der zweite Komplex umfasst Kugelschreiberzeichnungen, die Kiesler auf kleinen Blättern realisiert, die Blätter unregelmäßig ausreißt und wiederum auf größere Blätter kaschiert. Sie zeigen waben- oder höhlenartige Gebilde (Abb. 12 und 13).

Zurück in New York, setzt Kiesler die in Paris begonnenen Architekturzeichnungen fort, die er unter dem Titel *Tooth House* zu einem Konvolut von ca. 20 Zeichnungen zusammenfasst.[19] Kiesler entwickelt aus den, zum Teil den *Paris Endless*-Zeichnungen sehr ähnlichen, abstrakt-archiskulpturalen Durchdringungen von organischen und geometrischen Formen ein Einfamilienhaus mit einer frei geformten Schalenkonstruktion.

Auf einem Deckblatt (Abb. 14) verwendet Kiesler den Titel *Tooth House* selbst[20] und spielt damit auf die Hartgebilde des menschlichen Gebisses an.

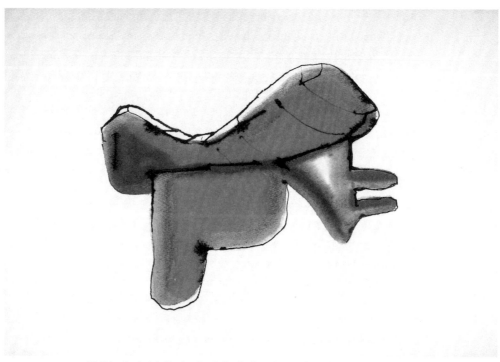

10/11—Frederick Kiesler, Study for *Endless House* [Paris Endless], 1947

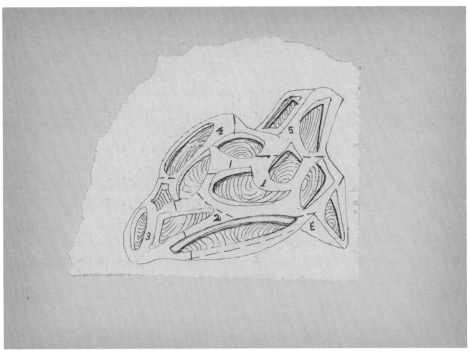

12/13—Frederick Kiesler, Study for *Endless House* [Paris Endless], 1947

which he also named *Paris Endless*.[17] Looking at this group of works, one can, in principle, discern two different complexes: the first comprises water-colors that allude to *Écriture Automatique* (Figs. 7, 8, 9, 10 and 11). Kiesler placed geometric shapes on the sheet. These were then filled with watercolor or simply just with ink. Since he had first dampened the sheet, the colors or the ink bled and thereby broke open the geometric shapes. Kiesler captured in contours the resulting flow of paint and added hatchings or further details to the newly created formations, giving them spatial depth and archi-tectural character. There is substantial evidence that Kiesler was familiar with the *écriture automatique* and its modification for the visual arts. Interest-ingly, Kiesler himself wrote an essay in which he explained the auto-matisms of his drawing work on the basis of his drawings for the *Endless House*. "Drafting is grafting vision on paper with lead, ink, or—or. Blindfolded skating rather than designing, […] Chance drawing and sculpting is an ability to let go, to be entirely tool rather than a guide of tools. It means to design with all one's body and mind and to not think of either while doing this."[18] Common to all the works is the interpenetration of geo-metric and organic structures. The second group of works comprises pen drawings that Kiesler made on small sheets of paper, tearing out the

Einerseits erinnert die Gliederung der Baukörper an den Aufbau eines menschlichen Zahns mit Zahnkrone, Zahnhals und Zahnwurzel, andererseits bezieht sich die Schale des Hauses auf den Zahnschmelz. Die *Tooth House*-Serie zeigt Kieslers Suche nach einer Form für sein *Endless*. In einigen Blättern greift er die Pariser Architekturstudien auf, welche sich durchdrin-gende geometrische Formen mit organischen Körpern abbilden und entwickelt aus ihnen zahnähnliche Gebäude (Abb. 15). Im Laufe des Entwurfs-prozesses entfernt sich Kiesler immer weiter von der Zahnform. Er verbiegt und krümmt die Kontur zu einem abgerundeten *U*. Es scheint, um bei der Metapher des Zahnes zu bleiben, als ob er die Krone eines Weisheits-zahnes entfernt und durch eine Wölbung die Zahnwurzeln miteinander verbindet. Die *Tooth House*-Serie beinhaltet einerseits Grundrisse, Schnitte und Ansichten, mit Zimmereinteilungen, der Verteilung verschiedener Wohnfunktionen, andererseits zeigen einige Blätter die Einbettung des Hauses in die umgebende Landschaft (Abb. 16).

Endless 1950 – von der Galerie ins Museum

Am 3. Oktober 1950 eröffnet in der New Yorker Kootz Gallery die Ausstellung *The Muralist and The Modern Architect*. Im Vorwort zum Katalog schreibt

sheets irregularly and then gluing them on larger sheets. They show honey-combs or cave-like formations.

Back in New York, Kiesler continued the architectural sketches that he had begun in Paris; giving them the title *Tooth House*, he grouped them together in a collection of approximately twenty drawings.[19] (Figs. 12 and 13) Some very similar to the *Paris Endless* drawings, it is from the abstract-archi-sculptural interpenetration of organic and geometric forms that Kiesler developed a single-family house with a freely formed shell construction.

On the cover sheet (Fig. 14), Kiesler wrote the title *Tooth House*[20], thus alluding to the hard formation of human teeth. On the one hand, the structure of the building reflects the structure of a human tooth with its crown, neck and root (Fig. 15), while, on the other hand, the shell of the house refers to the tooth enamel. The *Tooth House* shows Kiesler searching for a form for his *Endless*. On some sheets, he takes up the Parisian architectural studies, which depict interpenetrating geometric shapes and organic bodies, using them to develop a tooth-like building. In the course of the design process, Kiesler moved further and further away from the tooth-like form. He bent and curved the contour to create a rounded *U* shape. To stick to the metaphor of the tooth, it is as if he were removing the crown of a wisdom tooth and thus

14—Frederick Kiesler, Study for *Tooth House* (cover sheet), ca. 1948–50

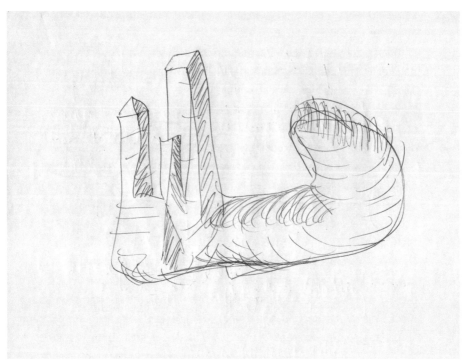

15—Frederick Kiesler, Study for *Tooth House*, ca. 1948–50

16—Frederick Kiesler, Study for *Tooth House*, ca. 1948–50

connecting the curvature of the tooth roots. On the one hand, the *Tooth House* series contains floor plans, sections and views, with room divisions and the distribution of various living functions, while on the other hand, several sheets show the house embedded in the surrounding landscape. (Fig. 16)

Endless 1950—from the gallery to the museum

On October 3, 1950 the exhibition *The Muralist and the Modern Architect* opened at the New York Kootz Gallery. In the preface to the catalog, Samuel L. Kootz writes: "Actually, creative architecture demands the murals and sculpture of the modern artist. Too frequently we see a magnificent concept in architecture leveled down in taste through the use of academic murals. The creative thrust of the architect requires an equally imaginative treatment by the muralist. To encourage the use of modern artists by architects and builders, we have secured the cooperation of a group of distinguished modern architects who planned projects for the artists and made models showing the use of the mural in their planning. Particularly worth noting is the variety of the projects and the unusual manner in which the murals are used."[21]

The artists featured in the exhibition were William Baziotes, Adolph Gottlieb, David Hare, Hans Hofmann and Robert Motherwell. They worked together with

Samuel L. Kootz: „Gegenwärtig verlangt kreative Architektur nach Wandmalerei und Skulpturen moderner Künstler. Nur allzu oft sehen wir, wie großartige Konzepte der Architektur durch lehrmeisterliche Wandmalerei herabgesetzt werden. Der kreative Schub des Architekten bedarf einer ebenso imaginativen Bearbeitung durch den Maler. Um Architekten und Bauunternehmer zu ermutigen, moderne Künstler miteinzubeziehen, haben wir die Zusammen-arbeit einer Gruppe ausgezeichneter moderner Architekten ermöglicht. Sie haben für die Künstler Projekte und Modelle entworfen, die uns zeigen, wie die Wandmalerei in ihre Planungen miteinbezogen wurde."[21]

Die Künstler der Ausstellung sind William Baziotes, Adolph Gottlieb, David Hare, Hans Hofmann und Robert Motherwell. Sie arbeiteten mit den Architekten Marcel Breuer, Walter Gropius/The Architects Collaborative, Philip Johnson, Jose Luis Sert, Paul Lester Wiener und Friedrich Kiesler zusammen. Er wäre gar nicht für die Teilnahme an dieser Ausstellung vorgesehen gewesen, behauptet Kiesler in jenem Interview mit Thomas Creighton, welches so aufschlussreich für Kieslers Selbstwahrnehmung ist. Er wäre nur durch die Einladung des Bildhauers David Hare zum Projekt gestoßen. Kiesler und der um mehr als 25 Jahre jüngere Bildhauer waren befreundet. In den späten 1940er Jahren kreuzen sich ihre Wege bei den verschiedensten Projekten

architects Marcel Breuer, Walter Gropius/The Architects Collective, Philip Johnson, Jose Luis Sert, Paul Lester Wiener and Frederick Kiesler. It was not planned that he would participate in this exhibition, as Kiesler claimed in the interview with Thomas Creighton, which says so much about Kiesler's self-perception. He only became part of the project as a result of an invitation from the sculptor David Hare. He and the sculptor, more than 25 years younger than him, were friends. In the late 1940s, their paths crossed in a variety of projects of the New York Surrealist community. David Hare was the editor of the art magazine *VVV*, in which Kiesler published the *Endless House* montage discussed above in 1944. Hare took part in the exhibition *Bloodflames 1947* at the New York Hugo Gallery, which was curated by Nicolas Calas and designed by Kiesler. That same year, Kiesler placed David Hare's sculpture *L'Homme Angoisse* in a central position of the *Salle de Superstition* in the *Exposition Internationale du Surréalisme* conceived by André Breton and Marcel Duchamp.[22]

His younger artist friend "gallantly returned a favor," as Kiesler later recalled. Hare asked Kiesler: "Could you design a house for me so that I can make sculpture in relation to it and we can exhibit together?" […] Kiesler's answer was that he could not design him any kind of house. "I can do only one

der New Yorker Surrealistengemeinde: So ist etwa David Hare der Herausgeber des Kunstmagazins *VVV*, in dem Kiesler 1944 die weiter oben besprochene *Endless House*-Montage veröffentlicht. Hare nahm an der von Nicolas Calas kuratierten und von Kiesler gestalteten Ausstellung *Bloodflames 1947* in der New Yorker Hugo Gallery teil, und Kiesler integriert im selben Jahr David Hares Skulptur *L'Homme Angoisse* an zentraler Stelle in die *Salle de Superstition* in der von André Breton und Marcel Duchamp konzipierten *Exposition Internationale du Surréalisme*.[22]

Sein jüngerer Künstlerfreund hätte sich mit der Einladung auf „galante Weise revanchiert", erinnert sich Kiesler später. Hare bittet Kiesler, für ihn ein Haus zu „entwerfen, damit ich dafür eine Skulptur errichten […] und wir gemeinsam ausstellen können?" Kieslers Antwort war, dass er ihm nicht irgendein Haus entwerfen könne. „Ich kann Dir nur eines anbieten und das wäre eine Einfamilien-Version meines *Endless House*, und da man das *Endless* von unten in der Nähe der Mitte betritt, ergibt das die Möglichkeit für einen wunderschönen, skulptural geformten Treppenaufgang."[23]

Der Einladung folgt ein intensiver künstlerischer Austausch, in dessen Verlauf Kiesler unter anderem das kleine *Endless House*-Modell anfertigt, das sich heute im MoMA, New York befindet,[24] und eine Serie von 20 bis 30

thing, and that is, I can make you a one-family version of the *Endless House*, and since one enters the *Endless* from underneath near the center, there is a chance of making a beautifully sculpted staircase."[23] The invitation was followed by an intensive artistic exchange, in the course of which Kiesler also created the small model of the *Endless House* which can be found today at the MoMA in New York[24], and a series of 20 to 30 drawings which Kiesler used primarily to illustrate the lighting of the *Color Clock*[25], as well as a series of model photographs that served Kiesler as a way to convey his ideas.

Together with his wife Jacqueline Lamba and their common son Merlin, David Hare spent the summer of 1950 at a house on Hewitt Pond in Minerva, Essex County, near the Canadian border. He invited Kiesler to come work with him on the joint project in the seclusion of the rural area. "When are you going to send me the drawings for your house? I have been waiting for them so that I can think of what to put in it,"[26] asked Hare of his artist friend in a letter dated June 20, 1950. Whether Kiesler actually sent the requested drawings, which ones they were and whether they still exist today, is difficult to answer. Lillian Kiesler entitled several of the sheets *Endless House for David*.[27] Two weeks later, a longer letter followed in which the sculptor apparently took up earlier discussions and tried to arrange the details of Kiesler's

Zeichnungen, die Kiesler zur Veranschaulichung vor allem der Beleuchtung durch die *Color clock* dienen,[25] sowie eine Serie an Modellfotografien, die Kiesler benutzte, um seine Ideen zu vermitteln.

David Hare verbringt den Sommer 1950 gemeinsam mit seiner Frau Jacqueline Lamba und dem gemeinsamen Sohn Merlin in einem Haus am Hewitt Pond in Minerva, Essex County nahe der Grenze zu Kanada und lädt Kiesler zur gemeinschaftlichen Arbeit in die ländliche Abgeschiedenheit ein.

„Wann schickst Du mir die Zeichnungen für Dein Haus? Ich warte auf sie, damit ich darüber nachdenken kann, was ich hineinstellen könnte",[26] bittet Hare seinen Kollegen in einem Brief, der mit 20. Juni 1950 datiert ist. Ob Kiesler die gewünschten Zeichnungen tatsächlich geschickt hat, um welche es sich handelt und ob sie heute noch erhalten sind, lässt sich nur schwer beantworten. Lillian Kiesler beschriftete einige Blätter mit *Endless House for David*.[27] Zwei Wochen später folgt ein längerer Brief,

in dem der Bildhauer offensichtlich an frühere Diskussionen anknüpft und Details zu Kieslers Aufenthalt zu regeln versucht. In diesem Brief wird auch die Art und Weise der Zusammenarbeit besprochen. Am 14. Juli vermerkt Stefi Kiesler in ihrem Kalendertagebuch Kieslers Abreise nach Minerva,[28] mit im Gepäck das Tonmodell (Abb. 17). Ende August fährt Kiesler noch einmal für

stay. In this letter, he also discussed the manner of their collaboration.
On July 14, Stefi Kiesler noted in her diary Kiesler's departure for Minerva[28],
with the clay model (Fig. 17) in his luggage. At the end of August, Kiesler
traveled to visit his artist friend for another 14 days.[29] In the interview with
Thomas Creighton, Kiesler addresses the difficulties of finding a suitable form
for presenting the sculptural staircase in his *Endless House*. "David
decided to enlarge the model to about five times its size (mine was only about
a foot long and eight or nine inches wide and seven or eight inches high)
because he had to enlarge it so that you could view the staircase inside.
However, although it was apparently the same shape and form, it was not the
same thing. Strange, we were both stunned and worried. The *Endless
House*, you see, isn't like a square house that is square anyway, no matter
how long or high. … Here the calculation of the inclinations of every part
must be exact, otherwise the coordination of the whole doesn't work."[30] The
result must have been disappointing, as both admitted that it would
have been better to not exhibit the large model with David Hare's staircase
sculpture. "Let's exhibit the little one, and at the side of it we will
have the staircase in a large scale,"[31] remembered Kiesler about the solution
that was found.

14 Tage zu seinem Künstlerfreund.[29] Im Interview mit Thomas Creighton
bespricht Kiesler die Probleme, eine geeignete Form für die Präsentation des
skulpturalen Stiegenhauses in seinem *Endless House* zu finden. „David
entschloss sich, das Modell auf das Fünffache zu vergrößern, (das Meinige
war nur einen Fuß lang, acht oder neun Zoll breit und sieben oder acht Inches
hoch). Er wollte es vergrößern, damit man sein Stiegenhaus darin betrachten
könne. Obwohl es augenscheinlich dieselbe Gestalt und Form hatte, war
es nicht das gleiche. Es war seltsam, aber wir beide waren erstaunt und be-
sorgt. Das *Endless House* […] ist nicht wie ein rechteckiges Haus, das
immer rechteckig aussieht ganz egal wie lang oder wie hoch es ist. …Hier
muss die Berechnung der Neigung einer jeden einzelnen Bahn ganz exakt sein,
sonst funktioniert die Koordination des Ganzen nicht mehr."[30] Das Ergebnis
dürfte ernüchternd gewesen sein, denn beide gestehen sich ein, dass es wohl
besser wäre, das große Modell mit David Hares Stiegenhaus-Skulptur nicht
auszustellen. „Lass uns das Kleine ausstellen, und daneben das Stiegenhaus
in größerem Maßstab,"[31] erinnerte sich Kiesler an die Lösung.

Vom ursprünglich vergrößerten Modell blieb nicht viel: eine Art Plattform –
Kiesler benutzte das Wort „Abschussrampe"[32] – die auf vier fragilen Beinen
ruht. In der Bodenplatte befindet sich eine Öffnung mit der Treppenskulptur

17—Frederick Kiesler, *Endless House*, model for Kootz Gallery, 1950

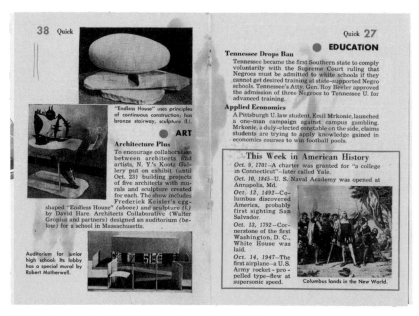

18—"Architecture Plus", in *QUICK News Weekly*, Oct. 9, 1950

David Hares. Der obere Teil der Schale, also die Wände und die Decke, wurde bis auf ein Wandelement mit einer Öffnung entfernt. Nur wenige Foto-dokumente geben über das Aussehen der Skulptur Auskunft. Eine Abbildung im *QUICK News Weekly*, October 9, 1950 (Abb. 18), eine Illustration im *Arts & Architecture* Magazins, sowie eine weitere Abbildung in Kieslers Artikel im *Interiors* Magazin. Hier ist dem Modell ein äußerst suggestives Foto gegenübergestellt (Abb.19), welches die Skulptur David Hares durch ein Fenster des Wohnzimmers betrachtet, und in ein atmosphärisches Spiel aus Licht und Schatten taucht.[33]

Es ist aber nicht nur die Ausstellung, die für diese Phase der Entwicklung des *Endless House* eine gewichtige Rolle spielt, sondern vielmehr noch die Begegnungen und Personen. Ganz besonders gilt dies für Arthur Drexler, der zuerst als Redakteur des Architekturteils des Interiors Magazin und später als Kurator sowie Direktor des Architekturdepartements im Museum of Modern Art in New York Kieslers *Endless* über mehr als zehn Jahre begleitet. Stefi Kiesler vermerkt in ihrem Kalendertagebuch mehrere Treffen ihres Mannes mit Drexler in den Wochen vor der Eröffnung.[34]

Drexler bietet Kiesler die Möglichkeit im Interiors Magazin einen aufwendig gestalteten Artikel zum *Endless House* zu veröffentlichen: Einem Überblick

19—*Endless House*, model for Kootz Gallery with sculpture by David Hare, 1950

Not much remained of the originally enlarged model: a kind of platform— Kiesler used the word "launching pad"[32]—which rested on four fragile legs. On the floor slab, there was an opening with David Hare's staircase sculpture. The upper part of the shell, that is the walls and ceiling, were removed with the exception of one wall element with an opening. Only a few photo documents give an impression of the appearance of the sculpture. An illustration in *QUICK, News Weekly, Oct. 9, 1950* (Fig. 18), another one in the *Arts & Architecture* magazine as well as a further depiction in Kiesler's article in the magazine *Interiors* (Fig. 19). Here the model was juxtaposed with a highly allusive photograph which views David Hare's sculpture through a window in the living room, immersing it in an atmospheric play of light and shadows.[33]

It was, however, not just the exhibition that played such a significant role for this phase in the development of the *Endless House* but also the encounters and individuals. This applies in particular to Arthur Drexler, who accompanied Kiesler's *Endless* for more than ten years, first as editor of the architectural section of the magazine *Interiors* and then as director of the architectural department at the Museum of Modern Art in New York. In her calendar-diary, Stefi Kiesler made a note of several meetings that her husband had with Drexler in the weeks before the opening.[34] Drexler

Drexlers unter dem Titel *Lighting restudied* folgt Kieslers Beitrag „The Endless House and Its Psychological Lighting", in dem er sein radikales, ganzheitliches, den Menschen als Subjekt der Architektur begreifendes Konzept vorstellt. Der Text stellt einen wesentlichen Beitrag zu Kieslers theoretischer Auseinandersetzung mit dem *Endless House* dar.[35]

Wie so oft bei Kiesler besticht der Artikel durch eine visuelle Argumentation, einer Abfolge von Zeichnungen und Fotografien (Abb. 20 und 21). Anhand der Zeichnungen erklärt Kiesler die unterschiedlichen Möglichkeiten der Beleuchtung, allen voran die *Color clock* (Abb. 22), einen Apparat aus prismatischen Glaskristallen, die in kraterähnlichen Öffnungen in der Außenschale angebracht sind und mit Hilfe von Konkav- und Konvexspiegel das einfallende Licht zuerst bündeln und dann wieder gestreut in den Innenraum leiten. Durch die optischen Eigenschaften des Prismas wird das weiße (Sonnen-)Licht farbig gebrochen und erzeugt, so Kiesler, eine farbige Tönung des Hausinneren.[36] In Kieslers Lichtregie gibt es aber auch Alternativen zur *Color clock*: Durch große, kreisrunde Öffnungen kann das Licht direkt einfallen. Auch abends, wenn das Licht flach, fast parallel über den Boden gleitet, taucht es die Wölbungen im Inneren in eine Abfolge von Schatten hinter Schatten.[37]

offered Kiesler the possibility to publish an elaborately designed article on the *Endless House* in the magazine *Interiors*. A survey by Drexler with the title *Lighting restudied* followed Kiesler's text "The Endless House and its Psychological Lighting", where he introduced his radical, holistic concept in which the human being was seen as the subject of architecture. The text represented a significant contribution to Kiesler's theoretical work on the *Endless House*.[35]

As so often with Kiesler, the article stood out for its visual argumentation, a sequence of drawings and photographs (Figs. 20 and 21). On the basis of the drawings, Kiesler explained the various possibilities of lighting, in particular the *Color Clock* (Fig. 22), a device consisting of prismatic glass crystals mounted in crater-like openings of the outer shell. By means of concave and convex mirrors, the incident light is first bundled and then dispersed into the interior space. By virtue of the optical properties of the prism, the white (sun) light is broken into colors, generating a colored "tint" of the interior of the house.[36] However, in Kiesler's light dramaturgy, there are also alternatives to the *Color Clock*. Light could enter directly through the large circular openings. Even in the evenings, when the light glides flatly, almost parallel to the floor, it dips the curves on the inside in a sequence

Die Fotografien stammen zu einem großen Teil von Percy Rainford.[38] Die Zeichnungen, die Kiesler zur Illustration dieses Artikels verwendet, zählen zu den künstlerisch stärksten Arbeiten des Künstlers aus dieser Zeit. Kiesler fertigt sie wahrscheinlich extra für den Artikel an, da sie sich sowohl in der künstlerischen Technik, als auch in ihrem hohen didaktischen Gehalt von den sonstigen Kugelschreiber- oder Bleistiftstudien zum *Endless House* unterscheiden. Kiesler richtet sich offensichtlich bewusst an ein breites Publikum. Er deutet mit einfachen, gekonnt energetisch gesetzten Linien, etwa Lichtstrahlen, die Ausdehnung der durch Lichtstreuung gewonnenen Farbatmosphäre und ganz allgemein die Dynamik des kontinuierlich fließenden Raumes an. Um die Dimensionen des Hauses lesbar zu machen, zeichnet er Menschen in seine Raumgebilde, ebenfalls ein Merkmal dieser einzigartigen Serie. Zum Teil sind Linien und Beschriftungen der Raumfunktionen auf Beiblättern aus Transparentpapier oder Azetatfolie angebracht, um den visuellen Eigenwert der Zeichnungen nicht zu zerstören.[39]

Zwei Jahre nachdem Kiesler die Einfamilien-Version seines *Endless House* erfolgreich in der Kootz Gallery ausstellt, organisiert Arthur Drexler, mittlerweile Kurator am Museum of Modern Art, eine Ausstellung, in der er unter dem Titel: *Two Houses: New Ways to Build* Richard Buckminster Fullers

and spot lighting, and the problems involved can be classified as (a) installation, (b) operation and (c) maintenance. The endless house is more economical to light than a conventional building because its volume is not boxed into rooms. Uninterrupted, overflowing, reflected on curving surfaces, the light multiplies itself, and even the minimal amount switched on only to enable us to see gives us physical information over a wider area.

The continuous, flowing, shell construction of the endless house is not a fancy sculptural idea nor is it the imitation of an egg. The spheroid shape derives from the social dynamics of two or three generations living under one roof. The

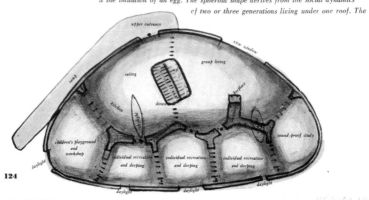

20/21—Frederick Kiesler's *Endless House* and its psychological lighting, *Interiors* Nov. 1950

from the side at an angle. Whereas the double-direct-indirect lighting scheme just describ...
is exhilarating and appropriately gay for social
gatherings, a single beam at the proper angle is
more congenial for concentration and study.

*Daylight raises different problems. We now have
at our disposal three technical means of controlling
daylight*: (1) *Dimensioning of the cut-outs—more
commonly referred to as windows—through which
daylight enters the building. We can make them
large or small, round or rectangular.* (2) *Shielding
the aperture or path of the light with a diffusing
skin of glass, plastic, or a translucent woven material.* (3) *Masking the aperture with one of any
number of disguises to temper or deflect the light
—shades, louvers, and shutters.*

*The light source itself is usually ignored. We do
not suggest an attempt to turn on the sun, but, although it has rarely been done by architects, it is
possible to send sunlight through a lens in order
to concentrate it, and pass it through convex mirror
reflex devices to diffuse it. The color clock of the
endless house illustrated on our introductory page
is designed to do these things, as well as to fill the
interior with color and make the dweller organically aware of the continuity of time.*

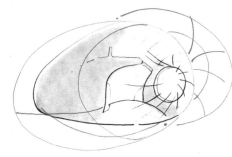

*At the top of this page we see the effect of tinting
the interior of the house with the light filters of the
color clock. The second drawing shows a completely different kind of daylight to be seen in
the endless house—a direct beam of sunshine
breaking through the six-foot circular opening—or
call it a round window—in the children's playroom.
The third drawing, a night view of the entrance as
one opens the door, illustrates the psychologically
evocative quality of the endless house. Light coming in parallel to the floor spills to the curving
partitions of the interior, transforming it into a
vast succession of shadows beyond shadows.*

*The apertures cut into the shell of the endless house
—the windows—admit more light and for longer
daily periods than if this curving shell were a vertical plane. The big view window of the living room
reverses its angle to the floor in the course of its
gradual curve, and also curves laterally.*

*The colored lines on the drawings represent (as
well as any two dimensional illustration can) the
psychological awareness of space beyond the physical partitions and walls of the endless house which*

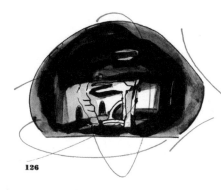

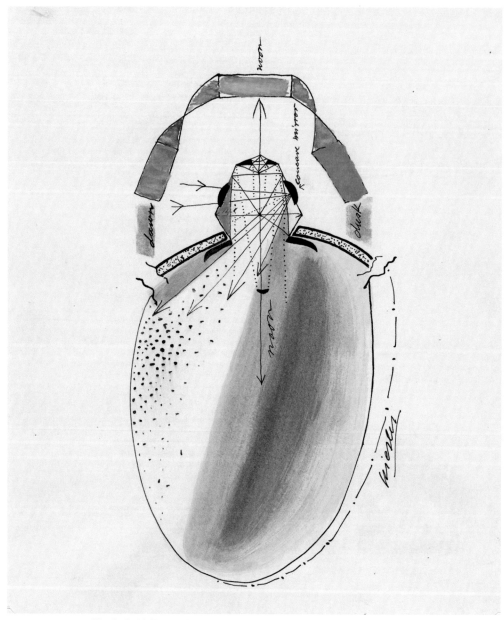

22—Frederick Kiesler, *Endless House*, Study for *Color Clock*, 1950

of shadow behind shadow.[37] Most of the photographs were made by Percy Rainford.[38] The drawings that Kiesler uses as illustrations for this article are among the artistically strongest works of the artist from this period. Kiesler probably created them especially for this article, since they differ from the other studies of the *Endless House* in pen or pencil, both in terms of artistic technique and their high didactic value. Kiesler was obviously targeting a broader audience. Using simple, skillfully and energetically placed lines, he alludes to light rays, the intensification of the color atmosphere resulting from the diffusion of light, and in general the dynamic of the continuously flowing space. In order to make the dimensions of the house legible, he draws persons in his spatial formations, also a feature of this unique series. In part, lines and markings indicating the spatial functions have been added on accompanying sheets of transparent paper or acetate foil, so as not to destroy the intrinsic visual value of the drawings.[39]

Two years after Kiesler exhibited the one-family version of his *Endless House* with great acclaim at the Kootz Gallery, Arthur Drexler, meanwhile curator at the Museum of Modern Art, organized a show with the title *Two Houses: New Ways to Build*, in which he confronted Richard Buckminster Fuller's *Geodesic Dome* with Kiesler's *Endless House*. He wanted to show how

Geodesic Dome mit Kieslers *Endless House* konfrontiert. Er will damit zeigen, wie zwei auf den ersten Blick unterschiedliche Herangehensweisen, die ingenieurstechnisch-wissenschaftliche und die skulptural-ästhetische, ähnliche Resultate der architektonischen Raumnutzung hervorbringen können."[40]

Kiesler fühlt sich allerdings in der Ausstellung missinterpretiert und sein *Endless House* falsch dargestellt. Er ist enttäuscht, dass keine Pläne seines Bauwerks gezeigt werden. Ohne Pläne wirke sein Haus „wie ein willkürliches Machwerk."[41] Wenngleich er die Gegenüberstellung der zwei Modelle begrüße, so wäre es verfälschend, sein *Endless House* nur als ästhetisches Objekt zu präsentieren. Kiesler moniert: „Es wurde zuallererst zur Befriedigung menschlicher Lebensbedürfnisse entwickelt, und dem entsprächen die Raumbereiche. Von diesen Bedingungen ausgehend, kam ich zu den Dimensionen, zur Form und zum Konstruktionsschema. Die Ästhetik kam danach und nicht als erster Gedanke."

In welcher Art Kiesler das *Endless House* Projekt in den Jahren nach der Ausstellung in der Kootz Gallery weiter verfolgt, ist schwer zu sagen. Belege dafür gibt es nicht. Lediglich eine kleine Kugelschreiber-Zeichnung, eine Art Kiesler'scher *Geodesic Dome* ist mit 9. November 1955 datiert (Abb. 23). Er muss aber auch an Modellen gearbeitet haben, denn im Kapitel „Towards

two, at first glance different approaches, the engineering technical-scientific one and the sculptural-aesthetic one, can produce similar results of space being used in an architectural sense.[40]

Kiesler, however, felt that he had been misinterpreted in the exhibition and his *Endless House* had been falsely portrayed. He was disappointed that no plans of his building had been presented. Without plans, he thought that his house looked like "an arbitrary concoction."[41] Even though he welcomed the juxta-position of two models, it was an adulteration to present his *Endless House* only as an aesthetic object. As Kiesler voiced his criticism: "It has primarily been conceived for the creation of satisfactory living conditions, the spatial areas needed for this purpose, and that from these conditions I had arrived at the dimensions, the form and the construction scheme. The aesthetic aspect comes with it and was not the primary thought."

It is difficult to say how Kiesler continued work on the *Endless House* project in the years following the exhibition at the Kootz Gallery. There is no evidence—only a small pen drawing, a sort of Kieslerian *Geodesic Dome* dated November 9, 1955 (Fig. 23). He must have also worked on models, though, as the chapter "Towards the Endless Sculpture, Saturday Afternoon, July 25, 1956" documents with a reminiscence of the evolution of his

the Endless Sculpture, Saturday Afternoon, July 25, 1956", einer als Dialog mit Stefi Kiesler verschriftlichten Erinnerung an die Entstehung seiner Skulptur *Cup of Prometheus* (Abb. 24), hält Kiesler fest, dass der erste Teil dieser Skulptur eigentlich als Modell für ein *Endless House* gedacht war: „[…] der erste Teil war ursprünglich ein Modell für das *Endless House*, ein aus Ton geformtes Stück Architektur, gebildet durch ein dreifaches Zusammenspiel von Schalen, ein Hohlraum in einen anderen gelegt, zerbrochenen Eierschalen gleich. Zusammen waren sie etwa eineinhalb Fuß [ca. 45 cm] lang und einen Fuß breit. Keine Skulptur, wohlgemerkt, sondern ein Stück Architektur."[42]

Da weder Kiesler noch seine Atelierassistenten Erfahrung im Umgang mit dem Material Ton haben, zerspringen die Tonschalen beim Trocknen. Alle Versuche, die Risse und Sprünge zu reparieren, schlagen fehl. Da Kiesler allerdings so viel Mühe und Zeit in das Modellieren der Schalenformen verwendet hat, will er es nicht einfach wegwerfen. So entschließt er sich, die verwendbaren Teile in Bronze gießen zu lassen, um zumindest einen Teil dieses *Endless House* dokumentieren zu können.

Als Kiesler den Guss nach zwei Monaten gezeigt bekommt, ist er mit dem Resultat zufrieden. „[…] die Sprünge waren fest mit Bronze gefüllt. Die Schalen-Architektur ruhte auf ihrem Rücken, sie schaukelte friedlich

23—Frederick Kiesler, Study for *Endless House*, Nov. 9, 1955

24—Frederick Kiesler, *The Cup of Prometheus* (detail), 1956–59

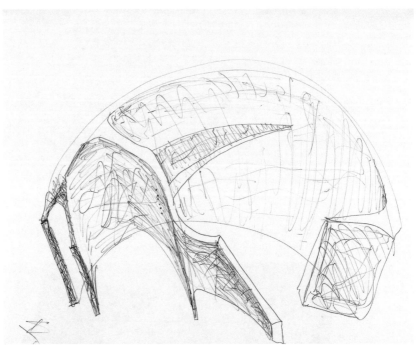

25—Frederick Kiesler, Study for *Endless House*, ca. 1955–60

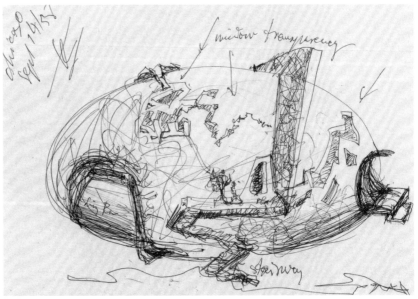

26—Frederick Kiesler, Study for *Endless House*, Sept. 14, 1958

sculpture *Cup of Prometheus* (Fig. 24), written down in a dialog with Stefi Kiesler. Here Kiesler notes that the first part of this sculpture was actually conceived as a model for the *Endless House*: "[…] the first unit was the original model for the *Endless House*, a piece of architecture done on clay and constituting a triple interplay of shells, one hollow laid within another, like broken eggshells. Altogether, they were about one and a half feet long and one foot wide. Not a sculpture, mind you, but a piece of architecture."[42]

Since neither Kiesler nor his studio assistant had any experience in working with clay, the clay shells burst when dried. All attempts to repair the cracks and fissures failed. Because Kiesler had spent so much time and energy modeling the shell forms, he didn't want to simply throw them away. He therefore decided to have the usable pieces cast in bronze, in order to be able to document at least part of this *Endless House*. When Kiesler was shown the cast two months later, he was happy with the result. "[…] the cracks had been filled solidly with bronze. The shell-architecture rested on its back, rocking peacefully like a cradle. I asked that it be lifted on its edge; why I don't know. That spontaneous demand was really the beginning of the endless sculpture […] it was no longer the shell of my *Endless House*. It acquired a new personality, the plasticity of a sculpture."[43]

wie in einer Wiege. Ich bat, sie auf einer ihrer Seiten aufzustellen. Warum? Ich weiß es nicht. Dieser spontane Wunsch war der Anfang der *Endless Sculpture*. [...] Sie war nicht mehr länger die Schale meines *Endless House*. Sie erwarb eine neue Persönlichkeit, die Plastizität einer Skulptur."[43]

Vergleicht man die Bronzeplastik mit der Bodenplatte des Modells von 1950, so kann man die Weiterentwicklung des Formvokabulars sehr gut erkennen. Dies wird umso deutlicher, wenn man in die Analyse jene *Endless House*-Zeichnungen miteinbezieht, die im Zusammenhang mit der Ausstellung in der Kootz Gallery entstanden sind und die Möglichkeiten der Raumunterteilungen ausloten. Im Vergleich mit den großformatigen Kugelschreiber-Zeichnungen, die man als zeichnerische Auseinandersetzung Kieslers mit den im Modell gewonnenen Formen bezeichnen könnte, wird einerseits die Verwandtschaft und andererseits die Entwicklungslinie noch deutlicher. (Abb. 25)

Endless 1959 – Vom Skulpturengarten zur *Visionary Architecture*

Wie ein Paukenschlag vertreibt eine Presseaussendung des New Yorker Museum of Modern Art vom 2. Februar 1958 die erneute Stille um Friedrich Kieslers *Endless House*. Das Department for Architecture and Design erhält

If one compares the bronze sculpture with the base plate of the model of 1950, the further development of the formal idiom can be very easily recognized. This becomes all the more evident when one also analyzes the *Endless House* drawings that were created in connection with the exhibition at the Kootz Gallery, in which he explored the possibilities of spatial divisions. Compared to the large-format ink drawings that can be described as Kiesler's work in drawing with the forms derived from the model, the affinity but also the line of development becomes even more evident. (Fig. 25)

Endless 1959—From the Sculpture Garden to *Visionary Architecture*

Like a bombshell, a press release of the New York Museum of Modern Art dated February 2, 1958 lifted the new silence surrounding Frederick Kiesler's *Endless House*. The Department for Architecture and Design received a 12 000 dollar grant from the D.S. and R.H. Gottesman Foundation to prepare an *Endless House* that was to be constructed in the original size (40 × 60 feet with a height of 25 feet) and erected in the museum's sculptural garden. The grant was to allow Kiesler to create work sketches, engineering plans and models.[44] Even if it cannot be exactly determined when Kiesler

von der D. S. und R. H. Gottesman Foundation eine Förderung in der Höhe von 12 000 Dollar für die Vorbereitung eines *Endless House*, das in Originalgröße (40 × 60 Fuß und einer Höhe von 25 Fuß) im Skulpturengarten des Museums errichtet werden soll. Die Dotierung würde es Kiesler ermöglichen, Arbeitszeichnungen, Ingenieurspläne und Modelle anzufertigen.[44] Wenngleich sich nicht genau klären lässt, wann Kiesler mit den Vorarbeiten beginnt – in der ersten Jahreshälfte ist das Architekturbüro Kiesler & Bartos vor allem mit den Planungen für den *Shrine of the Book* beschäftigt – so haben sich einige Blätter aus diesem Jahr erhalten, und am 11. Juni 1958 verfasst Kiesler sein bekanntes Gedicht *Life is short, Art is long, Architecture endless*.[45] Eine Studie für ein *Endless House* ist mit 14. September 1958 datiert (Abb. 26). Es ist eines der wenigen von Kiesler eigenhändig datierten Blätter und dürfte während seines Aufenthalts in Chicago bei der Graham Foundation, wahrscheinlich für die Diskussion mit den anderen Stipendiaten, angefertigt worden sein.[46]

Eine Werkgruppe, deren Entstehung sich sehr gut rekonstruieren lässt, kann von den heute noch existierenden Modellen gebildet werden. Insgesamt haben sich drei Modelle und zwei skulpturale Modellstudien erhalten. Sie sind allesamt im Winter 1958/59 entstanden. Kiesler entwickelte eine Meister-

began with the preparation work, in the first half of the year the architectural firm Kiesler & Bartos was mainly busy with planning the *Shrine of the Book*. Several sheets from this year still remain, and on June 11, 1958, Kiesler wrote his well-known poem entitled *Life is short, Art is long, Architecture endless*.[45] One study for an *Endless House* is dated September 14, 1958 (Fig. 26). It is one of the few sheets dated by Kiesler himself and it was probably created during his stay in Chicago at the Graham Foundation, for the discussion with other grant holders.[46]

A group of works whose production can be easily reconstructed can be created on the basis of models that still exist today. Altogether, three models and two model-like studies remain. They were all created in the winter of 1958/59. Kiesler developed an ingenious way of staging himself. He particularly liked to be photographed while working, be it at his desk or in the studio, as a snapshot or as a well-composed staging. It is therefore hardly surprising that Kiesler's work on the models was incredibly well-documented in photographs. (Fig. 27) This documentation provides important insights into their production and also makes it possible to create a chronology. The shots show the artist and his assistants cutting the wire arcs, modeling the basic structures or assembling the various grid shells. Since the

haftigkeit in der Selbstinszenierung. Besonders gerne ließ er sich bei der Arbeit fotografieren, ganz gleich ob am Schreibtisch oder im Atelier, ob als Schnappschuss oder als durchkomponierte Inszenierung. So verwundert es kaum, dass Kieslers Arbeit an den Modellen unglaublich dicht fotografisch dokumentiert wurde (Abb. 27). Diese Dokumentation liefert wichtige Einsichten in das Making-of und erlaubt darüber hinaus die Erstellung einer Chronologie. Die Aufnahmen zeigen etwa den Künstler und seine Assistenten beim Zuschneiden der Drahtbögen, beim Modellieren der Grundstrukturen oder beim Zusammenfügen der verschiedenen Gitterschalen. Da auf den Fotos zum Teil das Datum ihrer Entwicklung aufgedruckt ist, kann man Kieslers Arbeitsprozess heute gut rekonstruieren.

Den Anfang dieses Formfindungsprozesses bildet das tubenförmige Modell (Abb. 28), das sich heute im Besitz der Jason McCoy Gallery in New York befindet.[47] Auf den Fotos, die den Datumsvermerk „January 1959" tragen, erkennt man, dass die skulpturalen Studien zum *Endless House* (Abb. 29) schon mit Beton überzogen sind, während Kiesler die Arbeit am kleineren *Endless House* Modell beginnt.[48] Gleichzeitig fertigt Kiesler großformatige Kohlezeichnungen (Abb. 30) mit Studien zum *Endless House*.[49] Die Formfindung entsteht scheinbar in einem Wechselspiel der zeichnerischen Annäherung

27—Frederick Kiesler working on *Endless House* model, 1959

28—Frederick Kiesler, *Endless House*, sculptural study, 1958/59

29—Frederick Kiesler, *Endless House*, sculptural study, 1958/59

date of development was printed on some of the photographs, Kiesler's work process can be easily reconstructed today.

The beginnings of this form-finding process are marked by the tube-shaped model (Fig. 28) that is currently owned by the Jason McCoy Gallery in New York.[47] In photographs bearing the date "January 1959," one can see that the sculptural studies on the *Endless House* (Fig. 29) were already coated with cement, while Kiesler began working on the smaller *Endless House* model.[48]

At the same time, Kiesler created large-format charcoal drawings (Fig. 30) with studies on the *Endless House*.[49] The form-finding process appears to unfold in an interplay between first attempts at drawing and the spatial experimentation when modeling the cement-mesh wire objects. Moreover, Kiesler, in an interview for *CBS Camera Three*, explained the sequence of work steps and stated why he abandoned certain solutions while pursuing others in order to obtain those spatial dispositions that corresponded to his idea of a continuously flowing space. He also explained that he used the first model to test the division of space within the main shell but that he was not happy with the solution he found: "Here I tried reinforced concrete to divide a larger area into a smaller area, but that was not satisfactory because I know the wall is curved and tried to relate the floor, ceiling, and the wall in a different

und der räumlichen Erprobung beim Modellieren der Beton-Maschendraht-Objekte. Darüber hinaus erläutert Kiesler in einem Interview für *CBS Camera Three* die Abfolge der Arbeitsschritte und erklärt, warum er gewisse Lösungen verwirft und welche er weiterverfolgt, um jene räumlichen Dispositionen zu erhalten, die seiner Vorstellung des kontinuierlich fließenden Raumes entsprechen.

Unter anderem erklärt er, dass ihm das erste Modell dazu diente, die Raumteilung innerhalb der Hauptschale zu testen, aber dass er mit der gefundenen Lösung nicht zufrieden war: „[…] aber das war nicht befriedigend. Die Wand ist gekurvt […] aber es ist noch immer eine Wand und eine Abtrennung – eine harte Abtrennung".[50] In den skulpturalen Studien und mit dem kleineren Modell erarbeitet er dann jenes Formvokabular, mit dem er das große Modell gestaltet, das sich heute im Whitney Museum of American Art befindet.[51] Ein weiteres Modell ist heute nur über zwei Abbildungen bekannt. Interessanterweise entspricht die Gliederung seiner Baukörper jenem aus dem Whitney Museum, hat allerdings eine glatte Oberfläche.[52]

Das große Modell ist für Kiesler von eminenter Bedeutung, dient es ihm doch als Arbeitsgrundlage zur Erstellung der Pläne für das *Endless House* im

DEC · 58

30—Frederick Kiesler working on *Study for Endless House Shells*, 1958

way like we usually see it—it still is a wall and a division—a hard division."[50] In the sculptural studies and with the smaller model, he then developed the formal idiom that he used to design the large model still found today in the Whitney Museum of American Art.[51] A further model is only known today from two illustrations. Interestingly, the structure of his buildings corresponds to that from the Whitney Museum, only with a smooth surface.[52]

The large model was of eminent importance to Kiesler, as it served him as a basis for developing the plans for the *Endless House* found in the sculptural garden of the Museum of Modern Art. As already mentioned, it was very important to Kiesler to document the production process by photographing it. If one looks at the preserved photographs, one can see that the raw-mesh wire object that was not yet covered with cement assumed a very special place for Kiesler.

He often reported on this in his notes that were published posthumously, and even the number of remaining shots seem to corroborate this, since in the artist's estate one finds almost just as many shots of the unfinished wire structure as of the finished object. On February 25, Kiesler wrote to Arthur Drexler that he was almost finished with the wire model, but that he didn't want to show it until the whole thing was completely covered with cement.[53]

Skulpturengarten des Museum of Modern Art. Wie schon erwähnt, ist für Kiesler die fotografische Dokumentation des Making-of von großer Bedeutung. Betrachtet man die erhaltenen Fotografien, so fällt auf, dass das rohe, noch nicht mit Beton überzogene Maschendraht-Objekt für Kiesler einen ganz besonderen Platz einnimmt. Mehrfach berichtet er darüber in seinen posthum erschienenen Aufzeichnungen, und auch die Anzahl der erhaltenen Aufnahmen scheint das zu untermauern, denn es befinden sich im Nachlass des Künstlers beinahe so viele Aufnahmen der noch unfertigen Drahtstruktur wie vom fertiggestellten Objekt. Am 25. Februar schreibt Kiesler an Arthur Drexler, dass er mit dem Drahtmodell fast fertig ist, dass er es allerdings erst dann zeigen möchte, wenn es zur Gänze mit Beton überzogen ist.[53]

Die Arbeit an der Drahtstruktur für das große Modell dürfte die ersten Monate des Jahres 1959 in Anspruch genommen haben. Am 10. März berichtet Kiesler in *Inside The Endless House* über das Fotoshooting in seinem Studio, bei dem wohl ein Großteil der Aufnahmen entstehen, die das *Endless House*-Modell noch als Maschendrahtstruktur zeigen: „Ein neues Modell ist bereit, fotografiert zu werden." Wie schon 1952 arbeitet er auch diesmal mit Percy Rainford zusammen. „Für ihn ist die Realität im Glas der Kamera, und der Traum ist das Objekt davor, das außerhalb steht. [...]

It probably took him the first months of 1959 to work on the wire structure for the large model. On March 10, Kiesler, in *Inside the Endless House*, reported on the photo shoot at his studio. Most of the shots that were created still show the *Endless House* model as a chicken-wire structure. "A new model is ready to be photographed." As in 1952, he again worked with Percy Rainford. "For him, reality is on the glass of the camera, and the dream is the object which stands outside, in front of him. […] He is the only photographer I know who portrays with sharpness and exactitude what the camera sees, not his own eye.[…] The most difficult thing, of course, was the lighting of the *Endless*, which was only formed of wire mesh: the lights fell not only on the surface, but pierced through the mesh, making images like X-ray photographs, without body and form. […] The house looked like streaks of black smoke dispersed in curves and parabolas over an indefinite horizon. (I) directed the light so that it only hit the outer surface of the model without the light reaching the inside."[54]

Soon after, the work on the model must have been completed. In April, Kiesler and his staff worked on the plans, for which the measurements were taken from the model.[55] In May, Kiesler consulted with Severud, Elstad & Krueger, Engineers regarding the structural plans for the *Endless House* and

Er ist der einzige Fotograf, den ich kenne, der mit Schärfe und Exaktheit das portraitiert, was die Kamera sieht und nicht sein eigenes Auge. […] Das Schwierigste war, wie könnte es anders sein, das Ausleuchten des *Endless*, welches nur aus Maschendraht geformt war: Das Licht fiel nicht nur auf die Oberfläche, sondern durchbohrte das Gitter. Die entstandenen Bilder waren wie Röntgenaufnahmen, ohne Körper und Form. […] Das Haus glich Schlieren aus schwarzem Rauch, die sich in Kurven und Parabeln über einen unbestimmten Horizont verteilten. [Ich] dirigierte die Beleuchtung so, dass sie nur die äußere Oberfläche des Modells traf ohne dass das Licht ins Innere drang."[54]

Bald danach dürfte die Arbeit am Modell fertig gewesen sein, und im April erarbeitet Kiesler mit seinen Mitarbeitern die Pläne, deren Maße sie vom Modell abnehmen.[55] Im Mai lässt sich Kiesler von Severud, Elstad & Krueger, Engineers bezüglich der Statikpläne für das *Endless House* beraten und schickt Blaupausen (siehe „Vision und Ingenieurskunst", Medicus & Zillner, S. 258).[56]

Parallel zu den Arbeiten an den Bau- und Statikplänen entwickelt sich ein medialer Diskurs um das ambitionierte Projekt. Am 25. Mai erscheint im *TIME Magazine* ein Artikel über das *Endless House* (Abb. 31). Es trägt den Titel

sent blueprints (see "Vision and The Art of Engineering", Medicus & Zillner, p. 258).

In parallel to work on the construction and static plans, a discourse developed in the media on the ambitious project. On May 25, an article on the *Endless House* appeared in *TIME Magazine* (Fig.31).[56] The title was "Tough Prophet" and it featured a photograph of the model for illustration purposes. Both the title and the total view of the model in a shot that was composed from slightly below evoke the visionary character.[57]

The summer of 1959, for which the *Endless House* had originally been planned at the sculptural garden, was approaching and construction had still not begun. It was agreed to move it by one year. When exactly the decision was made is not easy to determine—a letter dated July 1 from Drexler to Kiesler ends with the sentence: "I feel that we have made some progress in clarifying the situation, and I hope that we will shortly be able to prepare a detailed budget for fund-raising purposes in order to have the house open to the public as early as possible in the summer of 1960."[58]

In order to rouse the public's interest in the project, Drexler and Kiesler apparently worked on organizing a media campaign. In the October edition of *Harper's Bazaar*, a short text appeared in the *Features and Fiction* section

"Tough Prophet" und ist mit einem Foto des Modells illustriert. Der Titel gemeinsam mit der in leichter Untersicht komponierten Gesamtaufnahme des Objektes evoziert den visionären Charakter.[57]

Der Sommer des Jahres 1959, für den man das *Endless House* ursprünglich im Skulpturengarten geplant hätte, rückt näher, und der Baubeginn steht weiterhin noch aus. Man einigt sich auf eine Verschiebung um ein Jahr. Wann genau der Beschluss gefasst wird, lässt sich schwer sagen, einen Brief vom 1. Juli an Kiesler schließt Drexler mit dem Satz: „Ich fühle, dass wir bei der Klärung der Situation weitergekommen sind, und ich hoffe, dass wir bald in der Lage sein werden, ein detailliertes Budget für das Fundraising zu haben, um das Haus so früh als möglich im Sommer 1960 der Öffentlichkeit zugänglich machen zu können."[58]

Um öffentliches Interesse für das Projekt wecken zu können, arbeiten Drexler und Kiesler anscheinend an einer Medienkampagne: So erscheint in der Oktober-Ausgabe des *Harper's Bazaar* in der Rubrik *Features and Fiction* ein Kurztext, der anhand von Richard Buckminster Fullers *Geodesic Dome* und Friedrich Kieslers *Endless House* neue Architekturkonzepte vorstellt, und im Januar 1960 greift Arthur Drexler selbst zur Feder, um Kieslers Architekturkonzept zu bewerben, diesmal in der *Vogue* mit einem Foto Irving Penns.[59]

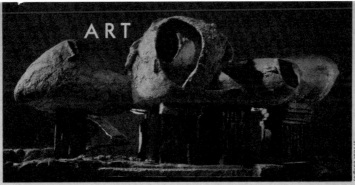

FREDERICK KIESLER'S "ENDLESS HOUSE"

Tough Prophet

The wellspring of any architectural masterpiece lies in its design; blueprints and bricks come later. Even such a titan as the late Frank Lloyd Wright had to wait years to see his "impossible" ideas bear fruit. And the more adventurous the pioneer, the longer the wait. One of the most adventurous of all is Manhattan's Frederick Kiesler, who at 62 has originated more ideas and seen fewer of them built than almost any other architect of his time.

For Scrolls, a Fountain. Coming to the U.S. from his native Vienna in 1926, Kiesler took up teaching at Columbia in the 1930s, amazed his students with suggestions that they develop spiral buildings, semicircular projection screens, "floating cities" wrapped in cocoonlike weather protectors, and "horizontal skyscrapers" suspended like bridges. In the 1940s he built great open sculptures and clusters of pictures "to relax inside" and designed striking stage sets for *No Exit* and *The Magic Flute.*

Small, spry, tough, intense, Kiesler got few commissions for his missionary work and asked for no favors. His credo, stated in the *College Art Journal:* "The artist must learn only one thing in order to be creative: not to resist himself, but to resist without exception every human, technical, social, economical factor that prevents him from being himself." Recently,

a former student of Kiesler, Armand Bartos, asked him to become a partner while remaining strictly Kiesler. Their collaboration resulted first in Manhattan's strange and elegant World House Galleries (TIME, Feb. 4, 1957). Now ground is being broken for the partners' full-scale project at the Hebrew University of Jerusalem: a gigantic shrine, to be entered from underground, and built around an 80-foot column of water, to house the Dead Sea Scrolls.

Back in 1923 Kiesler proposed the first actual shell house in history. The Pantheon in Rome is half a shell. Kiesler modeled a true shell, an egglike construction balanced on stilts and tensile all around—not just at the top and sides. Last year, 35 years after he proposed it, Kiesler was commissioned by Manhattan's Museum of Modern Art to carry out his still-revolutionary idea in model form. He secluded himself in his Greenwich Village loft, spent month after month brooding, sketching, constructing. The end result is bound to surprise even those who know him. Anchored to its supporting columns as lightly as a dirigible, Kiesler's "Endless House" looks more like a cloud than a building.

For People, Change. Entrance is up a winding ramp. Windows, to be filled with curving panes of Plexiglas, come wherever they naturally fall, between the ribs of the construction. Floors curve into walls and walls into ceilings, with no inter-

ruption and no corners. Designed for shoeless clambering, the interior is a plexus of balcony hideaways, ramps, hanging screens, near-flat areas with shelves for seats, and even a waterfall in the master bedroom. "Of course a building shouldn't be a box," Kiesler explained last week, perching by his model like a bird overlooking its nest. "It shouldn't be candy either—the candy engineering they're doing now. It needs to be flowing and opening, getting louder and softer, opening out and moving in. To be inside my Endless House will be like living inside a sculpture that is changing every second with the light."

Might it also be comfortable? Where would the refrigerator go? Won't those balconies be dangerous for children? How about privacy, heating and storage? Kiesler does have answers to these questions, though as an all-out idea man he can be impatient with too much insistence on the practical. Comfort is largely a matter of habit, he argues; his house might seem uncomfortable at first, not remain so. The curving lips of the interior overhangs make them fairly safe for children. There is visual privacy, though not the privacy that doors afford. The kitchen is to be built into one of the supporting pillars beneath. Radiant heating will keep the house snug. Storage space exists in abundance between the interior and exterior shells of the building.

Tentative plans have been made to

DISTANT REALM

THERE is no substitute for actuality, yet art books can do wonders in bringing home to space-bound men impossibly far realms of art. This spring, with the publication of *Japan: Ancient Buddhist Paintings,* the New York Graphic Society offered U.S. readers 32 color reproductions of masterpieces of Japanese religious art that are rolled up in scrolls, tucked away in mountain monasteries or otherwise unavailable to all but the most determined travelers.

Like all too many art books, *Japan* is expensive ($18), and its text contributes little or nothing to the pictures. But any one of the big (14 in. by 20 in.) color plates is worthy of a frame and a wall.

Strangest picture in the book, perhaps, is a 7th century

panel representing the willful martyrdom of a future Buddha. It illustrates the legend of a saintly youth who comes upon a family of starving tigers. Filled with pity, he flings himself down from the top of a cliff, offering his own body to feed the tigers' hunger. The story is told consecutively in a single picture, as in the case of some modern comic strips and many early Renaissance paintings. With Buddhist confidence in reincarnation on a higher plane, the youth gives himself up as simply as a candle flame pinched from its wick. He lies peacefully under the tigers' tearing fangs. The whole dark and wild episode is painted with the utmost delicacy, even serenity. It looks like the imaginary scenes that small boys find among the ashes of dying fires.

TIME, MAY 25, 1959

31—"Tough Prophet", *Time Magazine,* May 25, 1959

which presented new architectural concepts on the basis of Richard Buckminster Fuller's *Geodesic Dome* and Frederick Kiesler's *Endless House*. And in January 1960, Arthur Drexler took it upon himself to promote Kiesler's architectural concept, this time in *Vogue* magazine, with a photo taken by Irving Penn.[59]

The articles that appeared on Kiesler's *Endless House* were all illustrated with photographs of the model—not drawings or plans. Drexler and Kiesler were aware of the impact of these illustrations. What is more, the shots of the architect with his model were also skillfully self-fashioning. This becomes particularly clear in the illustrations that appeared in *Harper's Bazaar* and in *Vogue* , which are today among the best-known portrait shots of Kiesler. Even though both illustrations have the same subject—Kiesler with his model— the two shots could hardly be any more different. Hans Namuth shows Kiesler in front of the backside of the model. Dressed in black, he seems to emerge from the void of the atmospheric dark, in which the entire scene is dipped. The artist's head is supported by his hand and is positioned in front of the central window opening of the *Endless House* so that his head seems to be surrounded by a dark halo. Pensive, his forehead wrinkled, he addresses the viewer, resembling a prophet who announces the future of housing.

Die Artikel, die zu Kieslers *Endless House* erscheinen, sind allesamt mit Fotos des Modells illustriert, nicht mit Zeichnungen oder Plänen. Drexler und Kiesler sind sich der Wirkmächtigkeit dieser Abbildungen bewusst. Die Aufnahmen des Architekten mit seinem Modell sind darüber hinaus gekonnte Selbstinszenierungen. Besonders deutlich wird dies anhand der Illustra-tionen im *Harper's Bazaar* und in der *Vogue*, die heute zu den bekanntesten Portrait-aufnahmen Kieslers zählen. Obwohl die beiden Abbildungen das gleiche Sujet haben – Kiesler mit seinem Modell – könnten die zwei Aufnahmen nicht unter-schiedlicher sein. Hans Namuth zeigt Kiesler vor der Rückseite des Modells. Schwarz gekleidet scheint er aus dem Nichts des atmos-phärischen Dunkels zu kommen, welches die Szenerie umfängt. Der Künstler hat seinen Kopf auf die Hand gestützt und ist genau so vor der zentralen Fensteröffnung des *Endless House* platziert, dass sein Haupt scheinbar von einem dunklen Halo umfasst wird. Nachdenklich, die Stirn in Falten gelegt, adressiert er den Betrachter und wirkt wie ein Prophet, der die Zukunft des Wohnens verkündet.

Irving Penn inszeniert Kiesler bei der Arbeit. Der Künstler steht hinter seinem *Endless House* und scheint mit bloßen Händen Beton aufzutragen. Die beiläufig am Dach des Hauses abgestellte Schüssel weist das Modell als

Irving Penn staged Kiesler while he was working. The artist stood behind his *Endless House* and seemed to be applying cement with his bare hands. The bowl casually left on the roof of the house identifies the model as a yet-unfinished object which the artist would soon complete. Kiesler's gaze is directed from the image. He seems detached, tired. Penn staged Kiesler as a demiurge who lends the material of his creation definitive form.[60] Comparing these pictures with snapshots taken in Kiesler's studio in the winter months of December 1958 and January 1959, one sees how staged these works were.[61]

Aware of the allusive impact of the photographs, Kiesler noted on January 5, 1960 that the article in *TIME Magazine* had aroused curiosity in his *Endless*. "Pictures of my model appeared in *Harper's Bazaar* and *Vogue*, and yesterday in *Art in America*. It is spreading before I have even had a chance to build it. Typical of our time: artists and architects satisfying this hunger for novelty, and using for plastic inspiration flat photographs of something that hasn't yet been realized. A hint of what could be done creates a hullabaloo."[62]

On March 20, Kiesler was interviewed for the program *CBS Camera Three*. He explained the theory of his architectural concepts and used his models to describe the *Endless House*. A bundle of readers' letters testifies to the viewers' interest.[63] It was also discussed in the *New York Times* by Ada Louise

noch unvollendetes Objekt aus, das der Künstler in Bälde fertigstellen wird. Kieslers Blick ist aus dem Bild gerichtet. Er wirkt abgeklärt und müde. Penn inszeniert Kiesler als Demiurgen, der der Materie seiner Schöpfung die endgültige Form verleiht.[60] Wie sehr die Bilder Inszenierungen sind, erschließt sich im Vergleich mit den Schnappschüssen aus den Wintermonaten Dezember 1958 und Januar 1959 in Kieslers Atelier.[61]

Im Wissen um die suggestive Wirkmächtigkeit der Fotografien vermerkt Kiesler am 5. Januar 1960 reflektierend, dass der Artikel im *TIME Magazine* die Neugier an seinem *Endless* geweckt hätte. „Bilder von meinem Modell erschienen im Harper's Bazaar und in der Vogue und gestern in Art in America. Es verbreitet sich, bevor ich überhaupt die Chance hatte, es zu bauen. Typisch für unsere Zeit: Künstler und Architekten befriedigen diesen Hunger nach Neuem und verwenden flache Fotografien von etwas, das noch gar nicht realisiert wurde, zur plastischen Inspiration. Allein ein Hinweis auf das, was getan werden könnte, schafft ein Tohuwabohu."[62]

Am 20. März wird Kiesler für die Sendung *CBS Camera Three* interviewt. Er erläutert die Theorie seiner Architekturkonzepte und erklärt das *Endless House* anhand seiner Modelle. Ein Konvolut an Leserbriefen zeugt vom großen Interesse der Zuschauer.[63] Sie wird von Ada Louise Huxtable am 27. März 1960

32—Frederick Kiesler, Study for *Endless House*, ca. 1960

auch in der *New York Times* besprochen, wobei der Ton des Artikels nicht unkritisch, wenn nicht sogar zynisch ist. Die Autorin attestiert Kiesler zwar ein „einzigartiges Talent" und dass er ein „Meister der intellektuellen Überzeugungsarbeit [sei], ein Verkäufer seiner Ästhetik mit fast schon missionarischem Sendungsbewusstsein." Kiesler spräche zwar von der „Befreiung der Persönlichkeit", diese würde aber, so wie etwa in seiner Ausstellungsgestaltung für Peggy Guggenheim, „ins Chaos führen". Des Weiteren hält die Autorin fest, dass „der grundlegende Irrtum darin liegt, dass Mr. Kieslers Architekturbegriff nicht wirklich Architektur sei" und er unglücklicherweise die Gabe besitze „ständig das, was er sagt, durch das, was er tut, zu widerlegen. In die Praxis umgesetzt, werden seine Theorien häufig von ihrer Ausführung entkräftet."[64]

Von 12. April bis 1. Mai diesen Jahres stellt Kiesler gemeinsam mit John Cage, Julian Beck und Kenneth Rexroth in der New Yorker Great Jones Gallery aus. Kiesler zeigt Zeichnungen für sein *Endless House* (Abb. 32), Cage Notationen für *Fontana Mix* und *Music Walk*, Beck Entwürfe für Bühnenbilder und Rexroth Pastelle.[65] Für *ART News* gibt Kiesler ein Statement zur Ausstellung ab, in dem er seine Zeichnungen als „in den Raum geschrieben" umschreibt.

Huxtable on March 27, 1960, and the tone of the article was not uncritical, if not even cynical. The author credited Kiesler with being a "unique talent" and a "master of intellectual persuasion, a vendor of his own aesthetics with almost missionary zeal." To be sure, Kiesler spoke of the "liberation of the individual," but this "led to chaos," as in his exhibition design for Peggy Guggenheim, for example. Moreover, the author claimed that "the basic fault is to be found in the fact that Mr. Kiesler's notion of architecture was not really architecture" and he unfortunately had the talent to "constantly contradict what he says by what he does. Once they are implemented, his theories are often invalidated by their execution."[64]

From April 12 to May 1 of that year, Kiesler exhibited at the New York Great Jones Gallery together with John Cage, Julian Beck and Kenneth Rexroth. Kiesler showed drawings for his *Endless House* (Fig. 32), Cage notations for *Fontana Mix* and *Music Walk*, Beck designs for stage sets, and Rexroth pastels.[65] For *ART News*, Kiesler issued a statement on the exhibition, in which he described his drawings as "written into space."

The long wait for a decision regarding his *Endless House* at the Museum of Modern Art made Kiesler succumb to a state in which he felt emotionally torn. He played with the thought of withdrawing the project from the museum

Das lange Warten auf eine Entscheidung bezüglich seines *Endless House* im Museum of Modern Art versetzt Kiesler in einen Zustand innerer Zerrissenheit: Er spielt mit dem Gedanken, das Projekt dem Museum zu entziehen und nach Alternativen zu suchen. Kiesler trifft sich mit einem Freund, der Mitglied des Advisory Boards des MoMAs ist, und bespricht mit ihm die Gründe für die ewigen Verschiebungen. Er bekommt den Ratschlag, das Projekt zurückzu-ziehen. Daraufhin konzipiert Kiesler einen Brief für die Absage, nur um ihn nach einer neuerlichen Unterredung nicht abzuschicken.[66] Die überstürzt mit Herbert Mayer anberaumte Besprechung bezüglich des Baus eines *Endless House* nimmt Kiesler zwar wahr, aber nur um zu hören, dass der potenzielle Auftraggeber doch nicht so schnell ein *Endless House* benötige.[67]

Es wird knapp – „so früh als möglich im Sommer 1960" wollte man das *Endless House* im Skulpturengarten errichten, und dieser Termin rückt immer näher. Je später das Haus errichtet würde, desto kürzer würde es zu sehen sein, denn die Errichtung eines neuen Gebäudeflügels für das Museum of Modern Art würde die Ausstellung auf jeden Fall zeitlich begrenzen. Am 20. Mai trifft sich Kiesler mit Arthur Drexler und Renée d'Harnoncourt, um die Probleme zu erörtern. „Errichte es doch am Dach des neuen Museums-

and looking for alternatives. Kiesler later met with a friend, who was a member of MoMA's advisory board, and discussed with him the reasons for the constant delays. He was advised to withdraw the project. Subsequently, Kiesler drafted a letter to announce his decision, but decided not to mail it after another deliberation.[66]

Kiesler did take part in the discussion that had been scheduled with Herbert Meyer in great haste regarding the construction of an *Endless House*, but only to hear that the potential client did not need an *Endless House* so urgently after all.[67]

Time was short—"as early as possible in summer 1960" the *Endless House* was to be erected in the sculptural garden and this date was quickly approaching. The later the house was constructed, the shorter it would be on view, since the construction of a new wing of the Museum of Modern Art would certainly limit the exhibition time. On May 20, Kiesler met with Arthur Drexler and Renée d'Harnoncourt to discuss the problems: "Simply build it on the roof of the new museum wing," Drexler suggested— Kiesler could only conclude: "'Too late, the time is now… and now is too late, too,' I said. 'We agree,' the others answered."[68] Drexler then made the artist another offer in exchange. He would show the *Endless House* as a

flügels", schlägt Drexler vor – Kiesler kann nur resümieren: „‚Es ist zu spät, jetzt wäre die Zeit … und auch jetzt ist es schon zu spät', sagte ich ‚Da müssen wir dir zustimmen', antworteten die anderen."[68]

Drexler bietet dem Künstler daraufhin eine Rekompensation an. Er würde das *Endless House* als zentrales Projekt in der für den Herbst geplanten Ausstellung *Visionary Architecture* zeigen, als Modell in halbem Maßstab, damit die Besucher einen Eindruck von Kieslers Raumkonzept bekommen könnten. Er würde Kiesler zwei Kojen mit je 20 mal 21 Fuß anbieten. Kiesler reklamiert die Pläne seines *Endless Theater* von 1925 in die Ausstellung hinein, um sein *Endless* in einen historischen Kontext zu stellen.

Kiesler diskutiert den Vorschlag des Kurators mit seinem (Künstler-)Freund Salvatore Scarpitta: „Scarpita [sic] hielt mir einen glühenden Vortrag, warum ich nicht zustimmen sollte, ein zwergenhaftes Modell des *Endless* für die Ausstellung des Museum of Modern Art zu machen […]. Ich würde den rein architektonischen Anspruch meines Projekts auf das Niveau einer Theaterkulisse herabwürdigen, sagte er, und könnte damit nur den ordinären Geschmack der Öffentlichkeit befriedigen. […] Er schlug vor, dass ich den großen Raum dazu nutze, eine Super-Galaxy, eine plastische Idee, eine Abstraktion des *Endless House* zu bauen. […] Geben Sie ihnen besser einen

central project in the *Visionary Architecture* exhibition planned for the fall, presenting it as a model in a scale half the size, so that the visitors could get an impression of Kiesler's space concept. He would offer Kiesler two booths, each measuring 20 by 21 feet. Kiesler demanded that the plans for his *Endless Theater* of 1925 be included in the exhibition, so as to put his *Endless* in a historical context.

Kiesler discussed the curator's suggestion with his (artist) friend Salvatore Scarpitta: "Scarpita (sic) gave me a blistering lecture on why I should not agree to make a midget model of the *Endless* for the exhibition at the Museum of Modern Art, […] It would lower the purely architectural standard of my project to the level of a theatrical display, he said, and could only gratify vulgar public taste. […] He suggested that I use the larger space to build a super-galaxy, a sculptural idea, an abstraction of the *Endless House* (….) Give them a section, a cut-out piece of the total concept, but in full scale, rather than the total concept in miniature. Your work must always be hard and uncom-promised."[69]

The idea of the abstract sculptural presentation of an *Endless House Galaxy* was ultimately abandoned just as the performance of the theater-stage set miniature version was. The model was shown together with a wall-filling

Ausschnitt, einen Teil des ganzen Konzepts, aber dafür in voller Größe, als das ganze Konzept in Miniatur. Ihre Arbeit muss stets hart und kompro-misslos sein."[69]

Die Idee der abstrakt skulpturalen Präsentation einer *Endless House Galaxy* wird ebenso verworfen wie die Ausführung der theaterkulissenhaften Miniaturausgabe. Das Modell wird gemeinsam mit einer wandfüllenden Vergrößerung einer Innenaufnahme gezeigt und mit den Diazotypien der *Endless Theater*-Pläne als historischer Referenz des aktuellen Projektes ergänzt.[70]

Kieslers *Endless House* bekommt einen Ehrenplatz in der von Drexler kuratierten Schau *Visionary Architecture*, einer Ausstellung von Architektur-projekten des 20. Jahrhunderts, die „für eine Ausführung als zu revolu-tionär erachtet wurden" und die „radikale Lösungen für dringende soziale und ökonomische Probleme" versprächen.[71] Passagenweise liest sich die Presseaussendung zur Ausstellung wie ein Programm zu Kieslers Lebenspro-jekt, wenn etwa der Kurator des Weiteren ausführt, dass „die gesell-schaftliche Nutzung bestimmt, was visionär ist und was nicht. Visionäre Pro-jekte werfen ihre Schatten auf die reale Welt des Erlebens, der Kosten und Enttäuschungen voraus. Wenn wir erlernen können, was sie uns zu lehren haben, […] dann könnten Vision und Realität zusammenfallen."[72] Ein Leitmotiv

enlargement of an interior shot; as a historical reference to the current project, diazotypes of the *Endless Theater* plans were added.[70]

Kiesler's *Endless House* was given an honorary place in the *Visionary Architecture* show curated by Drexler, an exhibition of architectural projects of the 20th century that were considered "too revolutionary to be built" and promised "radical solutions for urgent social and economic problems."[71] Passages of the press release of the exhibition read like a program on Kiesler's life project when, for instance, the curator adds that "social usage determines what is visionary and what is not. Visionary projects cast their shadows over into the real world of experience, expense and frustration. If we could learn what they have to teach, we might exchange irrelevant rationalizations for more critical standards. Vision and reality might then coincide."[72] A key motif of the exhibition is that "architecture, too, has an existence prior to its becoming real, and there is a second history of an architecture unhampered by technical details and uncompromised by the whims of patrons, or the exigencies of finance, politics, and custom."[73]

Referring to the opening, Kiesler noted: "Today, on the day after the opening of the exhibition at the Museum of Modern Art, which is to open up possibilities for my building, the *Endless*, to be constructed—somewhere,

---

der Ausstellung ist, dass „auch die Architektur eine Existenz vor der Realität [hat] und es eine zweite Geschichte der Architektur gibt, die sich nicht von technischen Details behindern lässt, die sich trotz der Launen von Auftraggebern und finanziellen oder politischen Erfordernissen sowie den Gewohnheiten treu bleibt."[73]

Zur Eröffnung bemerkt Kiesler: „Heute, am Tag nach der Vernissage der Ausstellung im Museum of Modern Art, die meinem Gebäude, dem *Endless*, die Möglichkeiten eröffnen soll, gebaut zu werden – irgendwo, irgendwie – auf dem Wasser schwimmend oder hoch in der Luft. Es war augenscheinlich ein guter Start, einfach das Modell ausgestellt zu haben. [...] Mein Modell schwebte wie eine fliegende Untertasse aus Stahlbeton voller Löcher und Öffnungen zum Durchschauen, die Leute steckten ihre Köpfe hinein und wurden nicht schlau daraus."[74] Nach der Eröffnung besucht Kiesler P. J. Clarkes Bar mit einigen Freunden – vor allem Robert Rauschenberg und Jasper Jones „waren von der Genauigkeit meiner kurvilinearen Tuschentwürfe der Wiener Originalpläne [1924] für das *Endless* beeindruckt. Ihre Begeisterung ist wahrscheinlich mein größter Erfolg. [...] Ich habe immer gefühlt, dass sich der wahre Maßstab für den Erfolg nicht von der Reaktion der Öffentlichkeit oder der Kritiker, sondern von jener der

somehow—swimming on water or high up in the air. It was apparently a good start to simply have the model exhibited. […] My model drifted like a flying saucer made of reinforced concrete full of holes and openings to look through, the people stuck their heads in them and couldn't figure out what they were."[74] Following the opening, Kiesler visited P. J. Clarke's bar with several friends— and it was mainly "Bob Rauschenberg and Jasper Johns who were struck by the precision of my curvilinear concepts in ink of the original / 1924 Vienna plans for the *Endless*. Their enthusiasm is probably my greatest success […] I have always felt that the real measure of success does not derive from the reaction of the public or critics, but from that of one's colleagues."[75] In addition to the praise that came from several younger artist colleagues, Kiesler was probably also flattered by the recognition from critics. In one of the first reviews of the exhibition, he was named in a row with Leonardo da Vinci and as the only contemporary participant.[76]

A No-man's Land of Architecture

On January 10, 1961, the exhibition *Shell Sculptures and Galaxies* opened at the Leo Castelli Gallery, where Kiesler's *Galaxy Paintings* and the model-like sculptural studies for his *Endless House* were on display (Fig. 33 and 34). At

eigenen Kollegen herleitet."[75] Neben dem Lob seiner jungen Künstler- kollegen dürfte Kiesler auch die Anerkennung aus der Feder der Kritiker ge- schmeichelt haben. In einer der ersten Besprechungen der Ausstellung wird er in einer Reihe mit Leonardo da Vinci und als einziger zeitgenössischer Teilnehmer genannt.[76]

Ein Niemandsland der Architektur

Am 10. Januar 1961 eröffnet in der Leo Castelli Gallery die Ausstellung *Shell Sculptures and Galaxies*, in der Kieslers *Galaxy-Paintings* und die modellhaft skulpturalen Studien für sein *Endless House* gezeigt werden (Abb. 33 und 34). Anfang April resümiert Kiesler, dass leider nichts verkauft wurde, aber „[e]ine Lady aus Florida […] am letzten Samstagnachmittag meiner Show kurz vor dem Schließen in die Galerie [kam]. Es war ihr erster Besuch, sie fragte nach Mr. Castelli und erkundigte sich: ‚Was ist das?' Ihr Finger deutete auf etwas, das aussah wie eine Schalenskulptur aus Beton. Castelli antwortete: Das ist ein Modell des ‚Endless House, eine kleine Version.' Ein ‚Endless House'? Endlos … Darin würde ich gerne wohnen.'"[77] Das ist der Beginn eines weiteren Kapitels dieser endlosen Geschichte. Schon bald danach kommt es zum ersten Treffen Mary Sislers mit Kiesler. „Ich verhielt mich äußerst diskret. […]

33/34—Frederick Kiesler. *Shell Sculptures and Galaxies*, Castelli Gallery, New York 1961

the beginning of April, Kiesler concluded that, unfortunately, nothing had been sold, but "a Florida Lady appeared at the last hour of the last Saturday afternoon of my show. A newcomer to the gallery, she called for Mr. Castelli and said: 'What's that?' Her finger pointed to what seemed a shell sculpture in concrete. Castelli answered, 'it's a model for the *Endless House*, a small version'. 'An *endless house*? Endless… I would love to live in it,' she said."[77] That marked the beginning of a further chapter of this endless story. Soon after, Mary Sisler met with Kiesler for the first time. "I behaved with discretion. [...] I refrained from speaking about the *Endless House*. Nevertheless, a letter agreement was drawn up a week later."[78] In a letter dated March 30, 1961, Kiesler summed up the outcome of a meeting that he had had with a client the previous day. He explained his services and suggested methods of payment. He also mentioned the date for inspecting the building site on May 12 and noted that he was to begin his research and working studies on May 1.[79]

The possibility of being able to realize his life project after all the setbacks gave Kiesler a creative thrust. In addition to a large number of very free, expressive studies, there are also many very pragmatic plan sketches that pointed to an imminent realization (Figs. 35, 36, 37). The designs for the Museum of Modern Art served as a point of departure, with the abstract

Ich vermied es über das *Endless House* zu sprechen. Nichtsdestotrotz wurde eine Woche später eine Vereinbarung verfasst."[78] In einem Brief datiert mit 30. März 1961 fasst Kiesler die Ergebnisse eines Treffens mit seiner Auftraggeberin vom Vortag zusammen. Er erläutert seine Leistungen und schlägt Modalitäten bezüglich der Bezahlung vor. Er erwähnt auch einen Besichtigungs-termin des Baulandes am 12. Mai und hält fest, dass er am 1. Mai mit den Recherchen und Arbeitsstudien beginnen wird.[79]

Die Möglichkeit, sein Lebensprojekt nach all den Rückschlägen nun doch verwirklichen zu können, versetzt Kiesler einen produktiven Schub. Neben einer großen Anzahl an sehr freien, ausdrucksstarken Studien entstehen auch viele ganz pragmatische Planzeichnungen, die auf die bevorstehende Umsetzung hinweisen (Abb. 35, 36, 37). Als Ausgangspunkt dienen die Entwürfe für das Museum of Modern Art, wobei der abstrakte Charakter des 1:1-Modells für den Skulpturengarten der konkreten Planung für die Bewohnerin mit Alltäglichkeiten wie der Anordnung einer Küche, sanitären Einrichtungen und einer detaillierten Anordnung von Möbeln weicht.

Am 11. Mai bricht Kiesler gemeinsam mit seinem Freund und Galeristen Leo Castelli, mit seiner Assistentin (und späteren Frau) Lillian Olinsey und seinem Mitarbeiter Len Pitkowsky nach Palm Beach auf, um das Bauland

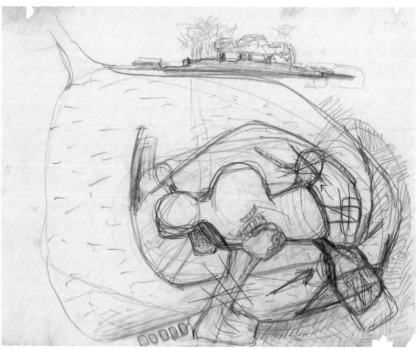

35—Frederick Kiesler, Study for *Mary Sisler House*, 1961

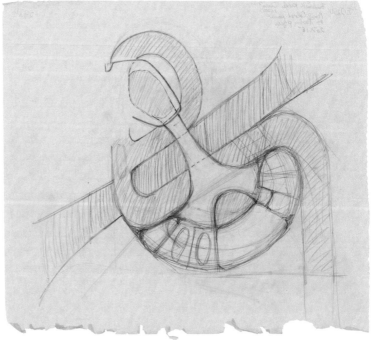

36—Frederick Kiesler, Study for *Mary Sisler House*, 1961

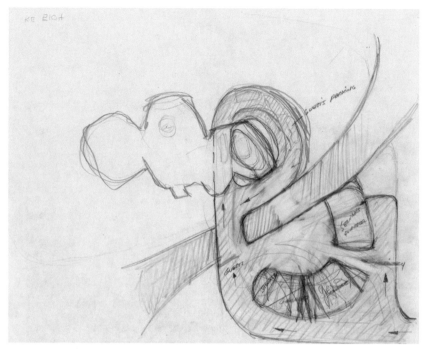

37—Frederick Kiesler, Study for *Mary Sisler House*, 1961

zu besichtigen. Diese Tour sollte zu einem der absurdesten Ereignisse im Leben des Künstlers werden. Dementsprechend umfangreich beschreibt er sie auch in seinem Journal. Mary Sisler empfängt ihre Gäste in ihrer mondänen in venezianischem Stil errichteten Villa. Kiesler fühlt sich, „berauscht, betrunken vor lauter Erwartung." Bei einem Glas Champagner lauscht die Runde den Worten der Gastgeberin: „Es ist das erste neue Konzept in der Architektur seit mindestens 500 Jahren, und ich liebe es einfach. Wissen Sie, wir sind 45 Meilen von Cape Canaveral entfernt, und von dort aus versuchen sie den Mond zu erreichen. Aber wenn wir das *Endless* auf meinem Grundstück gebaut haben, dann werden wir den Mond auf die Erde gebracht haben."[80]

Am Tag darauf setzt sich der Tross Richtung Bauland in Bewegung. Mit im Gepäck ein paar Gewehre, denn die Entscheidung über den Standort soll mit einem Tontaubenschießen gefeiert werden (Abb. 38). „Das Gebiet ist mit acht tümpelartigen Seen gesegnet, die Sie erweitern, vertiefen oder kombinieren können. So wie es Ihnen beliebt."[81] 3000 Morgen Land stehen Kiesler für sein *Endless* zu Verfügung. Mit der vielversprechenden Beschreibung der Auftrag-geberin im Kopf muss Kiesler wohl von einer parkähnlichen Landschaft geträumt haben. Mit dem tatsächlichen Zustand („Real Estate") konfrontiert, fällt Kiesler aus allen Wolken. So wunderbar die Worte Mary Sislers waren, so

38—Frederick Kiesler, skeet shooting at Mary Sisler's Florida estate, 1961

character of the 1:1 model deviating from the concrete plan for the resident in everyday aspects such as a layout of a kitchen, sanitary facilities and a detailed arrangement of furniture.

On May 11, Kiesler left together with his friend and gallery owner Leo Castelli, his assistant (and his later wife) Lillian Olinsey and his colleague Len Pitkowsky to Palm Beach to inspect the building site. This tour was to become one of the most absurd events of the artist's life. He also described it in great detail in his journal. Mary Sisler awaited her guests in her glamorous, elegant villa furnished in Venetian style. Kiesler felt "intoxicated as a result of all the expectations." While sipping a glass of champagne, the group listened to the host's words: "It is the first new concept in architecture for at least five hundred years, and I just love it. You know, we are forty-five miles from Cape Canaveral here, and we are trying to reach the moon from there. But when we build the *Endless* on my grounds, we will have brought the moon to earth."[80]

The next day, the party set off for the building site. A couple of firearms had been brought along as part of the luggage, since the decision regarding the site was to be celebrated with clay-pigeon shooting (Fig. 38). "An acreage blessed with eight swamp-like lakes which you can expand and deepen or combine. I leave it to you."[81] 3000 acres of land were available for Kiesler for

groß ist nun Kieslers Enttäuschung: „Das Land ist flach-gefegt, flach-geschliffen, flach-geschwemmt. Wüstenflecken. Grasflecken. Palmettenflecken. Verbrannte Baumstümpfe, vergebens. […] Ein Niemandsland der Architektur."[82] In einem Vortrag an der New York University findet Kiesler noch drastischere Worte: „Ich habe in meinem Leben niemals zuvor eine so verheerende und un-inspirierende Landschaft gesehen, und ich habe schon so einiges gesehen."[83]

Nach einer halben Stunde Fahrt auf der Suche eines idealen Standortes erspäht Kiesler einen Flecken für das *Endless House*. Ein Paar Zypressen und Pinien erscheinen wie eine Oase inmitten des öden Landes. Erleichtert verlässt der Tross die Fahrzeuge und beginnt mit dem Tontaubenschießen. Während Mary Sisler jede einzelne vom Himmel holt und Castelli jede verfehlt, lässt sich Kiesler eine Skizze seines *Endless House* geben. Er sucht sich ein Gestrüpp, steckt die Zeichnung auf einen Ast. Nun ist er an der Reihe. Er ver-langt nach einem Gewehr, legt an und zerschießt das *Endless House* (Abb. 39).[84]

„Die gesamte Gruppe lief herbei um zu sehen, was ich der Zeichnung angetan habe. Ich habe sie regelrecht umgebracht. Sie wurde mit unzählbar vielen Löchern durchsiebt. So als ob sie von einem Regen kosmischer Teilchen getroffen wurde."[85] Inmitten dieses „Niemandslandes der Architektur" erkennt Kiesler die wahren Beweggründe hinter dem Auftrag. Sein *Endless House*

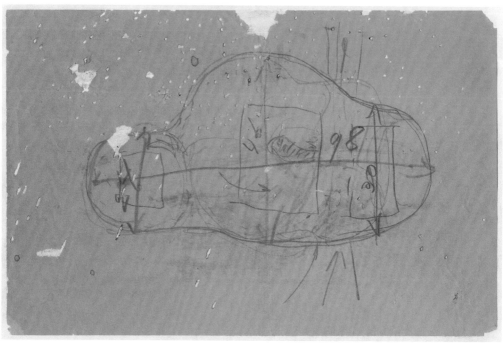

39—Frederick Kiesler, "Shot" *Endless House*, 1961 (detail)

his "Endless." With his client's very promising description in mind, Kiesler must have dreamed of a park-like landscape. But when he was confronted with the "real estate," Kiesler was completely flabbergasted. As wonderful as Mary Sisler's words had been, Kiesler's disillusionment was just as great. "The estate, the land is swept-flat, sanded-flat, flooded flat. Patches of desert. Patches of grass. Patches of palmettos. Burned tree trunks, forlorn. […] A no-man's land of architecture."[82] In a lecture he gave at New York University, he found even more drastic words: "I have never seen a more devastating looking and uninspiring landscape in my life, and I've seen quite many."[83]

After a half-hour drive in search of an ideal site, Kiesler discovered a spot for the *Endless House*. A couple of cypresses and pines looked like an oasis in the middle of a no-man's land. The party left the vehicles with relief and began with the clay-pigeon shooting. While Mary Sisler was able to hit each one from the sky and Castelli missed each one, Kiesler let someone give him a drawing of his *Endless House*. He looked for some brushwood, stuck the drawing onto a branch. Then it was his turn. He asked for a gun, aimed and shot the *Endless House* (Fig. 39).[84]

"The entire group ran over to see what I had done to the drawing. I had killed it squarely. It was riddled with numerable holes as though hit by a rain of

sollte wie ein voyantes Capriccio das Interesse potentieller Grundstückskäufer anlocken. Er hatte sich nur zu gerne täuschen lassen und diese *Ent-Täuschung* hatte sich nun mit dem Schuss entladen.

„Dann denken Sie gar nicht mehr daran, dass es [das *Endless House*] für Sie selbst ein idealer Wohnraum wäre? Verstehe ich richtig, dass es vor allem ein Magnet für Immobilienkäufer sein soll? Verstehe ich richtig, dass es eine Werbestrategie ist? Das ist nicht das, was ich mir vorgestellt habe, aber das muss wohl ein Missverständnis meiner selbst sein […] aber da ich mich schon so lange Zeit mit meinem *Endless* beschäftige, nahm ich an, dass auch jemand anderer, zumindest jemand wie Sie, das gleiche fühlen würde und es um seiner selbst willen haben wollte. Mir ist jetzt klar, dass ich wohl ständig geträumt habe. *Trompe-coeur*. Ich muss mich ent-schuldigen."[86]

Es wäre nicht Kiesler, wenn der Schuss das Ende seines *Endless House* gewesen wäre. Schon am nächsten Morgen stellt sich ihm die Frage: „bauen oder nicht bauen / to build or not to build", ob er das Projekt fallen lassen oder doch einen Kompromiss wagen solle. Es verwundert daher kaum, dass er einen Monat später ein detailliertes Programm für das Haus seiner Auftrag-geberin verfasst und noch im September an aufwendigen Plänen arbeitet

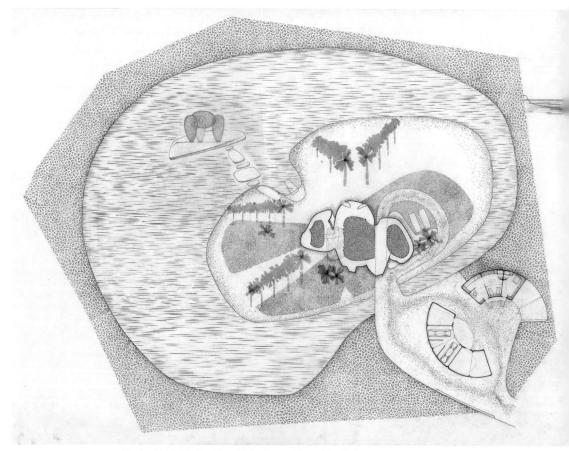

40—Frederick Kiesler, *Mary Sisler House* [Sheet No. 1], 1961

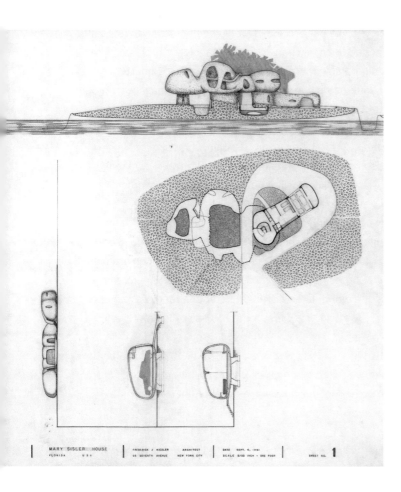

MARY SISLER HOUSE
FLORIDA   U S A
FREDERICK J KIESLER   ARCHITECT
56 SEVENTH AVENUE   NEW YORK CITY
DATE SEPT. 6, 1961
SCALE 3/32 INCH = ONE FOOT
SHEET NO. 1

cosmic particles."[85] In the midst of this "no-man's land of architecture," Kiesler recognized the real motivations for the commission. His *Endless House* was supposed to lure the interest of potential property buyers like a sort of voyant capriccio. He had let himself be deceived and this disillusionment had been discharged by a gunshot.

"Then you do not think of it any more as an ideal living quarters for yourself? Do I understand correctly it is to be chiefly a magnet for property buyers? Do I understand correctly—it is a promotion scheme, and that is not what I thought it to be, but naturally that must have been a misunderstanding of mine. [...] but being involved with my *Endless* for such a long time, I assumed others, one at least, one like you, would feel the same and like it for its own sake. I realize now I am continuously dreaming. *Trompe-coeur.* I apologize."[86]

It would not be Kiesler if the gunshot hadn't been the end of the *Endless House.* As soon as the next morning, he asked himself "to build or not to build," or to abandon the project or dare to reach a compromise. It is therefore hardly surprising that he wrote a detailed program for his client's house one month later, and in September already developed elaborate plans (Fig. 40).[87] The *Endless House* for Mary Sisler also remained

(Abb. 40).[87] Auch das *Endless House* für Mary Sisler bleibt ungebaut, wenngleich kein Brief, kein Schreiben eines Rechtsanwaltes, nicht einmal eine kleine Notiz mit einer definitiven Absage bekannt ist.

Nachspiel

Im Nachlass Friedrich Kieslers hat sich eine Mappe mit dem Titel *The Endless House. Frederick Kiesler, Architect. Prospectus for a museum of contemporary art in Cleveland* erhalten.[88] Neben einer fünfseitigen Beschreibung des Projektes enthält es auch Statements zu Friedrich Kiesler und seinem *Endless House.* Kiesler bedankt sich bei Reid B. Johnson, dem Begründer der Initiative. Die letzten Zeilen seines Briefes zeugen von Kieslers Wissen, dass es wohl die letzte Chance für sein *Endless House* wäre: „Viel Glück und Gott möge sich mit Ihnen beeilen."[89] Kiesler stirbt am 27. Dezember 1965, ohne seine schöpferische Grundidee realisiert zu haben. Die Statements im Prospekt, sie stammen unter anderem von Philip Johnson, Wallace Harrison, Paul Rudolph, Walter Gropius, Lewis Mumford, Arthur Drexler und Aline Saarinen, lesen sich wie ein vorweggenommener Nachruf auf Kieslers endloses und zugleich unvollendetes Lebensprojekt.[90]

unbuilt, although there is no knowledge of a letter, a written document from a lawyer, or even a small note with a definitive refusal.

Postlude

In Frederick Kiesler's papers, one finds a folder with the title *The Endless House. Frederick Kiesler, Architect. Prospectus for a museum of contemporary art in Cleveland.*[88] In addition to a five-page description of the project, there are also statements relating to Frederick Kiesler and his *Endless House*. Kiesler thanked Reid B. Johnson, who started the initiative. The last lines of his letter testify to Kiesler's knowledge that it would probably be the last chance for his *Endless House*: "Good luck and may God be with you."[89] Kiesler died on December 27, 1965 without his creative basic idea having been realized. The statements in the prospectus also stemmed from Philip Johnson, Wallace Harrison, Paul Rudolph, Walter Gropius, Lewis Mumford, Arthur Drexler and Aline Saarinen. They all read like an anticipated obituary of Kiesler's endless and, at the same time, unfinished life project.[90]

1 Creighton, Thomas: „Kiesler's Pursuit of an Idea", in *Progressive Architecture* 7 (1961), 104–123, 123. Die deutsche Fassung der Interviewpassage folgt einem Typoskript im Archiv der Friedrich Kiesler Stiftung, vermutlich für einen Dia-Vortrag, Typoskript, ÖFLKS, TXT 6999/0.

2 Zur Problematik der Quellenlage siehe *Friedrich Kiesler 1890–1965. Inside the Endless House*, hg. v. Dieter Bogner, (Wien: Böhlau, 1997), Ausstellungskatalog, 9; zu einer Chronologie des *Endless House*-Projektes und zur Literatur vgl. *Friedrich Kiesler: Endless House 1947–1961*, hg. v. Österreichische Friedrich und Lillian-Kiesler Privatstiftung und Museum für Moderne Kunst Frankfurt am Main (Ostfildern: Hatje Cantz, 2003). Kiesler war ein Meister der Selbstdarstellung. Interviews, Lebensläufe und autobiographische Texte bedürfen einer besonders kritischen Reflexion,

wenn man sie als Quellen heranzieht. Zur Bedeutung des Interviews mit Thoms Creighton vgl. Laura McGuire, „Introduction: The Architecture of an Idea", in Laura McGuire, *Space Within – Frederick Kiesler and the Architecture of an Idea* (PhD diss., The University of Texas in Austin, 2014), 1–22.

3 Thomas Creighton, „Kiesler's Pursuit of an Idea", 110, Illustrationen, Interviewtext auf 112; deutsche Fassung der Interviewpassage, vermutlich ein Dia-Vortrag, Typoskript, ÖFLKS, TXT 6999/0 [1]. Für eine konzise Analyse des Endless Theater vgl. Stephen Phillips, „Plastic Forms of Glassy Balloon Materials", in Stephen Phillips, *Elastic Architecture: Frederick Kiesler and his reserach practice—a study of continuity in the age of modern production*, (PhD diss., Princeton University, 2008), 23–54.

4 Marc Dessauce, *Machinations. Essai sur Frederick Kiesler,*

l'histoire de l'architecture moderne aux États-Unis et Marcel Duchamp (Paris: Sens & Tonka, 1996); Gunda Luyken, „Infra-geringe Verschiebungen. Beobachtungen zu den künstlerischen Konzepten von Marcel Duchamp und Frederick Kiesler", in *Impuls Marcel Duchamp // Where do we go from here? Poiesis I. Schriftenreihe des Duchamp-Forschungszentrums Schwerin* (Ostfildern: Hatje Cantz, 2011), 128–155; Gunda Luyken, „Frederick Kiesler und Marcel Duchamp. Rekonstruktion ihres theoretischen und künstlerischen Austausches zwischen 1925 und 1937" (PhD diss., Staatliche Hochschule für künstlerische Gestaltung, Karlsruhe, 2002), 69–131.

5 Der Katalog zur Ausstellung erwähnt nur die Pläne, nicht aber das Modell. Vgl. *International Theater Exposition*, (New York, 1926), Ausstellungskatalog, Katalognr. 41–46, 6. Fotos mit

1 Thomas Creighton: "Kiesler's Pursuit of an Idea", in *Progressive Architecture*, 7 (July 1961), 123.
2 On the problems related to the sources, cf. *Frederick Kiesler 1890–1965. Inside the Endless House*, ed. Dieter Bogner (Vienna: Böhlau, 1997), exhibition catalog, 9; on the chronology of the *Endless House* project and the literature, cf. *Friedrich Kiesler: Endless House 1947–1961*, ed. Österreichische Friedrich und Lilian-Kiesler Privatstiftung and Museum für Moderne Kunst Frankfurt am Main (Ostfildern: Hatje Cantz, 2003); Kiesler was a master of self-fashioning. Interviews, CVs and autobiographical texts require special critical reflection when consulted as sources. On the importance of the interview with Thomas Creighton, cf. Laura McGuire, "Introduction: The Architecture of an Idea", in Laura McGuire, "Space Within – Frederick Kiesler and the Architecture of an Idea"

(PhD diss., The University of Texas at Austin, 2014), 1–22.
3 Cf. Creighton, "Kiesler's Pursuit of an Idea", 110; illustrations, interview text on p. 112; For a concise analysis of the *Endless Theater*, cf. Stephen Phillips, "Plastic Forms of Glassy Balloon Materials", in Stephen Phillips, "Elastic Architecture: Frederick Kiesler and his research practice—a study of continuity in the age of modern production" (PhD diss., Princeton University, 2008), 23–54.
4 Marc Dessauce, *Machinations. Essai sur Fredrick Kiesler, l'histoire de l'architecture moderne aux États-Unis et Marcel Duchamp* (Paris: Sens & Tronka, 1996); Gunda Luyken, "Infrageringe Verschiebungen. Beobachtungen zu den künstlerischen Konzepten von Marcel Duchamp und Frederick Kiesler", in *Impulse Marcel Duchamp // Where do we go from here? Poiesis I. Schriftenreihe des Duchamp-*

Forschungszentrums Schwerin (Ostfildern: Hatje Cantz, 2011), 128–155; Gunda Luyken, "Frederick Kiesler und Marcel Duchamp. Rekonstruktion ihres theoretischen und künstlerischen Austausches zwischen 1925 und 1937" (PhD diss., Staatliche Hochschule für Gestaltung, Karlsruhe, 2002), 69–131.
5 The exhibition catalog mentions only the plans, but not the model, cf. *International Theater Exposition* (New York, 1926) exhibition catalog, cat. no. 41–46, 6; photographs with the model: ÖFLKS, PHO 813/0, PHO 2872/0, PHO 6447/0.
6 Dieter Bogner, "Architecture as Biotechnique. Friedrich Kiesler und das Space House von 1933", in *Visionäre & Vertriebene. Österreichische Spuren in der modernen amerikanischen Architektur*, ed. Matthias Boeckl (Berlin: Ernst & Sohn, 1995), 139–154; Beatriz Colomina, "De psyche van het bouwen. Frederick

dem Modell: ÖFLKS, PHO 813/0, PHO 2872/0, PHO 6447/0.
6 Dieter Bogner, „Architecture as Biotechnique. Friedrich Kiesler und das Space House von 1933", in *Visionäre & Vertriebene. Österreichische Spuren in der modernen amerikanischen Architektur*, hg. v. Matthias Boeckl (Berlin: Ernst & Sohn, 1995), 139–154. Beatriz Colomina, „De psyche van het bouwen. Frederick Kiesler's Space House", in *Archis* 2 (1996), 70–80. Laura McGuire, „Space House", in *Space House* (11/2012), hg. v. Monika Pessler (Wien: Österreichische Friedrich und Lilian Kiesler Privatstiftung, 2012).
7 Friedrich Kiesler, *Endless Space House*, ÖFLKS, TXT 594/0.
8 „[...] besides its solution as a One-Family-Shelter: (a) the Time-Space-Concept of architecture; (b) the Shell-Construction in continuous tension." In: Friedrich Kiesler, „Notes on Architecture. The Space-House. Annotations at

Random." in: *Hound and Horn* 2 (1934), 295.
9 ÖFLKS, SFP 813/0 und CLP 6466/0 unter Verwendung einer Illustration aus: „On Correalism and Biotechnique. A Definition and Test of a New Approach to Building Design", in *Architectural Record* 9 (1939), 67; sowie ÖFLKS, SFP 6668/0–4 (Skizzen mit ausklappbaren Ausschnitten).
10 „[...] both of these projects were designed by Kiesler, 'Structures in continuous tension' to facilitate pre- and fabrication in moulds for plastics, as well as to shelter those 'continuous mutations' of the life-force, which seem to be part of the 'practical' as well as of the magical." Vgl. Friedrich Kiesler, „Endless House" (Photomontage), in *VVV* 4 (1944), 60–61.
11 „[...] of the hemispheres, which are infinite and divided by an infinite number of lines in such a way that every man has always one of these lines between his

feet. Men shall speak and touch and embrace each other while standing in different hemispheres, and shall understand each other's language.' da Vinci." Ebenda.
12 Friedrich Kiesler, „Manifeste du Corréalisme", in *L'Architecture d'Aujourd'hui* 2 (1949), 79–105.
13 Eva-Christina Kraus, „Exposition internationale du Surréalisme" (PhD diss., Universität für angewandte Kunst, Wien, 2010); *Breton Duchamp Kiesler. Surreal Space 1947* (14/2013), hg. v. Monika Pessler (Wien: Österreichische Friedrich und Lillian Kiesler-Privatstiftung, 2013).
14 „L'architecture de la pièce figurant deux ellipses ouverts, en forme de ruban, l'une verticale, l'autre horizontale. La respiration de la pièce se faisait par les brachies de ces anneaux, oscillant entre compression et la dilation." Vgl. Kiesler, „Manifeste du Corréalisme", 79–105.

Kiesler's Space House", in *Archis* 11 (1996), 70–80; Laura McGuire, "Space House", in *Space House*, (11/2012), ed. Monika Pessler (Vienna: Austrian Frederick and Lillian Kiesler Private Foundation, 2012).

7　Frederick Kiesler, *Endless Space House*, undated, ÖFLKS, TXT 594/0.

8　Frederick Kiesler, "Notes on Architecture. The Space-House. Annotations at Random", in *Hound and Horn* 2 (1934), 295.

9　ÖFLKS, SFP 813/0 and CLP 6466/0 based on an illustration from: "On Correalism and Biotechnique. A Definition and Test of a New Approach to Building Design", in *Architectural Record* 9 (1939), 67; as well as ÖFLKS SFP 6668/0–4 (sketches with pull-out parts).

10　Cf. Frederick Kiesler, "Endless House" (Photomontage) in: *VVV* 4 (1944), 60–61.

11　"… of the hemispheres, which are infinite and divided by an infinite number of lines in such a way that every man has always one of these lines between his feet. Men shall speak and touch and embrace each other while standing in different hemispheres, and shall understand each other's language. Da Vinci", ibid.

12　Frederick Kiesler, "Manifeste du Corréalisme", in *L'Architecture d'Aujourd'hui* 2 (1949), 79–105.

13　Eva-Christina Kraus, "Exposition international du Surréalisme" (PhD., University of Applied Arts, Vienna, 2010); *Breton Duchamp Kiesler. Surreal Space 1947* (14/2013), ed. Monika Pessler (Vienna: Austrian Frederick and Lillian Kiesler Private Foundation, 2013).

14　"L'architecture de la pièce figurant deux ellipses ouverts, en forme de ruban, l'une vertical, l'autre horizontale. La respiration de la pièce se faisait par les brachies de ces anneaux, oscillant entre compression et la dilation", cf. Frederick Kiesler, "Manifeste du Corréalisme", 79–105.

15　Hans Arp, "L'oeuf de Kiesler et la sale des Superstitions", in *Cahiers d'Art* XXII (1947), 281–284; based on a typescript dated "Aout 1947", ÖFLKS, TXT 7289, (3-page).

16　May 27, 1947 – Sept. 21, 1947, cf. Stefi Kiesler, Calendar Diary 1947, calendar week 21 and 31, ÖFLKS, MED 862/0.

17　Approx. 40 different sheets, mostly water color, pencil and ink on paper or ball-point pen and pencil on paper, ÖFLKS, box_mpf_06.

18　Frederick Kiesler, "Hazard and the Endless House", in *Art News* 7 (1960), 48.

19　20 drawings on 16 sheets, approx. same dimensions (21.5 × 28 cm), ÖFLKS, box_sfp_14, Folder Tooth Draw 1–3, ball-point pen on paper, some with drawings on both sides. Undated but probably created in 1948/49. On the back side "Tooth House" or

15　Hans Arp, „L'oeufe de Kiesler et la salle des Superstitions", in *Cahiers d'Art* XXII (1947), 281–284, zitiert nach einem mit „Août 1947" datierten Typoskript, ÖFLKS, TXT 7289, (3-seitig).

16　27. Mai 1947 – 21. September 1947, vgl. Stefi Kiesler, Kalender 1947, KW 21 und 38, ÖFLKS, MED 862/0.

17　Ca. 40 verschiedene Blätter zumeist Aquarell, Bleistift und Tusche auf Papier bzw. Kugelschreiber und Bleistift auf Papier, ÖFLKS, box_mfp_06.

18　Friedrich Kiesler, „Hazard and the Endless House", in *Art News* 7 (1960), 48. (Übersetzt aus dem Englischen)

19　20 Zeichnungen auf 16 Blättern, annähernd gleiche Maße (21,5 × 28 cm), ÖFLKS, box_sfp_14, Folder Tooth Draw 1–3, Kugelschreiber auf Papier, teilw. beidseitig bezeichnet. Undatiert, wohl aber in den Jahren 1948/49 entstanden. Auf der Rückseite von Lillian Kiesler mit „Tooth House" oder „David's Endless" bezeichnet und mit 1948 datiert.

20　Deckblatt *Tooth House*, ÖFLKS, SFP 431/0.

21　*The Muralist and The Modern Architect* (New York: Kootz Gallery, 1950), Ausstellungskatalog; Kieslers persönliches Exemplar: ÖFLKS, KIES 040. (Übersetzt aus dem Englischen)

22　David Hares *L'homme-angoisse* ist auf ca. zehn Fotografien der *Salle de Superstition* zu sehen. ÖFLKS, box_sfp_29, Folder: EXP47_PHO_02.

23　Creighton, „Kiesler's Pursuit of an Idea", 114. (Übersetzt aus dem Englischen)

24　Friedrich Kiesler, Model für ein *Endless House*, 1950, Ton (50,8 × 29,2 × 15,2 cm), MoMA Inv.-Nr.: MC 25.

25　Ein Großteil dieser Zeichnungen befindet sich heute im Museum of Modern Art, New York (MoMA, Inv.-Nr.: SC.20.1966-SC.42.1966).

26　„When are you going to send me the drawings for your h[ous]e? I have been waiting for them so that I can think of what to put in it." David Hare an Friedrich Kiesler, 20. Juni [1950, Poststempel 23. Juni 1950], ÖFLKS, LET 1255/0.

27　Z.B. ÖFLKS, SFP 566/0–568/0, SFP 571/0–574/0; insgesamt tragen ca. 30 Blätter den Vermerk. Lillian Kiesler ordnete den Nachlass ihres Mannes mit großer Kenntnis und Hingabe. Dennoch unterliefen ihr bei der Identifikation einzelner Blätter kleinere Fehler.

28　Stefi Kiesler, Kalender, 1950 KW 27, „July 14: 10 a.m. K. to David Hare's Minerva, N.Y." ÖFLKS, MED 863/0.

29　Ebenda, KW 33, „August 24: K. arrives at David Hare's Hewitt" und 1950 KW 35 „September 5 by [sic] Hares arrived back at midnight."

30　Creighton, „Kiesler's Pursuit of an Idea", 114. (Übersetzt aus dem Englischen)

"David's Endless" written by Lillian Kiesler and dated 1948.

20 Cover sheet for "Tooth House", ÖFLKS, SFP 431/0.

21 *The Muralist and the Modern Architect* (New York: Kootz Gallery 1950), exhibition catalog, Kiesler's personal copy, ÖFLKS, KIES 040.

22 David Hare's *L'homme-angoisse* can be seen on approx. ten photos of the *Salle de Superstition*, ÖFLKS, box_sfp_29, Folder: EXP47_PHO_02.

23 Creighton, "Kiesler's Pursuit of an Idea", 114.

24 Frederick Kiesler, *Endless House*, Model, 1950, clay (50.8 × 29.2 × 15.2 cm), MoMA, inv. no.: MC 25.

25 A large number of these drawings can be found today at the Museum of Modern Art, New York (MoMA, inv. no.: SC.20.1966-SC.1966).

26 David Hare to Frederick Kiesler, June 20 (1950, post stamp June 23, 1950), ÖFLKS, LET 1255/0.

27 For example: ÖFLKS, SFP 566/0–568/0, SFP 571/0–574/0; altogether approx. 30 sheets are labeled this way. Lillian Kiesler classified her husband's papers with great insight and devotion. Nonetheless, she made some small mistakes while identifying individual sheets.

28 Stefi Kiesler, Calendar Diary, 1950 calendar week 27, " July 14: 10 a.m. K. to David Hare's Minerva, N.Y." ÖFLKS, MED 863/0.

29 Ibid. 1950 calendar week 33, "August 24: K. arrives at David Hare's Hewitt" and 1950 calendar week 35 "September 5 by (six) Hares arrived back at midnight."

30 Creighton, "Kiesler's Pursuit of an Idea", 114.

31 Ibid., 104–123.

32 "I made the model with a 'launching pad,'" ibid., 114

33 "The Muralist and The Modern Architect", in *Arts & Architecture* 4 (1951); *Quick. News Weekly,* Oct. 9, 1950; Frederick Kiesler, "The Endless House and its Psychological Lighting", in *Interiors* 4 (1950), 129.

34 Stefi Kiesler, Calendar Diary, 1950 calendar week 37, "September 19, [...] 9.30 Mr. Drexler from Interiors Mag. (interview for Magazine), September 26, 2.30 Drexler here, September 27, 8h Drexler here." Kiesler must have met Drexler during the exhibition; there are no earlier entries in Stefi Kiesler's calendar diary.

35 Kiesler, "The Endless House and its Psychological Lighting", 122–129.

36 Ibid.

37 Ibid.

38 On the collaboration of Kiesler and Percy Rainford, but for a completely different project, cf. Herbert Molderings, *Marcel Duchamp im Alter von 85 Jahren. Eine Inkunabel der konzeptuellen Fotografie* (Cologne: Verlag der Buchhandlung Walther König, 2013).

31 Ebenda.

32 „I made the model with a 'launching pad'", ebenda.

33 „The Muralist and The Modern Architect", in *Arts & Architecture* 4 (1951); *Quick. News Weekly,* Oct. 9, 1950; Friedrich Kiesler, „The Endless House and its Psychological Lighting", in *Interiors* 4 (1950), 129.

34 Stefi Kiesler, Kalender, 1950 KW 37, „September 19, [...] 9.30 Mr. Drexler from Interiors Mag. (interview for Magazine), September 26, 2.30 Drexler here, September 27, 8h Drexler here." Kiesler muss Drexler im Zuge der Ausstellung kennengelernt haben, denn in Stefi Kieslers Kalender finden sich keine früheren Einträge unter dem Namen „Drexler".

35 Kiesler, „The Endless House and its Psychological Lighting", 122–129.

36 Ebenda, 122.

37 Ebenda, 126.

38 Zum Zusammenwirken Kieslers und Percy Rainfords, allerdings für ein gänzlich anderes Projekt, vgl. Herbert Molderings, *Marcel Duchamp im Alter von 85 Jahren. Eine Inkunabel der konzeptuellen Fotografie* (Köln: Verlag der Buchhandlung Walther König, 2013).

39 Ein Großteil dieser Zeichnungen befindet sich heute im Museum of Modern Art, New York (MoMA, Inv.-Nr.: SC.20.1966-SC.42.1966), zwei Blätter in der Friedrich Kiesler Stiftung, ÖFLKS, SFP 621/0 und SFP 622/0.

40 *Envisioning Architecture. Drawings form The Museum of Modern Art*, hg. v. Mathilda McQuaid (New York: The Museum of Modern Art, 2002); 26; Press release MoMA (ÖFLKS, TXT 7002/0).

41 „[...] I can only state the fact that is [it] has primarily been conceived for the creation of satisfactory living conditions, the spatial areas needed for this purpose, and that from these conditions I had arrived at the dimensions, the form and the construction scheme. The estehtic [!] aspect comes with it and was not the primary thought." Friedrich Kiesler an Arthur Drexler vom 14. Sept.1952, ÖFLKS, LET 983/0.

42 Friedrich Kiesler, *Inside The Endless House. Art People and Architecture. A Journal* (New York: Simon and Schuster, 1966), 21. (Übersetzt aus dem Englischen)

43 Ebenda, 22. (Übersetzt aus dem Englischen)

44 Presseaussendung vom 2. Februar 1958, „GRANT GIVEN TO MUSEUM FOR ARCHITECTURAL PROJECT", ÖFLKS, TXT 616/0. In einem Brief vom 5. Februar 1958 bedankt sich Kiesler bei Armand Bartos. (Bartos, der zu dieser Zeit ein gemeinsames Architekturbüro mit Kiesler unterhielt, war Mitglied des Vorstandes der Gottesman Foundation).

45 Im Nachlass haben sich mehrere Versionen erhalten; ÖFLKS, TXT 623/0 mit Annotationen, ÖFLKS, TXT 6552/0 Reinschrift.

39 A large number of these drawings can be found today in the collections of the Museum of Modern Art, New York, (MoMA, inv. no.: SC.20.1966-SC.42,1966), two sheets at the Frederick Kiesler Foundation, ÖFLKS, SFP 621/0 and SFP 622/0.

40 *Envisioning Architecture. Drawings from The Museum of Modern Art*, ed. Mathilda McQuaid (New York, 2002), exhibition catalog, 26; press release MoMA (ÖFLKS, TXT 7002/0).

41 "[…] I can only state the fact that (it) has primarily been conceived for the creation of satisfactory living conditions, the spatial areas needed for this purpose, and that from these conditions I had arrived at the dimensions, the form and the construction scheme. The esthetic (!) aspect comes with it and was not the primary thought." Frederick Kiesler to Arthur Drexler on Sept. 14, 1952, ÖFLKS, LET 983/0.

42 Frederick Kiesler, *Inside the Endless House. Art People and Architecture. A Journal* (New York: Simon and Schuster, 1966), 21.

43 Ibid., 22.

44 Press release from Feb. 2, 1958, "GRANT GIVE TO MUSEUM FOR ARCHITECTURAL PROJECT", ÖFLKS, TXT 616/0. In a letter from Feb. 5, 1958, Kiesler thanked Armand Bartos (Bartos, who at the time ran an architectural firm together with Kiesler, was a member of the board of directors at the Gottesman Foundation.)

45 In Kiesler's estate, one finds several versions: ÖFLKS, TXT 623/0 with annotations, ÖFLKS, TXT 6552/0 final copy.

46 In the literature, the drawing is attributed to an *Endless House* for Chicago, cf. *Friedrich Kiesler. Architekt Maler Bildhauer. 1890–1965*, ed. Dieter Bogner (Vienna: Löcker, 1988), 151. (The drawing was owned by Lilian Kiesler; it is not known where it is today.)

Kiesler was in Chicago that year in September, cf. Frederick Kiesler to William Hartmann (Graham Foundation), Aug. 14, 1958 (LET 3489/0)—"I am leaving for Europe for consultations and will come back specially to meet you in Chicago, September 8. I'm invited to stay privately by Mr. W. Reich. (Wilhelm Reich). […] My main reason for writing you today is that I'd be very grateful if you would find me a large room or a studio for doing some sculptural work and design planning during my stay in Chicago." Kiesler's letter refers to a letter from the Graham Foundation in which the grant holders were asked to be present in Chicago from September 7 to 28. Cf. ÖFLKS, LET 3480/0.

47 Jason McCoy, Inc., New York: FK 914 (mesh wire and cement, 38.1 × 66 × 25.4); Jason McCoy, Inc. FK 532 (mesh wire and cement; 144.8 × 154.9 × 99.1 cm); collection of Gertraud and Dieter

46 In der Literatur wird die Zeichnung einem *Endless House* Projekt für Chicago zugeschrieben, vgl. *Friedrich Kiesler. Architekt Maler Bildhauer. 1890–1965*, hg. v. Dieter Bogner (Wien: Löcker, 1988), 151. (Die Zeichnung befand sich im Besitz von Lillian Kiesler, der heutige Verbleib ist unbekannt.) Kiesler hielt sich im September des Jahres in Chicago auf; vgl. Friedrich Kiesler an William Hartmann [Graham Foundation], 14. August 1958 (LET 3489/0) – „I am leaving for Europe for consultations and will come back specially to meet you in Chicago, September 8. I'm invited to stay privately by Mr. W. Reich. [Wilhelm Reich]. […] My main reason for writing you today is that I'd be very grateful if you would find me a large room or a studio for doing some sculptural work and design planning during my stay in Chicago." Kieslers Brief bezieht sich auf ein Schreiben der Graham Foundation, in dem

die Anwesenheit der Stipendiaten in Chicago von 7. bis 28. September erbeten wird. Vgl. ÖFLKS, LET 3480/0.

47 Jason McCoy, Inc., New York: FK 914, (Maschendraht und Beton, 38,1 × 66 × 25,4 cm); Jason McCoy, Inc.: FK 532 (Maschendraht und Beton; 144,8 × 154,9 × 99,1 cm); Sammlung Gertraud und Dieter Bogner, Dauerleihgabe an die ÖFLKS, MOD 05/0. Jason McCoy betreute für Lillian Kiesler den Nachlass und war Mitglied im Gründungsvorstand der Friedrich Kiesler Stiftung. Bei Errichtung der Stiftung einigte man sich darauf, dass die skulpturalen Objekte aus dem Nachlass des Künstlers bei Jason McCoy verblieben.

48 ÖFLKS, box_pho_11, Folder EH_59 _PHO_PRODUKTION_3; *From Chicken Wire to Wire Frame. Kiesler's Endless House* (07/2010), hg. v. Monika Pessler (Wien: Österreichische Friedrich

und Lillian Kiesler Privatstiftung, 2010).

49 ÖFLKS, PHO 669/0; zu Kieslers *Galaxies* vgl. *The Space In Between. Kiesler's Galaxies* (03/2009), hg. v. Monika Pessler (Wien: Österreichische Friedrich und Lillian Kiesler Privatstiftung, 2009).

50 „Here I tried ??? reinforced concrete to divide a larger area into a smaller area, but that was not satisfactory because I know the wall is curved and tried to relate the floor, ceiling, and the wall in a different way like we usually see it—it still is a wall and a division—a hard division." Vgl. Interview, „CBS Camera Three", ÖFLKS, TXT 7005/0, 3.

51 Model für ein *Endless House*, 1959, Beton, Maschendraht und Plastik, (90,5 × 247 × 100,5 cm), Whitney Museum of American Art, New York; Gift of Mrs. Lillian Kiesler, Accession number 89.9.

52 Vgl. ÖFLKS, PHO 770/0; Borsick, Helen: „Fame is Endless", in *Plain*

Bogner, permanent loan to the ÖFLKS, MOD 05/0. Jason McCoy was put in charge of the estate by Lillian Kiesler and was a member of the board of founding directors of the Frederick Kiesler Foundation. When the foundation was established, it was agreed that the sculptural objects from the artist's estate would remain with Jason McCoy.

48 ÖFLKS, box_pho_11, Folder EH_59_PHO_PRODUKTION_3; *From Chicken Wire to Wire Frame. Kiesler's Endless House* (07/2010), ed. Monika Pessler (Vienna: Austrian Frederick and Lillian Kiesler Private Foundation, 2010).

49 ÖFLKS, PHO 669/0; on Kiesler's "Galaxies" cf. *The Space in Between. Kiesler's Galaxies* (03/2009), ed. Monika Pessler (Vienna: Austrian Frederick and Lillian Kiesler Private Foundation, 2009).

50 Cf. Interview, "CBS Camera Three", ÖFLKS, TXT 7005/0, p. 3.

51 *Endless House*, Model, 1959, cement, wire mesh and plastic, (90.5 × 247 × 100.5 cm), Whitney Museum of American Art, New York; Gift of Mrs. Lillian Kiesler, Accession number 89.9.

52 Cf. ÖFLKS, PHO 770/0; Helen Borsick, "Fame is Endless", in *Plain Dealer*, Feb. 5, 1967, the clipping shows no page number (CLP 614/0).

53 Frederick Kiesler to Arthur Drexler, letter of Feb. 25, 1959, ÖFLKS, LET 505/0. In a letter of Feb. 16, 1959 Kiesler thanked the director of the Museum of Modern Art, Renée d'Harnoncourt for a studio visit, ÖFLKS, LET 2208/0.

54 Kiesler, *Inside the Endless House* (March 10, 1959, "Rainford of Triple VVV"), 194.

55 Header, dated NOV. 1958 – APR. 26. 1959; ÖFLKS, PLN 240/0 and PLN 241/0.

56 Meeting, ÖFLKS, TXT 3815/0; Kiesler to Severud, May 21, 1959, ÖFLKS, LET 503/0.

57 *TIME Magazine*, May 25, 1959,

newspaper excerpt without page number, ÖFLKS, CLP 6691/0.

58 From a letter, Arthur Drexler to Frederick Kiesler, dated July 1, 1959, ÖFLKS, LET 3157/0.

59 "New Concepts of Architecture", in *Harper's Bazaar*, Oct. 1959, pp. 182. The photograph with Kiesler is printed on 183. See also Arthur Drexler, "Frederick Kiesler and his Endless House", in *Vogue* 1 (1960), 114–115.

60 There are several variants of this setting. One of them shows Kiesler with a bare torso, which once again underlines the staging of himself as a demiurge. ÖFLKS, PHO 771/0 (Kiesler with cape), PHO 807/0 (Kiesler with bare torso), PHO 808/0 (Kiesler with bowl).

61 *Studio and Workshop. Frederick Kiesler as a Master of Self-Fashioning* (18/2014), ed. Peter Bogner (Vienna: Austrian Frederick and Lillian Kiesler Private Foundation, 2014).

Dealer, Feb. 5, 1967, Zeitungsausschnitt ohne Seitennummer (ÖFLKS, CLP 614/0).

53 Friedrich Kiesler an Arthur Drexler, Brief vom 25. Februar 1959, ÖFLKS, LET 505/0. In einem Brief von 16. Februar 1959 bedankt sich Kiesler beim Direktor des Museum of Modern Art, Renée d'Harnoncourt für einen Atelierbesuch, ÖFLKS, LET 2208/0.

54 Kiesler, *Inside the Endless House* („Rainford of Triple VVV", 10. März 1959), 194ff.

55 Plankopf, mit Datierung NOV. 1958 – APR. 26. 1959; ÖFLKS, PLN 240/0 und PLN 241/0.

56 Meeting, ÖFLKS, TXT 3815/0; Kiesler an Severud, 21. Mai 1959, ÖFLKS, LET 503/0.

57 *TIME*, 25. Mai 1959, Zeitungsausschnitt ohne Seitenangabe, ÖFLKS, CLP 6691/0.

58 Aus einem Brief Arthur Drexlers an Friedrich Kiesler vom 1. Juli 1959, ÖFLKS, LET 3157/0.

59 „New concepts of architecture", in *Harper's Bazaar* 2975 (1959), 182f. Das Foto mit Kiesler ist auf 183 abgedruckt. Sowie: Arthur Drexler, „Frederick Kiesler and his Endless House", in *Vogue* 1 (1960), 114–115.

60 Von diesem Setting gibt es mehrere Varianten. Eine davon zeigt Kiesler mit nacktem Oberkörper, was die Inszenierung als Schöpfergott noch einmal untermauert. ÖFLKS, PHO 771/0 (Kiesler mit Cape), PHO 807/0 (Kiesler mit nacktem Oberkörper), PHO 808/0 (Kiesler mit Schüssel).

61 *Atelier und Werkstatt. Friedrich Kiesler als Meister der Selbstinszenierung* (18/2014), hg. v. Peter Bogner (Wien: Österreichische Friedrich und Lillian Kiesler Privatstiftung, 2014).

62 Kiesler, *Inside The Endless House*, 243; vgl. Philip Johnson, „Three Architects", in *Art in America* 1 (1960), 70–75;

Endless House auf der Doppelseite 74–75.

63 ÖFLKS, box_txt_101, Folder EH Camera Three.

64 Ada Louise Huxtable, „ARCHITECTURE ON TV. 'Greatest Non-Building Architect of Our Times' Expounds His Ideas", in *New York Times*, 27. März 1960, Zeitungsausschnitt ohne Seitennummer, ÖFLKS, CLP 6696/0.

65 Vgl. Einladungsfolder, abgebildet in: Fred W. McDarrah, *The Artist's World in Pictures. The New York School* (New York: Shapolsky Publishers, 1988); 87; „These are Drawings written into space." Vgl. „Form is a Language", in *ART News* 2 (1960), (Statement by Frederick Kiesler), 34. Für den Tag der Eröffnung findet man den Eintrag „Opening Party" in einem Kalender Friedrich Kieslers. ÖFLKS, MED 6635/0.

66 Kiesler, *Inside The Endless House* („Herbert Mayer-Endless House", April 20, 1960), 267f.; Briefversionen vom 20. April

62 Kiesler, *Inside the Endless House* ("Two Letters", Jan. 5, 1960), 243; cf. Philip Johnson, "Three Architects", in *Art in America* 1 (1960), 70–75; Endless House on double-paged spread 74–75.

63 ÖFLKS, box_txt_101, Folder EH Camera Three.

64 Ada Louise Huxtable, "ARCHITECTURE ON TV. 'Greatest Non-Building Architect of Our Times' Expounds His Ideas", in *New York Times*, March 27, 1960 (ÖFLKS, CLP 6696/0).

65 Cf. invitation folder, reproduced in Fred W. McDarrah, *The Artist's World in Pictures. The New York School* (New York: Shapolsky Publishers, 1988), 87; "These are Drawings written into space." Cf. "Form is a Language", in *ART News* 2 (1960), (Statement by Frederick Kiesler), 34; For the day of the opening, one can find the entry "Opening Party" in one of Frederick Kiesler's diaries. ÖFLKS, MED 6635/0.

66 Kiesler, *Inside the Endless House* ("Herbert Mayer-Endless House" April 20, 1960), 267; letter versions from April 20, 1960 (draft), ÖFLKS, LET 3169/0_N5; May 3, 1960, ÖFLKS, LET 3169/0_n1+N2; and May 17, 1960, ÖFLKS.

67 "Oh Fred, Don't do that. I don't want you to lose the opportunity of doing it there on account of me, and besides, you know, I'm not in a hurry", ibid. ("Herbert Mayer-Endless House", April 20, 1960), 267.

68 "'Too late, the time is now… and now is too late', I said. 'We agree,' the others answered", ibid., 278 ("Decisions Sudden", Friday, May 20), 1960, and ibid., 267f. ("Herbert Mayer-Endless House", April 20, 1960).

69 Ibid. ("Scarpita Endless House", Thursday May 26, 1960), 281.

70 McQuaid, *Envisioning Architecture*, illustration on page 27.

71 "Visionary Architecture, an exhibition of 20th Century projects considered too revolutionary to be built […]", cf. for this and other quotes: Press Release no. 108, For Release: Thursday, Sept. 29, 1960, ÖFLKS, research material.

72 Ibid.

73 Ibid.

74 Kiesler, *Inside the Endless House* ("'Endless House' Opening at M.M.A.", Sept. 28, 1960), 299.

75 Ibid., 300–302.

76 "It begins with a historical section in which Leonardo da Vinci appears as an early theorist of the perfect city, and concludes with full-scale enlargements of Frederick Kiesler's Endless House, so installed that you can imagine walking into it." CLP 6804/0, John Canaday, "Dreamers at Work", in *New York Times* (undated, press clipping without page number).

77 Kiesler, *Inside the Endless House* ("The Object and the Objective", April 1, 1961), 417.

78 Ibid.

1960 (Draft), ÖFLKS, LET 3169/0_ N5; 3. Mai 1960, ÖFLKS, LET 3169/0_N1+N2; und 17. Mai 1960, ÖFLKS, LET3169/0_N3.

67 "Oh Fred, Don't do that. I don't want you to lose the opportunity of doing it there on account of me, and besides, you know, i'm not in a hurry." Kiesler, *Inside The Endless House* ("Herbert Mayer-Endless House", 20. April 1960), 267f.

68 "'Too late, the time is now… and now is too late, too' I said. 'We agree,' the others answered." ("Decisions Sudden", Freitag 20. Mai 1960), ebenda, 277ff.

69 Ebenda ("Scarpita Endless House", Donnerstag, 26. Mai 1960), 281.

70 Matilda McQuaid, *Envisioning Architecture*, Abbildung auf 27.

71 "Visionary Architecture, an exhibtion of 20th Century projects considered too revolutionary to be build […]", vgl. für diese und die weiteren Zitate: Press Release No. 108, For Release:

Thursday, Sept 29, 1960, ÖFLKS, Recherchematerial.

72 Ebenda. (Übersetzt aus dem Englischen)

73 Ebenda. (Übersetzt aus dem Englischen)

74 Kiesler, *Inside The Endless House* ("Endless' Opening at M. M. A.", September 28, 1960), 299.

75 "Bob Rauschenberg and Jasper Johns, who were struck by the precision of my curvilinear concepts in ink of the original /1924 Vienna plans [sic] for the 'Endless.' Their Enthusiasm is probably my greatest success, because, although these crest-riding talents are naturally possessed by their own ideas and successes, they broke down facing this work, with delight in their defeat. I have always felt that the real measure of success does not derive from the reaction of the public or critics, but from that of one's colleagues. And so it was now", ebenda, 300–302.

76 "It begins with a historical section in which Leonardo da Vinci appears as an early theorist of the perfect city, and concludes with full-scale enlargements of Frederick Kiesler's Endless House, so installed that you can imagine walking into it." CLP 6804/0, John Canaday, Dreamers at Work, in *New York Times* [o.D.].

77 "A Florida Lady appeared at the last hour of the last Saturday afternoon of my show. A newcomer to the gallery, she called for Mr. Castelli and said, 'What's that?' Her finger pointed to what seemed a shell sculpture in concrete. Castelli answered, 'It's a model for the 'Endless House,' a small version.' 'An endless house? Endless … I would love to live in it,' she said. […] 'Who is the architect? Is he in New York?'" Kiesler, *Inside The Endless House* (1. April 1961), 417.

78 "We met on the twentieth at La Fonda del Sol. I behaved with discretion. […] I refrained from

79 Frederick Kiesler to Mary Sisler,
   March 30, 1961, ÖFLKS, LET
   1946/0.
80 Kiesler, *Inside the Endless House*
   ("Near Palm Beach, Palm Beach",
   May 14, 1961), 437.
81 Ibid.
82 Ibid., 438.
83 ÖFLKS, TXT 6775/0, sheet N07.
84 Kiesler, *Inside the Endless House*
   ("Near Palm Beach, Palm Beach",
   May 14, 1961), 442.
85 Ibid.
86 Ibid., ("Wednesday / Three days
   later"), 444.
87 "Program for Mary Sisler's House
   on the W.S. Bar Ranch, Hobe
   Sound, Florida", 4 pages on 4
   sheets; ÖFLKS, LET 1955/0. Plan
   material in ÖFLKS, box_ofp_09
   (Misc 02).
88 ÖFLKS, MED 614/0.
89 Friederick Kiesler to Reid B.
   Johnson, July 16, 1965, ÖFLKS,
   LET 496/1.
90 ÖFLKS, TXT 615/0.

speaking about the 'Endless
House.' Nevertheless, a letter
agreement was drawn up a
week later." Ebenda.
79 Friedrich Kiesler an Mary Sisler,
   30. März 1961, ÖFLKS, LET
   1946/0.
80 Kiesler, *Inside The Endless House*
   ("Near Palm Beach, Palm Beach",
   14. Mai 1961), 437.
   (Übersetzt aus dem Englischen)
81 Ebenda. (Übersetzt aus dem
   Englischen)
82 "The estate [Kursivstellung im
   Original] The Land is swept-flat,
   sanded-flat, flooded flat. Patches
   of dessert. Patches of grass.
   Patches of palmettos. Burned
   tree trunks, forlorn. [...]
   A no man's land of architecture."
   Ebenda, 438.
83 "I have never seen a more devastating looking and uninspiring
   landscape in my life, and I've
   seen quite many." ÖFLKS, TXT
   6775/0, Blatt N07.
84 "I aimed, and shot the 'Endless
   House'", Kiesler, *Inside The

Endless House ("Near Palm
Beach, Palm Beach", 14. Mai
1961), 442.
85 "The entire group ran over to see
   what I had done to the drawing.
   I had killed it squarely. It was
   riddled with numerable holes as
   though hit by a rain of cosmic
   particles." Ebenda.
86 Ebenda ("Wednesday / Three
   days later"), 444.
87 "Programm for Mary Sisler's
   House on the W.S. Bar Ranch,
   Hobe Sound, Florida", 4 Seiten
   auf 4 Blättern; ÖFLKS, LET
   1955/0. Planmaterial in ÖFLKS,
   box_ofp_09 (Misc 02).
88 ÖFLKS, MED 614.
89 "Goodluck and God speed with
   you." Friedrich Kiesler an Reid B.
   Johnson, 16. Juli 1965, ÖFLKS,
   LET 496/1.
90 ÖFLKS, TXT 615/0.

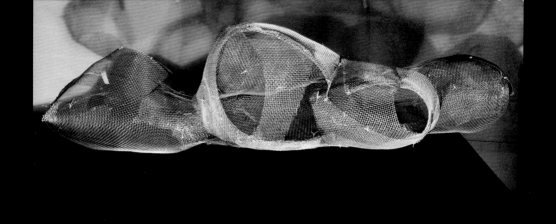
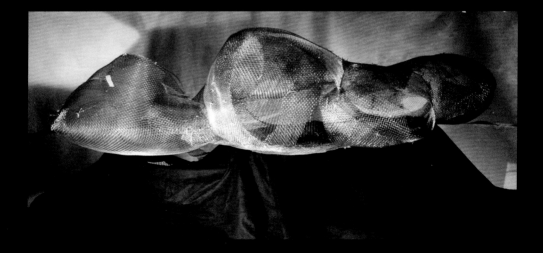

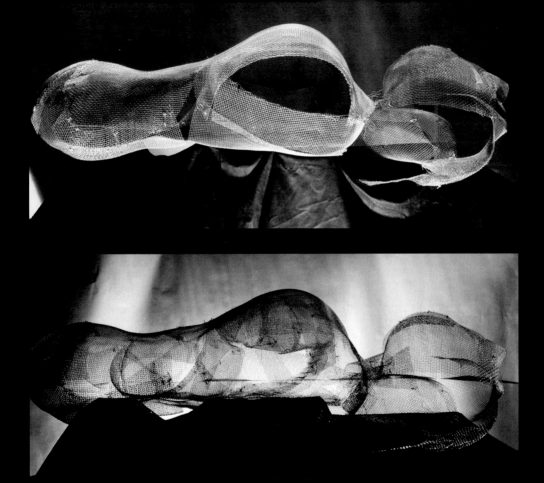

Spheres and Shells.
The Construction
of the *Endless House*

Florian Medicus

Sphären und Schalen.
Zur Konstruktion
des *Endless House*

"It is possible to set physical limits to space, but space itself is
limitless and intangible. Space dissolves in darkness and in infinity.
It is necessary to take action before space can become visible: it
must acquire form and boundary."
—Sigfried Giedion[1]

Berlin

The years between 1913 when Frederick Kiesler left the Vienna Academy
of Fine Arts without a degree and 1923 when, by then in Berlin, he
created what was to become the legendary set design for Karel Čapek's piece
R.U.R (Fig. 1) can only be filled with all sorts of speculation. The only thing
that can be stated with certainty is that Kiesler and Stephanie Frischer were
married at the Vienna synagogue in 1920. There is only little evidence for
his work as an "academic painter." And what about Kiesler's collaboration with
Adolf Loos? Just a persistent rumor? From 1921, Kiesler was often in Berlin.
But what was he doing there? What did he see, whom did he meet? Up
until the end of 1922, it is hard to say, but from then on "everything Kiesler
did fell on fertile ground (that can be traced)."[2]

There is evidence that, even before his studies at the Vienna Academy of

„Es ist möglich, Raum abzugrenzen.
Seinem Wesen nach ist er grenzenlos und unfassbar.
Er erlischt im Dunkel, und er kann sich im Unendlichen verflüchtigen.
Es braucht Media, um ihn sichtbar zu machen:
Er muss abgegrenzt und geformt werden."
– Sigfried Giedion[1]

Berlin

Die Jahre zwischen 1913, als Friedrich Kiesler die Wiener Akademie der
bildenden Künste ohne Diplom verlässt und 1923, als er in Berlin das
legendär gewordene Bühnenbild zu Karel Čapeks Science-Fiction-Stück *W.U.R*
(der deutsche Titel von *R.U.R*, Abb. 1) umsetzt, sind nur durch allerhand
Mutmaßungen auszufüllen. Als gesichert gilt lediglich die Hochzeit Kieslers
mit Stephanie Frischer in der Wiener Synagoge 1920. Nur wenig belegt ist
seine Arbeit als „akademischer Maler"; und Kieslers Mitarbeit bei Adolf Loos?
Ein hartnäckiges Gerücht. Ab 1921 war Kiesler allerdings immer wieder in
Berlin; aber was er dort macht, was er sieht, wen er trifft? Bis Ende 1922
wissen wir es nicht wirklich, ab dann „fiel alles, was Kiesler tat, auf
fruchtbaren (und nachvollziehbaren) Boden".[2]

1—Frederick Kiesler, *R.U.R.*, stage design, Berlin 1923

Fine Arts, he had shown an interest in and an affinity for the architecture of
Otto Wagner and his school. It is therefore probable, if not very likely, that
Kiesler soon had contacts with artists and architects in Berlin. There is also
evidence that, thanks to the writer Alfred Döblin, Kiesler was able to get to
know Herwarth Walden and his gallery *Der Sturm*, where works by László
Moholy-Nagy were exhibited in spring 1922 and later by Kurt Schwitters.[3] It is
therefore at least conceivable that Kiesler saw the much-acclaimed *First
Russian Art Exhibition* at the Galerie van Diemen in October of that year and
would have thus also seen works by Malevich, Rodchenko, Kandinsky,
Lissitzky, Gabo, Popowa and Tatlin. It is also possible that Kiesler, through the
intervention of the sociable Mr. Walden, had contact with the *Gläserne Kette*
or the *Novembergruppe* and therefore had the opportunity to meet Arp,
Feininger, Dix, Grosz, Pechstein, Kollwitz, Oud, Stam, Weill, Breuer, Finsterlin,
Hilberseimer, Mies, Taut and Mendelsohn. From March 1921, Hugo Häring,
for instance, was also in Berlin. Häring was the later secretary of the architects' organization *Der Ring*, which included Behrens, Mendelsohn, Mies van
der Rohe (who in the meantime had married Heinrich Wölfflin's former fiancé!),
Pölzig, Max and Bruno Taut. This group showed an almost natural affinity to
Scharoun, Gropius and Meyer. At that time, the war-torn metropolis of Berlin

Belegt ist, dass Kiesler noch von seiner Zeit an der Wiener Akademie her
dem baukünstlerischen Wirken Otto Wagners und seiner Schule interessiert
gegenüber- und nahestand, und es ist demnach gut möglich, um nicht zu
sagen sehr wahrscheinlich, dass Kiesler auch in Berlin rasch Künstler- und
Architektenbekanntschaften geschlossen hat. Belegt ist auch, dass Kiesler
über den Schriftsteller Alfred Döblin Herwarth Walden und dessen Galerie
Der Sturm kennenlernte, wo im Frühjahr 1922 Arbeiten von László Moholy-
Nagy, dann von Kurt Schwitters gezeigt wurden.[3] Es wäre also immerhin
denkbar, dass Kiesler im Oktober desselben Jahres die vielbeachtete *Erste
Russische Kunstausstellung* in der Galerie van Diemen gesehen hat, und
damit u.a. Arbeiten von Malewitsch, Rodtschenko, Kandinsky, Lissitzky, Gabo,
Popowa und Tatlin. Es wäre zudem möglich, dass Kiesler über den umtriebi-
gen Herrn Walden auch Kontakt zur *Gläsernen Kette* oder *Novembergruppe*
bekam und damit Zugang zu Arp, Feininger, Dix, Grosz, Pechstein, Kollwitz,
Oud, Stam, Weill, Breuer, Finsterlin, Hilberseimer, Mies, Taut oder Mendelsohn.
Ab März 1921 war beispielsweise auch Hugo Häring in Berlin, der spätere
Sekretär der Architektenvereinigung *Der Ring*, bestehend aus Behrens,
Mendelsohn, Mies van der Rohe (mittlerweile verheiratet mit der ehemaligen
Verlobten Heinrich Wölfflins!), Pölzig, Max und Bruno Taut mit einem fast

was a fertile ground for remarkable cultural forces, from which hope for a radical renewal of society was born in the early 1920s.

This attitude was reflected in a striking way by the *Arbeitsrat für Kunst* (AfK—Work Council for Art), which postulated that its goal was to unite all arts under the wings of a great architecture. "From now on, the artist as the designer of public feeling is alone responsible for the visible guise of a new state."[4] The difficult and also uncertain circumstances of the early Weimar Republic influenced and fomented ideas, alliances, manifestos, futurist aspirations and in part bizarre social experiments, all of which were full of energy and hope—much like in the young Soviet Union. And Frederick Kiesler as the only Austrian in this avant-garde movement found himself in the midst of all the action: "Arrive on Monday with finished sketches" (telegram sent to Eugen Robert).[5]

From today's perspective, we can now see the decisive transition from the 19th century to a new era less through the perspective of the horrors of World War 1 and more influenced by the 1920s, which despite all the material shortages were rich in creative terms.[6] First in the artistic avant-garde and a short time later also in architecture, the more recent popular ideas of a non-Euclidean, dynamic geometry (Gauss, Riemann) and of space and time

natürlichen Näheverhältnis zu Scharoun, Gropius und Meyer. In der ausgezehrten Metropole Berlin regten sich Anfang der 1920er-Jahre also ganz bemerkenswerte Kulturkräfte und mit ihnen die Hoffnung auf eine radikale Erneuerung der Gesellschaft.

Eindrücklich formuliert wurde diese Haltung durch den Arbeitsrat für Kunst (AfK), der postulierte, dass das erklärte Ziel ein „Zusammenschluss aller Künste unter den Flügeln einer großen Baukunst sei. Denn fortan ist der Künstler allein als Gestalter des Volksempfindens verantwortlich für das sichtbare Gewand des neuen Staates".[4] Die schwierigen und zudem unsicheren äußeren Umstände der frühen Weimarer Republik also bedingten und förderten, ähnlich wie in der jungen Sowjetunion, kraft- und hoffnungsvolle Ideenwelten, allerhand Zusammenschlüsse, Manifeste, post-futuristische Allüren und teils bizarre Sozialexperimente mit Friedrich Kiesler als einzigem österreichischen Avantgarde-Teilnehmer quasi mittendrin: „Ankomme Montag mit fertigen Skizzen" (Depesche an Eugen Robert).[5]

Mit der uns heute verfügbaren Distanz sehen wir die entscheidende Passage vom 19. Jahrhundert in eine neue Zeit weniger durch den furchtbaren Ersten Weltkrieg, als vielmehr die trotz aller Knappheit sprühenden 1920er-Jahre begründet.[6] Die neueren, durchaus populären Vorstellungen einer nicht-

(Poincaré, Einstein) prompted a turn to technology on the one hand and to organicism on the other. As well as in Mendelsohn, this could also be seen in Taut or Häring (when, for instance, Behne writes, "The perfect house for him [Häring] would be one that grows by itself out of the ground like an organic plant."[7]). And precisely this in part poetic, in part fantastic-magical world of ideas could have provided decisive foundation for the *Endless House* to be addressed here. And we say "could have" because Kiesler later proved to be ingenious in blurring or covering over all traces with too much cement. For me, it is also inexplicable how Kiesler and Bernard Rudofsky in spite (or perhaps precisely because?) of all the apparent overlaps could later "overlook" each other to such an extent.

As for possible roots of the *Endless House*, there does in any case seem to be a striking affinity to the German Expressionists, even if Kiesler's ideas showed greater proximity to Soviet constructivism and in particular to De Stijl (through Doesburg). But hadn't Bruno Taut, as early as 1914, written: "Making the building a living organism, recognizing first and foremost its functional and constructive preconditions and allowing the right form to emerge by itself as a necessary consequence and in subordination of the individual itself, a form that both breathes and lives, that is the goal."[8] Or as Hugo Häring, who,

euklidischen, dynamischen Geometrie (Gauss, Riemann) und von Raum und Zeit (Poincaré, Einstein) bedingen zuerst in künstlerischen Avantgarden, bald darauf in der Architektur eine Hinwendung zum Technischen einerseits und zum Organischen andererseits; nach Mendelsohn auch bei Taut oder Häring (wenn etwa Behne schreibt, „Das vollkommene Haus wäre ihm [Häring] jenes, das von selbst aus dem Boden wüchse wie eine organische Pflanze."[7]). Und eben diese, teils poetische, teils phantastisch-magische Gedankenwelt könnte mittelbar ganz entscheidende Grundlagen für das hier zu behandelnde *Endless House* gehabt haben. Konjunktiv deswegen, weil Kiesler auch später sowohl im Verwischen, als auch im übermäßigen Betonen von allfälligen Spuren meisterlich blieb. Unerklärlich ist mir in diesem Zusammenhang etwa, wie sich Kiesler und Bernard Rudofsky trotz (oder gerade wegen?) all der augenscheinlichen Schnittpunkte später derart *übersehen* konnten.

Im Hinblick auf mögliche Wurzeln des *Endless House* jedenfalls scheint ein Näheverhältnis zu den Deutschen Expressionisten recht offensichtlich, wenn die Ideenwelt Kieslers auch vorerst dem sowjetischen Konstruktivismus und vor allem über Doesburg dem De-Sijl näherstand. Aber hatte nicht Bruno Taut schon 1914 geschrieben: „Den Bau zu einem lebendigen Organismus zu machen, zuallererst seine funktionellen und konstruktiven Voraussetzungen

as already mentioned, was anti-functional in his thinking, put it even years later: "One of the attempts to break with the compulsion to design in rectangularity towards the house as an organ?"[9] Here we must also recall the doubly fantastic drawings by Hermann Finsterlin (Fig. 2 in the catalog to the exhibition *Visionary Architecture*, MoMA, 1960: "Finsterlin's plan for a building of unspecified purpose anticipates projects by Frederick Kiesler"[10]), who, in turn, showed a strong affinity to Erich Mendelsohn, a towering figure almost forgotten today. The visionary thrust reflected in his wonderful drawings relatively soon began to merge with actual, that is, built reality (as exemplified by the Einstein Tower!).

Mendelsohn

In 1919, Mendelsohn presented the sketches, entitled "Architecture out of iron and reinforced concrete", he had made in a Russian bunker on boards—first to Paul Cassirer in Berlin. Both in these really impressive drawings and in his lectures, Mendelsohn assumed that a new architecture would be defined by the new materials (reinforced concrete in particular!). Yet unlike the French school of Auguste Perret ("A & G Perret, constructeurs" and not "architectes!" and also his student Le Corbusier), Mendelsohn

zu erkennen und daraus in notwendiger Konsequenz und Unterordnung des eigenen Individuums wie von selbst die passende Form entstehen zu lassen, die gleichsam atmet und lebt, das ist das Ziel",[8] oder wie es Hugo Häring, der – wie schon erwähnt – eine anti-funktionale Denkweise vertrat, noch Jahre später formulierte: „Einer der Versuche zur Los-lösung aus dem Gestaltzwang der Rechtwinkligkeit in Richtung auf das Haus als Organ?"[9] Man muss an dieser Stelle auch an die in doppelter Hinsicht phantastischen Zeichnungen Hermann Finsterlins erinnern (Abb. 2, im Katalog zur Ausstellung *Visionary Architecture*, MoMA, 1960 etwa: „Finsterlins Plan für ein Bauwerk ohne spezi-fischen Zweck nimmt Projekte von Friedrich Kiesler vorweg."[10]), der wiederum Erich Mendelsohn sehr nahestand. Überhaupt Mendelsohn, ein Gigant eigentlich und heute fast vergessen, bei dem sich Visionär-Forderndes im Sinne von wunderbaren Zeichnungen schon relativ früh mit faktischer, also gebauter Realität (etwa dem Einsteinturm) zu decken beginnt!

Mendelsohn

Mendelsohn hatte 1919 zuerst bei Paul Cassirer in Berlin seine Skizzen aus dem Unterstand in Russland unter dem Titel *Architektur aus Eisen und Eisenbeton* auf großen Tafeln gezeigt. Sowohl in diesen so einprägsamen

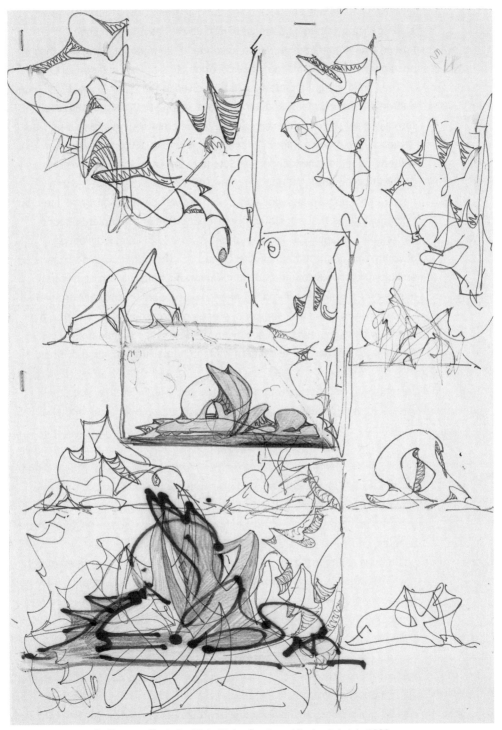

2—Hermann Finsterlin, *Bird with two heads*, architectural sketch, 1920

envisaged reinforced concrete being used in the future not for a load-bearing "skeleton" but, rather, as a monolithic sculpture, as a spatial shell, "and flowing sculptural qualities will be ascribed to the material along with the possibility of overcoming the classical opposition of load and support."[11]

The "architectural phantasies" that evolved in the years 1914–17 provided a strong foundation for Mendelsohn's later works; both thematically and formally, they show a surprising affinity to the architectural understanding of someone like Antonio Sant'Elia. In his manifesto of 1914, the latter had written: "What is called modern architecture is just a poor mix of a great array of stylistic elements that only serve to clad the skeleton of the modern house. […] I oppose and disdain: […] 4. The vertical and horizontal lines, the cylindrical forms that are static, heavy, oppressive and completely counter to our new sensitivity. 5. The use of massive, voluminous, long-lasting, obsolete and costly materials. And declare: 1. That futurist architecture is an architecture of calculation, of bold audacity and simplicity, an architecture of reinforced concrete, of iron, of glass, of cardboard, of textile fibers and all available ersatz materials for wood, stone and brick that allow the greatest elasticity and lightness to be achieved."[12] As the cited manifesto shows,— here as well as there—the concern was the future, the industrial dynamic. It

Zeichnungen als auch in seinen Vorträgen geht Mendelsohn davon aus, dass die neuen Materialien (Eisenbeton besonders!) eine neue Architektur bestimmen würden. Anders als die französische Schule von Auguste Perret (*A & G Perret, constructeurs* und nicht *architectes!* und auch seinem Schüler Le Corbusier) aber sieht Mendelsohn den künftigen Einsatz des Stahlbetons nicht in Form eines tragenden Skeletts, sondern als monolithische Plastik, als Raumschale, „und es werden dem Material fließend-plastische Eigenschaften und die Möglichkeit zugeschrieben, den klassischen Gegensatz von Last und Stütze zu überbrücken."[11] (Abb. 3)

Die in den Jahren 1914–17 entstandene Reihe von *Architekturphantasien* sind die starke Basis für Mendelsohns spätere Arbeiten, thematisch und formal der Architekturauffassung etwa eines Antonio Sant'Elia überraschend nahe. Dieser hatte ja in seinem Manifest von 1914 geschrieben: „Als moderne Architektur wird eine miese Mischung verschiedenster Stilelemente bezeichnet, die lediglich dazu dient, das Skelett des modernen Hauses zu verkleiden. […] Ich bekämpfe und verachte: […] 4. die senkrechten und waagrechten Linien, die zylindrischen Formen, die statisch, schwerfällig, erdrückend sind und völlig gegen unsere neue Empfindsamkeit verstoßen. 5. den Gebrauch von wuchtigen, voluminösen, dauerhaften, veralteten und kostspieligen Materialien. Und

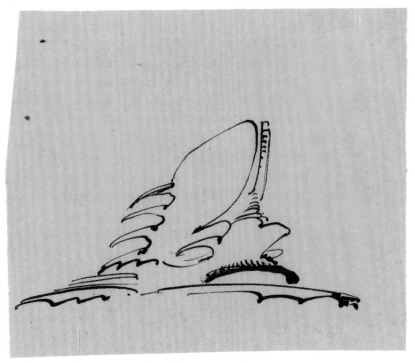

3—Erich Mendelsohn, *Gartenpavillon für Hermann*, 1920

verkünde: 1. daß die futuristische Architektur eine Architektur der Berechnung, der verwegenen Kühnheit und der Einfachheit ist, eine Architektur des
Stahlbetons, des Eisens, des Glases, der Pappe, der Textilfaser und
aller verfügbaren Ersatzmaterialien für Holz, Stein und Ziegel, die erlauben,
größtmögliche Elastizität und Leichtigkeit zu erlangen."[12] Es ging in den
gezeichneten Postulaten hier wie dort um die kommende, die industrielle
Dynamik; es ging um nichts weniger, als um die eindeutige Bestimmung
konstruktiver und ästhetischer Konzepte künftiger, also mithin möglicher
Architekturen. Mendelsohn meinte schließlich, „erst der Beton ermögliche es
der Architektur endlich in Fluss zu kommen, und dies war, ihm zufolge,
überhaupt Sinn der neuen Konstruktion des Eisenbetons," wie sich Julius
Posener erinnert (Abb. 3).[13]

Beton

Und dabei war genau das bereits geschehen: Der Beton und die in ihm
geführten Kräfte waren bereits in Fluss gebracht worden. Denn ganz anders
als Joseph August Lux in seiner 1910 erschienenen *Ingenieurästhetik*
befürchtet hatte, dass nämlich der Beton eine neue Ära des (schweren)
Steinbaues und damit einen Rückschritt hinter die modernen Entmaterial-

was about nothing less than the clear definition of constructive and aesthetic concepts of future that is also possible architecture. As Mendelsohn concluded: "Only concrete would make it possible for architecture to finally come into *flow*" and this was, in his view, actually the meaning of the new construction of reinforced concrete, as Julius Posener recalls (Fig. 3).[13]

Concrete

And, as it turns out, this is precisely what had already happened. Concrete and the forces it carried had already been brought into flow. Very different to what J. A. Lux had feared in his *Engineer's Aesthetics* that appeared in 1910, namely that concrete would exemplify a new era of (heavy) stone construction and thus a step backwards from the modern dematerialization tendencies of (light) iron constructions.[14] The Swiss concrete virtuoso[15] Robert Maillart had succeeded in transcending the load-bearing principle of classical tectonics by means of his beamless ceilings. Unlike Hennebique and Perret before him, Maillart first celebrated reinforced concrete as a monolithic building material in a storage building (Giesshübelstrasse, Zurich, 1910) and then in 1912 in the filter building—a building [...] in which the forces flowed from the ceiling into the (mushroom head) supports.

isierungstendenzen der (leichten) Eisenkonstruktionen beschreiben würde[14], war es dem Schweizer Beton-Virtuosen[15] Robert Maillart gelungen, das Träger-Stütze-Prinzip klassischer Tektonik durch seine unterzugslosen Decken zu überwinden. Anders als Hennebique und Perret zuvor bespielt Maillart zuerst in einem Lagerhaus (Giesschübelstrasse, Zürich, 1910) und dann 1912 im Filtergebäude Rorschach den eisenbewehrten Beton als monolithischen Baustoff, in dem die Kräfte fließend aus der Decke in die (Pilzkopf-)Stützen abgeleitet werden.

Bedenkt man, dass noch wenige Jahre zuvor eine heftige Debatte über Eisenkonstruktionen und die Frage nach deren architektonischem Gehalt geführt worden war (Labrouste, Semper über Viollet-le-Duc und Choisy, van de Velde, Behrens bis Gropius) und der Architekt Richard Lucae noch 1870 geschrieben hatte, dass sich „die Schönheit der Bausysteme nur im Überschuss an Masse über das zum Tragen notwendige Material"[16] zeige, so sieht man den Beton leichter und schneller in der Architektur ankommen als das Eisen in den langen Jahrzehnten zuvor. Maillart verlieh seiner Zuversicht wie folgt Ausdruck, dass „sich also der Ingenieur von der durch die Tradition der älteren Baustoffe gegebenen Formen löse, um in voller Freiheit und mit dem Blick aufs Ganze, die zweckmäßige Materialausnutzung

Considering that only a few years earlier a heated debate had taken
place on iron constructions and their architectural significance (Labrouste,
Semper to Viollet-le-Duc and Choisy, van de Velde, Behrens to Gropius)
and the architect Richard Lucae had still written in 1870 that "the beauty of
construction systems (is reflected) only in the excess of mass over the
material necessary for supporting it,"[16] one sees that concrete arrived more
easily and faster than iron in the long decades before. Maillart expressed
his optimism as follows: that "the engineer liberates himself from the forms
given through the tradition of older building materials, so as to aim at a
practical use of material with full freedom and a view to the totality. Perhaps
then, as in the construction of airplanes and automobiles, we will achieve
a new style that does justice to the material."[19]

But let's return once again to Erich Mendelsohn. As already mentioned,
he had proceeded in his early and so important years from the conviction
that reinforced concrete "is able to eliminate the difference between support
and load" and the related opposition between the "active" and the infill
elements in a construction. The building should be "monolithic, not articulated,
and its appearance neither the skeleton nor the somehow architecturally
structured building shape but rather the free, sculpturally shaped surface

zu erzielen. Vielleicht erreichen wir dann, wie im Flugzeug- und Automobilbau
auch Schönes, einen neuen materialgerechten Stil."[17]

Noch einmal zurück zu Erich Mendelsohn. Dieser war, wie schon erwähnt,
in seinen frühen und so bedeutsamen Jahren davon ausgegangen, dass
Stahlbeton „den Unterscheid zwischen Stütze und Last aufzuheben vermöge"
und den damit zusammenhängenden Gegensatz zwischen aktiven und
füllenden Teilen am Bau. Der Bau sollc „monolithisch sein, nicht artikuliert,
und seine Erscheinungsform sei weder das Skelett, noch irgendeine
architektonisch gegliederte Bauform, sondern die frei-plastische geformte
Oberflächenstruktur."[18] Mendelsohn hatte genau das versucht, als
er ab 1919 in Potsdam am Einsteinturm (Abb. 4) baute, allein: die Ausführung
in „reinem" Stahlbeton war (noch) nicht möglich. Die Zeit war damals,
wie Finsterlin später schreiben sollte, „noch weniger reif als heute in Bezug
vor allem auf Material wie auf die Ausführungskräfte".[19] So steht der Turm zwar
auf einem freigeformten Betonsockel, musste darüber aber klassisch auf-
gemauert und fein verputzt werden, um den gewünschten Eindruck eines homo-
genen Körpers zu vermitteln. Die herrliche Formenwelt in Mendelsohns
Zeichnungen wies, wie so oft in diesen Tagen über die faktischen Möglichkeiten der Materialisierung hinaus, aber ist es nicht, mit Benjamin gesprochen,

4—Erich Mendelsohn, Einsteinturm, Potsdam 1921

5—Frederick Kiesler, *Endless House*, model, New York 1959

structure."[18] This is precisely what Mendelsohn had attempted in building the Einstein Tower (Fig. 4) from 1919 onwards: the construction in "pure" reinforced concrete was not (yet) possible. The age was, as Finsterlin was to describe it, "still less ripe than today with respect primarily to the material as well as to the construction forces."[19] While the tower rests on a free-formed concrete base, it had to be classically rendered in a fine coat of plaster in order to convey the desired impression of a homogeneous body. As so often in those days, the wonderful world of forms in Mendelson's drawings pointed beyond the actual possibilities of materialization but, to quote Benjamin, hasn't it always been "one of the most important tasks of art to create a demand that cannot yet be fully satisfied?"[20]

"Never again!", Mendelsohn is reported to have said when students asked him about the Einstein Tower. "We had to turn to shipbuilders to have the formwork made," to which he added: "But it's a good thing that this building got built."[21]

Endless House

As we know, Frederick Kiesler's *Endless House* was never built. However, thanks partly to Kiesler's gregarious personality, it was soon "the most

„von jeher eine der wichtigsten Aufgaben der Kunst gewesen, eine Nachfrage zu erzeugen, für deren volle Befriedigung die Stunde noch nicht gekommen ist?"[20]

„Nie wieder!", soll Mendelsohn, von Studenten auf den Einsteinturm ange-sprochen, gesagt haben; „Da haben wir ja Schiffbauer herbeirufen müssen, um die Schalung zu machen." Als Nachsatz: „Und doch ist es gut, dass dieser Bau steht."[21]

Endless House

Friedrich Kieslers *Endless House* steht bekanntlich nicht; es war jedoch durch Kieslers umtriebige Art schon bald „das berühmteste ungebaute Haus, das existiert"[22] und blieb, vielleicht gerade deswegen, ein so hartnäckiger Mythos in der langen Kette radikaler, jedoch ungebauter Architekturvisionen des 20. Jahrhunderts. Auch wenn Gropius der Meinung war, dass es ganz wesentlich wäre, Kieslers Architektur in die Realität zu übersetzen[23], sollte es bei den mehr oder weniger bekannten Zeichnungen, Plänen, den oft lyrischen Begleittexten, Fotos und Modellen bleiben (Abb. 5). Es stellt sich jedoch wieder (und wie bei so vielen anderen Projekten auch) die Frage, ob die Verwirklichung des *Endless House* der Vision nicht mehr geschadet als Gutes getan hätte? Hätte man, frei nach Robert Musil, in der Umsetzung

famous unbuilt house in existence"[22] and remained, perhaps precisely
for that reason, such an obstinate myth in the long chain of radical but unbuilt
architectural visions of the 20th century. Even though Gropius believed
that it was absolutely essential to translate Kiesler's architecture into reality[23],
it was never to develop beyond the more or less known drawings, plans,
the accompanying (often poetic) texts, photographs and models (Fig. 5). Here,
once again, (as in so many other projects) we could ask whether the
realization of the *Endless House* wouldn't have perhaps done more harm than
good. To paraphrase Robert Musil, wouldn't strictly scientific evidence
have been gained at the expense of the dream and poetic myth which would
be lost in the process? Is it legitimate and meaningful at all to deploy the
technological possibilities of today to deal with architectural history of a given
time in order to confirm (or refute) the visionary approaches by at least
making their constructional feasibility tangible? However, looking at the works
of our esteemed students (IoA Student Works, pp. 282), you are left with
the impression that there are activities with far less meaning.

Here a brief digression. A few years ago, an association founded by the
Berlin Rudolf Springer Gallery took it upon itself to organize the realization of
Vladimir Tatlin's 400-meter-high *Monument of the III. International* on the

zwar den streng wissenschaftlichen Nachweis gewonnen, dafür aber den
Traum verloren und somit den poetischen Mythos ruiniert? Was wäre es denn
heute: ein pflegebedürftiges Relikt, ein quasi-ikonischer Gift-Shop oder einfach
eine etwas sonderbar gestaltete Smoothie-Bar? Andererseits wäre es natürlich
legitim zu fragen, warum man sich jetzt – und sei es nur als akademisches
Denkmodell – mit den uns zur Verfügung stehenden Mitteln und Möglichkeiten
über zeitgebundene Architekturgeschichten hermacht? Hätte man es damals
bauen können, wenn ja, wie und woran ist es gescheitert? Und wie würden wir
es heute bauen? Würde es gleich aussehen und das gleiche bedeuten?
Wohl eher nicht, aber was und wie dann? Relativ gelassen aber darf ich hier
auf die Arbeiten unserer StudentInnen (IoA Studentenarbeiten, S. 282)
verweisen, die schon zweimal den schönen Nachweis erbrachten, dass es weit
langweiligere und mithin sinnlosere Beschäftigungen gibt!

Kleiner Einschub: Vor einigen Jahren hatte sich ein Verein um den Berliner
Galeristen Rudolf Springer der tatsächlichen Realisierung von Vladimir
Tatlins 400 Meter hohem *Monument der III. Internationalen* auf dem Gelände
des 2008 eingestellten Flughafens Tempelhof verschrieben. Ein
gewisses Näheverhältnis zur *Paris Bar* darf angenommen werden, wobei die
Unternehmung durchaus ernsthaft geführt worden war (Vorstatik, Kosten-

grounds of Tempelhof airport, which had been shut down in 2008. It can
be assumed that there was a certain tie to the *Paris Bar*, but the whole project
was certainly carried out professionally (preliminary structural analysis,
cost estimates, etc.). According to Springer, had the political and economic
situation been more favorable there would have been a really good
chance to construct the monument.[24] If it hadn't been for the crisis, would it
have actually seen the light of day?

By way of comparison, let's imagine that Frederick Kiesler had been able
to prove his spatial theory by building a 1:1 model (planning began at
the start of 1958, "with a view toward the eventual construction of the house
in the Museum's garden"[25]). One can safely assume that the reception
of the project today would be more one-dimensional and thus simpler. And
perhaps the building would have the same fate as the wonderful works
by Melnikov, Wesnin, Ginsburg or Golossov, whereas the transportable Russian
avant-garde is filling exhibition venues all over the world.

It is indeed remarkable that for his *Endless House* Frederick Kiesler
adopted a scale that was almost modest in terms of his visionary structures.
This is all the more surprising, since his personal affinity to the avant-garde
of the young Soviet Union and later to De Stijl would rather suggest large-scale

schätzung etc.) und hätte, wie Springer meinte, unter günstigeren politischen
und wirtschaftlichen Vorzeichen tatsächliche Realisierungschancen gehabt.
Was wäre nur geworden, wenn nicht die Krise …?

Nochmals stellen wir uns vor, Friedrich Kiesler hätte den Nachweis seiner
räumlichen Theorie im Maßstab 1:1 tatsächlich erfüllen können oder müssen
(Planungsstart 1958, „mit Aussicht auf die tatsächliche Konstruktion des
Hauses im Garten des Museums"[25]): Sehr wahrscheinlich wäre dem Objekt
ein ähnlich trauriges Schicksal beschieden wie den so wunderbaren Bauten
Melnikovs, Wesnins, Ginsburgs oder Golossows, während zur gleichen
Zeit die transportable *Russische Avantgarde* weltweit Ausstellungshäuser füllt.

Bemerkenswert aber war und ist, dass sich Friedrich Kiesler mit seinem
Endless House einem für visionäre Strukturen fast bescheidenen Maßstab
zuwendet. Das ist umso überraschender, als seine persönliche Nähe zur Avant-
garde der jungen Sowjetunion und später zu De Stijl eher groß-maßstäbliche
Interventionen in Fortführung der *Raumstadt* nahegelegt hätte. Aber ebenso
wie etwas früher Buckminster Fuller, wählt Kiesler das Einfamilienhaus als
radikalste Zelle, als entscheidenden Baustein der Zukunft. Dieter Bogner hat
in seinem schönen Essay „Inside the Endless House" von 2001 bereits auf
diesen Umstand hingewiesen.[26] Und hatte Kiesler nicht bereits 1947 im

interventions as a continuation of the "spatial city." But just like Buckminster
Fuller some time before him, Kiesler adopted the single-family house as
the most radical cell, as the decisive building block of the future. Dieter Bogner
already pointed this out in his essay *Inside the Endless House*.[26] And
hadn't Kiesler already written in 1947, in connection with the *Paris Surrealist
Exhibition* , that "he was juxtaposing the mystery of hygiene, which is the
superstition of functional architecture, with the reality of a magical architecture. […] The house liberated from traditional aesthetics had become
a living being."[27] Here we feel immediately reminded of Taut and Häring. Also,
the fact that the *Endless House* rests on such strange, shapeless
supports certainly continues his earlier postulate on the "space city" (*Raumstadt*) of 1925, in which he wanted to "free himself from the earth and
overcome the static axis."[28] Yet Kiesler was unable (or unwilling?) to completely break with the "floating syndrome of modernity", even if this fact
also entailed significant limitations for a socio-dynamic and intrinsically flexible
conception. What Femke Bijlsma wrote about Steven Holl's "horizontal
skyscraper" (sic!) in Shenzen apparently still holds today: "Give a building legs
and something magical happens."[29] Even if the plans from June 1959 show
the building rising up over a pool, it did not rest on massive cores, but I will not

Rahmen der Pariser Surrealistenausstellung geschrieben, er „setze
dem Mysterium der Hygiene, das der Aberglaube funktionaler Architektur ist,
die Wirklichkeit einer magischen Architektur entgegen. […] Das von der
traditionellen Ästhetik befreite Haus ist zu einem Lebewesen geworden,"[27] so
fühlen wir uns doch gleich an Taut und Häring erinnert! Auch dass das
Endless House auf so sonderbar-unförmigen Kernen aufsitzt, führt wohl sein
früheres Postulat zur *Raumstadt* von 1925 weiter, in dem er sich „von
der Erde loslösen und die statische Achse aufgeben wollte."[28] Kiesler konnte
oder wollte sich dem bodenflüchtigen „Schwebesyndrom der Moderne"
(Adolf Max Vogt) doch nicht ganz entziehen, wenngleich dieser Umstand auch
entscheidende funktionale Einschränkungen für eine sozial-dynamische
und in sich flexible Konzeption mit sich brachte. Und auch heute noch scheint
zu gelten, was Femke Bijlsma zu Steven Holls „horizontalem Wolkenkratzer"
(sic!) in Shenzen geschrieben hat: „Gib einem Gebäude Beine und etwas
Magisches geschieht,"[29] was an dieser Stelle aber nicht weiter vertieft werden
soll auch weil die Pläne vom Juni 1959 zwar das Volumen über einem Pool
erhoben zeigen, ohne aber auf derart klobigen Kernen zu sitzen. Wichtiger
schien mir, auf den geistigen wie materiellen Fundus und die recht
offensichtliche Nähe Kieslers zu den Deutschen Expressionisten hinzuweisen,

dwell on this here. In my view it seems more important to refer to the legacy of the German Expressionists and Kiesler's obvious affinity to this impressive as well as critical sphere, which led even Henry-Russell Hitchcock to make the following statement in 1962: "Expressionism has never been completely dead. It only went underground, it continued to have a clandestine effect, before rising up again."[30]

Shells

Already the first picture of the *Endless House* (1950)—still formally related to the *Endless Theater* and *Space House*—shows a spherical shell construction (Fig. 6), which was continually transformed over the following years until it became a large biomorphic shape and was elaborated taking into account the growing importance of the interior. To the outside, the form was not intended to have either an aesthetic or symbolic effect. The *Endless House* was meant to be sensual, "to resemble the female body more than male architecture with its corners and edges."[31] By means of the shell, both a valid expression of the time and of new materials and (processing) techniques—plastic, glass and reinforced concrete—, Kiesler describes a possible rearrangement of the house system as an enveloping, organically flowing space, shaped by the

eine ebenso eindrucksvolle wie kritische Sphäre, die selbst Henry-Russell Hitchcock 1962 sagen ließ: „Der Expressionismus ist niemals ganz tot gewesen. Er ist nur in den Untergrund gegangen, er wirkte heimlich weiter, um dann wieder emporzusteigen."[30]

Schalen

Schon die erste Darstellung des *Endless House* (1950) – dem *Endless Theatre* und *Space House* formal noch nahe stehend – beschreibt eine sphärische Schalenkonstruktion (Abb. 6), die über die folgenden Jahre kontinuierlich zu einer biomorphen Großform verändert und vor allem hinsichtlich der zunehmenden Bedeutung des Innenraumes präzisiert wurde. Die Form sollte dabei (nach außen) weder ästhetischen noch symbolischen Vermittlungsmerkmalen unterliegen. Das *Endless House* wollte sinnlich sein, „dem weiblichen Körper mehr gleichen als der männlichen Architektur mit ihren Ecken und Kanten."[31] Durch die Schale, sowohl gültiger Ausdruck der Zeit und durch Einsatz neuer (Verarbeitungs-)Techniken – Plastik, Glas und vorgespanntem Beton –, beschreibt Kiesler eine zumindest mögliche Neuordnung des Systems Haus als einhüllenden, organisch-fließenden Raum, geformt von immanent-sozialer Dynamik, ohne Abtrennungen, Stützen und Fundierung.

immanent social dynamics without separations, supports and foundation. Delimiting elements such as floor, wall and ceiling create visually continuous transitions that were to respond to demands for utmost flexibility of the interior,[32] or put differently: as a "twisting, continuously curved ribbon wrapped around itself."[33] Over the years, Kiesler collected material on thin-walled shell constructions and was convinced: "A new construction method has not yet been reached. We are in transition from conglomeration to simplification. Next simplified method of building: the die-cast unit—not a die-cast part of roof, floor, wall or column, but a continuous unit overcoming the four-fold division of column, roof, floor, wall. Such construction I call a shell-monolith. Easily erected. Weight minimalized. Mobile. Separation into floor, walls, roof, columns is eliminated."[34]

At times, the *Endless House* was also envisioned as an isolated concrete shell with a rough coat of plaster (very recently, Gerd Zillner discovered an important plan by engineers in an archive (Figs. on pp. 262/263), which points very reliably to the existence of a "Shotcrete" shell) (Fig. 7); the already mentioned pre-stressing of the concrete would have made little sense. Like folded structures, the shells are surface-active structure systems, which, in keeping with the elegant-endless flow in the contemporary expression,

Begrenzende Elemente wie Boden, Wand und Decke schaffen optisch kontinuierliche Übergänge, die den Forderungen nach höchster Flexibilität des Innenraums Rechnung tragen sollen,[32] oder anders gesagt: als ein „drehendes, ununterbrochen geschwungenes Band, das um sich selbst gewickelt ist."[33] Dafür sammelte Kiesler über Jahre hinweg Unterlagen zu dünnwandigen Schalenkonstruktionen und war sich sicher: „Eine neue Konstruktionsmethode ist noch nicht erreicht worden. Wir befinden uns in einer Übergangsphase von der Ansammlung zur Vereinfachung. Die nächste vereinfachte Baumethode: die Druckgusseinheit – nicht einzelne Teile aus Druckguss für Dach, Boden, Wand oder Pfeiler, sondern eine durchgehende Einheit, die die vierfache Aufteilung von Pfeiler, Dach, Boden, Wand überwindet. Diese Konstruktion nenne ich Schalen-Monolith. Schnell errichtet. Sehr leichtgewichtig. Mobil. Die Trennung in Boden, Wand, Dach, Pfeiler wird verdrängt."[34]

Gedacht war das *Endless House* dann zeitweise als isolierte und wiederum rau verputze Betonschale (zuletzt fand Gerd Zillner im Archiv einen bedeutsamen Plan der Ingenieure (siehe Abb. S. 262/263), der sehr zuversichtlich auf eine gerippte „Shotcrete"-Schale verweist, Fig. 7); die bereits erwähnte Vorspannung des Betons hätte dabei nur wenig Sinn gehabt.

6—Frederick Kiesler, *Endless House*, model, New York 1959

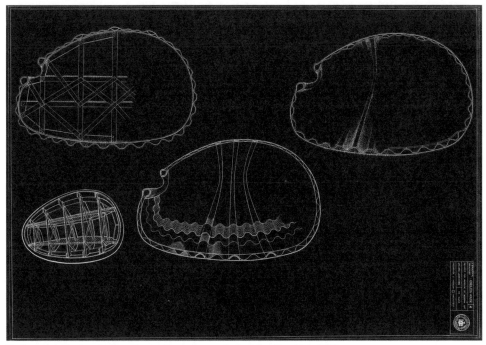

7—Frederick Kiesler, *Endless House*, three structural principles, New York 1956

8—Robert Maillart, Gunit-Cementhall, Zurich 1939

seemed to be consistent. "Since we have created reinforced concrete, we are now able to create buildings in endless spatial formations—lateral, vertical, in all directions and in all sizes that we aspire to. The column is dead,"[35] as wrote Kiesler. With the *Endless House*, perhaps he meant an architectural, or even constructive, vision in a biomorphic-ecological-economical-social sense. Especially since Kiesler, in all modesty, also spoke about having invented a new principle of construction (!) which he referred to as "continuous tension" and whose advantages, in comparison to the traditional masonry construction were, he said, lower costs, lower density, better fire-resistance and easier maintenance.[36] Kiesler's accompanying writings and comments are a specialty which he had developed in the Berlin years, especially since he "always saw his creative acts as being so fundamentally new and promising that he wanted to explain and justify them to the world,"[37] as Barbara Lesák has noted in a different context.

Yet what is strange is that Kiesler's idea of a multi-layer structure clearly runs counter to the notion of sculptural homogeneity. Kiesler had, however, familiarized himself with the means and possibilities of contemporary concrete constructions and so we can assume that he was familiar with the light (monolithic!) structural shell constructions designed, for instance, by Robert

Wie Faltwerke sind Schalen flächenaktive Tragsysteme, was im Sinne elegant-endlosen Fließens und im zeitgemäßen Ausdruck nur konsequent scheint. „Da wir den Stahlbeton geschaffen haben, sind wir nun in der Lage, Gebäude in grenzenlosen Raumformationen zu schaffen – lateral, vertikal, in jede Richtung und in jedem Ausmaß, das wir anstreben. Die Säule ist tot!",[35] schrieb Kiesler und meint mit dem *Endless House* vielleicht doch eine bau-technische, um nicht zu sagen konstruktive Vision vor der biomorph-ökologisch-ökonomisch-sozialen? Zumal Kiesler in aller Bescheidenheit auch davon sprach, ein neues Bauprinzip (!) erfunden zu haben, das er „kon-tinuierliche Spannung" nannte, und dessen Vorzüge er dem traditionellen Mauerwerksbau gegenüber in Kostenersparnis, Dichtheit, Feuerfestigkeit und leichter Instandhaltung darstellte.[36] Die Begleitschriften und Kommentare Kieslers sind eine Spezialität, die er sich in den Berliner Jahren angewöhnt hatte, zumal er seine „Schaffensakte immer als so fundamental neu und zukunftsweisend ansah, dass er sie der Welt begründen und erklären wollte"[37], wie Barbara Lesák in anderem Zusammenhang bemerkte.

Sonderbar aber ist Kieslers Idee des mehrlagigen Aufbaus, der dem Gedanken skulpturaler Homogenität beziehungsweise der monolithischen Schale doch merklich zuwiderläuft. Zudem dürfen wir davon ausgehen, dass

Maillart (cement hall in Zurich, 1939, Fig. 8), or Eduardo Torroja in Spain *(Hipódromo de la Zarzuela*, 1941), as well as Felix Candela's buildings in Mexico (Fig. 9). In 1950, the latter had founded the Cubiertas Ala, which specialized in the production of thin concrete shell constructions. These and similar buildings also deeply inspired Kiesler's and Bartos' *Shrine of the Book* and seems to have confirmed them (e.g. Basílica de Nuestra Señora de Guadalupe of 1959). And, of course, Pier Luigi Nervi had proved, to great international acclaim, concrete's great compositional/design potential when used appropriately. Even Lebbeus Woods pointed to these "traces of engineers"[38], although his assessment omits a general development in architecture from the mid-1950s onward: In these years, Le Corbusier also became organic (Chandigarh, Ronchamp, Philips), and Niemeyer designed his wonderful spatial curves, meandering free-form surfaces for Luciano Baldessari in Milan (1952). Saarinen built the "Trans World Airline Terminal" (1956–62) right in front of Kiesler's doorstep, as it were, and one shouldn't forget André Bloc's synthetic "sculptures habitacles" of the early 1960s or the much- underestimated Giovanni Michelucci with his bizarre "Chiesa dell'Autostrada del Sole" (from 1960 onward). (In the lovely book by Ulrich Conrads and Hans G. Sperlich *Phantastische Architektur* [Phantastic

Kiesler die leichten Schalentragwerke etwa von Robert Maillart (Zementhalle in Zürich, 1939, Abb. 8), von Eduardo Torroja in Spanien (z. B.: Hipódromo de la Zarzuela, 1941) ebenso kannte wie die Bauten Felix Candelas in Mexiko (Abb. 9). Letzterer hatte 1950 die auf die Herstellung dünner Betonschalen spezialisierte *Cubiertas Ala* gegründet, deren Bauten auch Kieslers und Bartos' *Shrine of the Book* nachhaltig inspiriert und bestätigt haben dürften (z. B.: Basílica de Nuestra Señora de Guadalupe von 1959). Und natürlich hatte Pier Luigi Nervi unter internationalem Aufsehen gezeigt, welche gestalterischen Möglichkeiten Beton bei entsprechender Handhabung eröffnet. Auch Lebbeus Woods hat auf diese „Ingenieur-Spuren" hingewiesen[38], wenngleich er in seiner Einschätzung eine generelle Architektur-Entwicklung ab Mitte der 1950er-Jahre ausspart: Denn auch Le Corbusier wurde in diesen Jahren organisch (Chandigarh, Ronchamp, Philips), Niemeyer entwarf seine wunderbaren Raumkurven, mäandernde Freiformflächen bei Luciano Baldessari in Mailand (1952), John Johansen experimentierte, beauftragt von der American Concrete Association am *Spray House* (ab 1954), Saarinen baute quasi vor Kieslers Haustüre den *Trans World Airline Terminal* (1956–62) ohne André Blocs synthetische *sculptures habitacles* der frühen 1960er-Jahre zu vergessen oder den vielfach unterschätzten Giovanni Michelucci mit seiner

9—Felix Candela, Los Manantiales, Mexico City 1958

10—Eero Saarinen, TWA-Terminal, New York (under construction, ca. 1960)

irrwitzigen *Chiesa dell'Autostrada del Sole* (ab 1960). (In dem schönen
Buch von Ulrich Conrads und Hans G. Sperlich *Phantastische Architektur*,
Hatje, 1960 findet man die organische Fülle, den optimistischen Überschwang
dieser Zeitspanne sehr gut dokumentiert. Interessant am Rande: In der
deutschen Erstausgabe kommt Kieslers *Endless House* noch nicht vor; dafür
umso prominenter im französischen Nachdruck aus dem gleichen Jahr
[Delpire éditeur]!)

  Es ist also ganz offensichtlich, dass dem Baustoff Beton – gedanklich
ab 1915, faktisch ab 1935 – nicht nur eine gänzlich neue Rolle zugedacht,
sondern mit ihm im Sinne organischer Formgebung in leichten, dünnen
Schalen auch umgesetzt wurde. Vor allem durch die großen Ingenieure war es
möglich geworden, sich endgültig vom Kanon des Stütze-Last-Prinzips
zu lösen und damit nichts weniger zu schaffen als Bauten im strengen Sinne
eines architektonischen Ereignisses. Diese gebauten Ereignisse folgen
in Bezug auf die Wirksamkeit als flächenaktive Tragsysteme einer gewissen
Logik der Form. Geometrische Grundlagen können natürlich angepasst
und überlagert werden, was im konkreten Fall des *Endless House* wohl zumindest zu unterschiedlichen Schalenstärken in Abhängigkeit von Lage
und Belastung und Einschränkungen im gedanklichen *Einschneiden* von

Architecture] Hatje, 1960, one finds the organic plenitude, the great
optimism of this period well-documented. An interesting note: in the first
German edition, Kiesler's *Endless House* is not featured, but it then
appears all the more prominently in the French reprint from the same year
[Delpire éditeur]!)

It is therefore quite clear that the building material concrete was not only
given a completely new role (in theory from 1910 onward, in reality from 1935
onward). It was also implemented in keeping with organic forms in light thin
shells. This had become possible mainly because of the great engineers who
had once and for all broken with the support-load principle and thus created
nothing less than constructions in the strict sense of an architectural event. In
terms of efficiency as surface-active structural frames, these built events were
based on a certain logic of form. Geometric foundations can, of course, be
adapted and superimposed, which in the concrete case of the *Endless House*
would have resulted in shells of various thicknesses, depending on the
position and the load and limitations in the intellectual "cutting" of openings.
But this would not have accounted for failure—neither then nor today!
Here I would much rather claim that, with the proper use of shotcrete—as for
example in 1926 in Dischinger's Zeiss-Planetarium in Jena—1959 the

Öffnungen geführt hätte. Damals wie heute aber wäre das kein
Versagensgrund! Viel lieber würde ich hier behaupten wollen, dass das
Endless House bei entsprechender Vorbe-reitung in Spritzbeton – wie schon
1926 bei Dischingers Zeiss-Planetarium in Jena – 1959 gut und gern
realisierbar gewesen wäre. Man hätte mit dieser Technik sogar eine gewisse
Dichtheit und die lebendige Oberfläche der Modelle herstellen können. Wir
wissen sogar von Saarinen, dass auch die Zimmerleute für den aufwendigen
Schalungsbau vorhanden waren (Abb.10); dort einem Kritiker zufolge sogar
„von Enthusiasmus ergriffen durch die Vorstellung möglicherweise zum ersten
Mal ihre eigene individuelle Arbeit an einem fertiggestellten Gebäude zu sehen,
wenn es enthüllt wird – etwas, das bei einem Schalungsbau gewissermaßen
nie passiert."[39]

Die Radikalität des *Endless House* bezieht sich über die konstruktive Vision
hinaus aus der möglichen Transformation einer kommenden Wirklichkeit.
Insofern ist die Idee der Materialisierung in Stahlbeton aber nicht wirklich
ereignisorientiert, bedenken wir Slavoj Žižeks grundlegende Definition eines
Ereignisses: „dass es nicht innerhalb der Welt geschieht, sondern eine
Veränderung des Rahmens ist, durch den wir die Welt wahrnehmen und uns
in ihr bewegen."[40] Freigeformter Beton aber war weitläufig vorhanden und

Endless House could certainly have been built. This technique would even have made it possible to recreate a certain compactness and the living surface of the models. From Saarinen, we even know that there were carpenters available who could have made the elaborately constructed formwork (Fig. 10); there they were, according to a critic, 'stirred to enthusiasm by the prospect of being able to see, for the first time perhaps, their own individual work in the completed building as it was uncovered— something that virtually never happens with formwork"[39].

What made the *Endless House* so radical was the possible transformation of a coming reality. In this sense, the idea of materialization of reinforced concrete is not really geared to the event if we take into account Slavoj Žižek's basic definition: "that it does not take place within the world but, instead, is a change of the framework through which we perceive the world and move in it."[40] In this light, Kiesler's reference to "plastic/synthetics" at the beginning of the American "Plastic Age" was more consistent, yes, even more appropriate to the visionary ideal of form and content (Fig. 11). *[Didn't El Lissitzky, in connection with his "Wolkenbügel" of 1925, describe materials that had not yet been invented but are now part of worldwide building standards?]* With regard to these considerations, the video "The Monsanto

stellt somit, weder in gedanklicher noch in materieller Hinsicht, eine „Ver-änderung des Rahmens" dar. Insofern wäre Kieslers Hinweis auf „Kunststoff" zu Beginn des amerikanischen *Plastic Age* konsequenter, um nicht zu sagen dem visionären Anspruch von Form und Inhalt angemessener gewesen (Abb. 11). (Hatte nicht auch El Lissitzky im Zusammenhang mit seinem *Wolkenbügel* von 1925 Materialien beschrieben, die noch nicht erfunden waren, heute jedoch zum weltweiten Baustandard gehören?) Im Bezug auf diese Überlegungen empfehlen sich anbei und schon aus humoristischem Interesse das Video *The Monsanto House of the Future* (1957) oder die gesammelten Cartoons des wunderbar-wahnwitzigen Tex Avery.

Tatsächlich haben sich gewisse Vorgriffe und technologische Facetten in den heutigen Planungs- und Produktionsumständen nicht nur etabliert, sondern geben vielerorts Anlass zu immer kühneren Materialisierungskon-zepten. Bezogen auf das *Endless House* wäre es heute durchaus vor-stellbar, eine Kleinserie davon in einer der riesigen Fräs- und Werkshallen internationaler Schiffswerften anfertigen zu lassen; entsprechende Über-arbeitung und konstruktive Optimierung vorausgesetzt. Konsequenterweise müssten wir uns das *Endless House* aktuell aber aus dem 3D-Printer vor-stellen, ein Druck wie aus *einem Guss*!

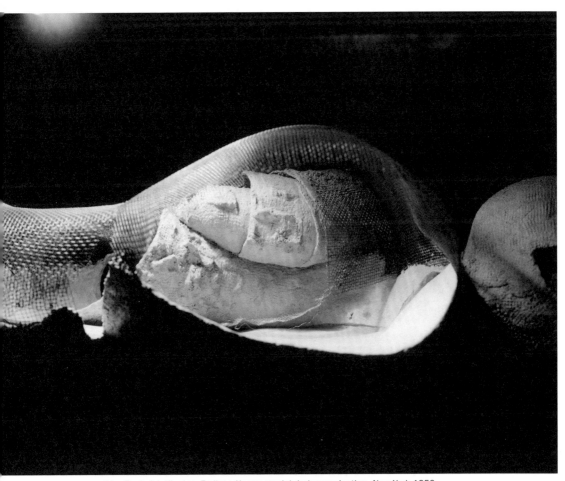

11—Frederick Kiesler, *Endless House*, model during production, New York 1959

12—Justo Garcia Rubio, Bus station in Casar de Cáceres, Spain 1998

House of the future" (1957) is recommended viewing, as are the collected cartoons by the wonderfully crazy Tex Avery.

Indeed, certain steps and technological facets have not just become established in today's planning and production; in many quarters, they have given rise to ever-bolder concepts of materialization. In relation to the *Endless House*, today a small series of them could conceivably be constructed in one of the huge production halls of international shipyards, provided that the construction is appropriately processed and optimized. It would, however, make more sense to imagine today's *Endless House* emerging from a 3D-printer, a print cast from "one mold!"

The somewhat simpler, but nonetheless appealing, variant could be a primary construction (that is vector- instead of surface-active) made of steel, one that has been formally and constructively optimized and that would be supported by reinforced concrete cores if desired. A structure that is invariably irregular could also allow for certain liberties in the (surface) design and possible access that could only do justice to Kiesler's sparse statements regarding "windows and doors" or "circulation." Formally analogous examples of architecture such as the Kunsthaus Graz (Cook/Fournier), the stations of the Innsbruck Hungerburgbahn (Zaha Hadid), the Ordos-Museum (MAD) or the

Die etwas banalere, aber gleichsam reizvolle Variante könnte eine formal und konstruktiv optimierte Primärkonstruktion (also vektor- statt flächen-aktiv) aus Stahl sein, die auf Stahlbetonkernen auflagert, sofern das überhaupt gewünscht ist. Eine zwangsläufig irreguläre Struktur ließe auch gewisse Freiheiten der (Oberflächen-)Gestaltung und möglicher Ab- und Anschlüsse offen, die den spärlichen Aussagen Kieslers zu *Fenstern und Türen* oder *Erschließung* wohl nur entgegenkämen. Formale Architektur-analogien wie das Kunsthaus Graz (Cook/Fournier), die Stationen der Innsbrucker Hungerburg-bahn (Zaha Hadid), das Ordos-Museum (MAD) oder die vielfältigen Virtuositäten des Zürcher Büros *Design to Production* zeigen, wie sehr aktuelle Planungs- und Fertigungstechniken der Realisierung derartiger Projekte Vorschub leisten. Und selbst wenn zuletzt der Eindruck entstand, dass die große Party des Parametrismus und der wilden, freien Oberflächen schon wieder zu Ende ist: Wesentlich bleibt die Entwicklung der Möglichkeiten, denn wie schrieb Arthur Drexler anlässlich der Ausstellung *Visionary Architecture*, 1960 auch in Bezug auf das E*ndless House* so schön: „In der Vergangenheit war es ausgeschlossen, solche Projekte aus einem oder beiden der zwei folgenden Gründe zu verwirklichen: Sie waren in technischer Hinsicht unmöglich auszuführen in jener Zeit, in der sie geplant

diverse ingenious creations of the Zurich firm "Design to Production" show to what extent very modern planning and manufacturing technologies have facilitated the realization of such projects. And even if, ultimately, the impression arose that the great party of parametricism and of wild, free surfaces is already over again, what remains significant is the development of possibilities, for as Arthur Drexler put it so nicely on the occasion of the 1960 *Visionary Architecture*, also with regard to the *Endless House*: "In the past, such projects were unbuildable for one or both of two reasons: they may have been technically impossible to execute at the time they were designed or society could find neither the justification nor the money for their construction. Today, virtually nothing an architect can think of is technically impossible to realize..."[41]

If someone were to have the (certainly appealing) idea of wanting to place the *Endless House* or even its later version *Sisler House* in their garden, with adequate funds it would not fail for reasons of construction or engineering. As such, the building would simply not refer to the image of a more promising new future order; also, it would no longer be an anti-functionalist statement and thus—outside of its time—completely contrary to what Kiesler intended. Let's leave the old images as they are! But let's still take them, in spite of

wurden, oder die Gesellschaft konnte weder eine Rechtfertigung bieten, noch das Geld für die Konstruktion aufbringen. Heute ist praktisch nichts, das sich ein Architekt vorstellen kann, technisch unrealisierbar."[41]

Nur für den Fall also, jemand käme auf die durchaus reizvolle Idee, sich das *Endless House* oder auch seine spätere Fassung, das *Sisler House*, in den Garten stellen zu wollen: An Konstruktion oder Bautechnik wird es heute bei entsprechender Budgetierung nicht scheitern. Nur wird das Objekt als solches wohl nicht mehr auf das Bild einer hoffnungsvollen Neuordnung der Zukunft verweisen, es wäre auch kein anti-funktionalistisches Statement mehr und damit – so außerhalb seiner Zeit – wohl ganz entgegen Kieslers Absichten. Eine kritische Distanz empfiehlt: Lassen wir die alten Bilder gut sein! Aber nehmen wir sie, trotz allem, doch zum Anlass, eigene überhaupt zu wollen und dann auch zu schaffen (Abb. 12)! Denn wie fasste Mies so knapp wie scharf zusammen: „Baukunst ist raumgefasster *Zeitwille*. Lebendig. Wechselnd. Neu."[42]

everything, as an occasion to want our own and to thus also create them (Fig. 12)! Just as Mies summed up so succinctly and incisively: "Architecture is the will of a certain time articulated in space. Alive. Alternating. New."[42]

1 Sigfried Giedion, *The Eternal Present: The Beginnings of Art. A Contribution on Constancy and Change* (New York: Bollingen Foundation, 1962), 514.
2 Barbara Lesák, "Die Theaterbiographie des Frederick J. Kiesler", in *Frederick Kiesler. Theatervisionär – Architekt – Künstler*, ed. Barbara Lesák and Thomas Trabitsch (Vienna: Christian Brandstätter Verlag, 2013), 25. (Translated from German)
3 Cf. Harald Krejci, "Die Beziehungen Friedrich Kieslers zu Berlin", in *Wien-Berlin. Kunst zweiter Metropolen* (Munich/London/New York: Prestel, 2013), 256. (Translated from German)
4 ed. Manfred Schlösser, *Arbeitsrat für Kunst: Berlin 1918–1921* (Berlin: Akademie der Künste,

1980), 87. (Translated from German)
5 Cf. Lesák, "Die Theaterbiographie des Frederick J. Kiesler", 25.
6 Cf. Jürgen Osterhammel, *Die Verwandlung der Welt. Eine Geschichte des 19. Jahrhunderts* (Munich: C.H. Beck, 2009), 1286. (Translated from German)
7 Adolf Behne, *Der moderne Zweckbau* (Munich: Drei Masken Verlag, 1926). (Translated from German)
8 Bruno Taut, "Das Problem des Opernbaus", *Sozialistische Monatshefte* 20 (1914), 355–357. (Translated from German)
9 See Matthias Schirren, *Hugo Häring. Architekt des Neuen Bauens* (Ostfildern: Hatje Cantz, 2001), 234. (Translated from German)

10 See The Museum of Modern Art, Press Release for *Visionary Architecture*, accessed July 15, 2015, http://www.moma.org/momaorg/shared/pdfs/docs/press_archives/2734/releases/MOMA_1960_0132_108.pdf?2010.
11 Julius Posener, "Erich Mendelsohn (1969)", in *Aufsätze und Vorträge 1931–1980* (Braunschweig/Wiesbaden: Viehweg & John, 1981), 175f. (Translated from German)
12 Antonio Sant'Elia, "Die futuristische Architektur – Manifest, 1914", in *Der Lärm der Strasse. Italienischer Futurismus 1909–1918*, ed. Norbert Noris (Milan: Mazotta, 2001), 380ff. (Translated from German)

1 Sigfried Giedion, „Ewige Gegenwart" (Köln: DuMont, 1964), 388.
2 Barbara Lesák, „Die Theaterbiographie des Frederick J. Kiesler", in *Frederick Kiesler. Theatervisionär – Architekt – Künstler*, hg. v. Barbara Lesák und Thomas Trabitsch (Wien: Christian Brandstätter Verlag, 2013), 25.
3 Vgl. Harald Krejci, „Die Beziehungen Friedrich Kieslers zu Berlin", in *Wien-Berlin. Kunst zweiter Metropolen* (München/London/New York: Prestel, 2013), 256.
4 *Arbeitsrat für Kunst: Berlin 1918–1921*, hg. v. Manfred Schlösser (Berlin: Akademie der Künste, 1980), 87.
5 Vgl. Lesák, „Die Theaterbiographie des Frederick J. Kiesler", 25.
6 Vgl. Jürgen Osterhammel, „Die Verwandlung der Welt. *Eine Geschichte des 19. Jahrhunderts*" (München: C.H. Beck, 2009), 1286.
7 Adolf Behne, „Der moderne Zweckbau" (München: Drei Masken Verlag, 1926).

8 Bruno Taut, „Das Problem des Opernbaus", *Sozialistische Monatshefte* 20 (1914), 355–357.
9 Siehe Matthias Schirren, *Hugo Häring. Architekt des Neuen Bauens* (Ostfildern: Hatje Cantz, 2001), 234.
10 Siehe The Museum of Modern Art, Presseaussendung für *Visionary Architecture*, letzter Zugriff: 15.07.2015, http://www.moma.org/momaorg/shared/pdfs/docs/press_archives/2734/releases/MOMA_1960_0132_108.pdf?2010.
11 Julius Posener, „Erich Mendelsohn (1969)", in *Aufsätze und Vorträge 1931–1980* (Braunschweig/Wiesbaden: Viewweg & John, 1981), 175f.
12 Antonio Sant'Elia, „Die futuristische Architektur – Manifest, 1914", in *Der Lärm der Strasse. Italienischer Futurismus 1909–1918*, hg. v. Norbert Noris (Mailand: Mazotta, 2001), 380ff.
13 Julius Posener, „Vorlesungen zur Geschichte der neuen Architektur", *ARCH+* 48 (1985), 9.

14 Joseph August Lux, „Ingenieurästhetik" (München: Gustav Lammers, 1910), 46f.
15 Wie man Robert Maillart anlässlich einer Ausstellung an der ETH in Zürich (1996) nannte.
16 Vgl. Sokratis Georgiadis, Nachwort zu *Bauen in Frankreich* von Sigfried Giedion (Berlin: Gebrüder Mann, 2000).
17 Robert Maillart, „Gestaltung des Eisenbetons", in *Robert Maillart*, hg. v. Max Bill (Zürich: Verlag für Architektur, 1947), 13f.
18 Julius Posener, „Architektur oder Konstruktion", in *Aufsätze und Vorträge 1931–1980*, (Braunschweig/Wiesbaden, 1981), 213.
19 Hermann Finsterlin an Louise Mendelsohn, in *Finsterlin* (Ostfildern: Hatje Cantz, 1988), Ausstellungskatalog, 52.
20 Walter Benjamin, „Das Kunstwerk im Zeitalter seiner technischen Reproduzierbarkeit" (Frankfurt am Main: Suhrkamp, 1996), 341.

13 Julius Posener, "Vorlesungen zur Geschichte der neuen Architektur", *ARCH+* 48 (1985), 9. (Translated from German)

14 Joseph August Lux, *Ingenieur-ästhetik* (Munich: Gustav Lammers, 1910), 46f. (Translated from German)

15 As Robert Maillart was referred to on the occasion of an exhibition at the Zurich ETH (1996).

16 Cf. Sokratis Georgiadis, afterword to *Bauen in Frankreich* by Sigfried Giedion (Berlin: Gebrüder Mann, 2000). (Translated from German)

17 Robert Maillart, "Gestaltung des Eisenbetons", in *Robert Maillart*, ed. Max Bill (Zurich: Verlag für Architektur, 1947), 13f. (Translated from German)

18 Julius Posener, "Architektur oder Konstruktion", in *Aufsätze und Vorträge 1931–1980*, (Braunschweig/Wiesbaden, 1981), 213. (Translated from German)

19 Hermann Finsterlin to Louise Mendelsohn, in *Finsterlin*

(Ostfildern: Hatje Cantz, 1988), exhibition catalog, 52. (Translated from German)

20 Walter Benjamin, *Das Kunst-werk im Zeitalter seiner technischen Reproduzierbarkeit* (Frankfurt am Main: Suhrkamp, 1996), 341. (Translated from German)

21 Posener, "Erich Mendelsohn (1969)", 178.

22 See Helen Borsick, "Fame Is Endless", *The Plain Dealer*, Feb. 5, 1967.

23 *Friedrich Kiesler. Architekt, Maler, Bildhauer, Schriftsteller, Bühnen-bildner, Designer*, ed. Peter Weirmair (Innsbruck: Allerheiligen Presse, 1975), 85.

24 Rudolf Springer in a conversation with Florian Medicus, Berlin, June 2008.

25 See The Museum of Modern Art, Press Release for *Visionary Architecture*.

26 Dieter Bogner, "Inside the Endless House", in *Frederick J. Kiesler. Endless Space*

(Ostfildern: Hatje Cantz, 2001), exhibition catalog, 11–26.

27 Cf. Frederick Kiesler, "Manifeste du Corréalisme", in *L'Architecture d'Aujourd'hui* 2 (1949), 79–105. (Translated from French.)

28 Frederick Kiesler, *Contemporary Art Applied in the Store and its Display* (New York: Brentano's, 1930), 48.

29 Femke Bijlsma, "Footloose", in *MARK* 26 (2010), 108.

30 After Bruno Zevi in *Erich Mendelsohn* (Berlin: Akademie der Künste, 1968), exhibition catalog.

31 Frederick Kiesler, "The 'Endless House': A Man-Built Cosmos", in *Inside the Endless House*, ed. Dieter Bogner (Vienna: Böhlau, 1998), 136. The text is also published in the present book on the pages 230–235.

32 See also: Bogner, "Inside the Endless House", 11–26.

33 See The Museum of Modern Art, Press Release for *Visionary Architecture*.

21 Posener, „Erich Mendelsohn (1969)", 178.

22 Siehe Helen Borsick, „Fame Is Endless", *The Plain Dealer*, Feb. 5, 1967. (Übersetzt aus dem Englischen)

23 „Friedrich Kiesler. Architekt, Maler, Bildhauer, Schriftsteller, Bühnenbildner, Designer", hg. v. Peter Weirmair (Innsbruck: Allerheiligen Presse, 1975), 85.

24 Rudolf Springer im Gespräch mit Florian Medicus, Berlin, Juni 2008.

25 Siehe The Museum of Modern Art, Presseaussendung für *Visionary Architecture*.

26 Dieter Bogner, „Inside the Endless House", in *Frederick J. Kiesler. Endless Space* (Ostfildern: Hatje Cantz, 2001), Ausstellungskatalog, 11–26.

27 Vgl. Frederick Kiesler, „Manifeste du Corréalisme", in *L'Architecture d'Aujourd'hui* 2 (1949), 79–105. (Übersetzt aus dem Französischen)

28 Friedrich Kiesler, „Vitalbau – Raumstadt – Funktionelle Architektur", in *De Stijl* 10&12 (1925), 144.

29 Femke Bijlsma, „Footloose", in *MARK* 26 (2010), 108.

30 Nach Bruno Zevi in *Erich Mendelsohn* (Berlin: Akademie der Künste, 1968), Ausstellungs-katalog.

31 Frederick Kiesler, „The 'Endless House': A Man-Built Cosmos", in *Inside the Endless House*, hg. v. Dieter Bogner (Wien: Böhlau, 1998), 136. Der englische Originaltext ist im vorliegenden Band abgedruckt auf den Seiten 230–235.

32 Siehe dazu auch: Bogner, „Inside the Endless House", 11–26.

33 Siehe The Museum of Modern Art, Presseaussendung für *Visionary Architecture*.

34 Frederick Kiesler, „Notes on Architecture: The Space House", in *Hound & Horn* 2 (1934), 296.

35 Frederick Kiesler, „Notes on Architecture as Sculpture", in

Inside the Endless House, hg. v. Dieter Bogner (Wien: Böhlau, 1998), 140.

36 Frederick Kiesler, „Short Statements about the Endless House, Pertaining to the Questions Usually Asked", in *Friedrich Kiesler: Endless House 1947–1961* (Ostfildern: Hatje Cantz, 2003), Ausstellungskatalog, 93.

37 Siehe Lesák, „Die Theaterbio-graphie des Frederick J. Kiesler", ab Seite 19.

38 Vgl. Lebbeus Woods, „Frederick J. Kiesler: Out of Time", in *Frederick J. Kiesler. Endless Space* (Ostfildern: Hatje Cantz, 2001), Ausstellungskatalog, 63–66. (Übersetzt aus dem Englischen)

39 „Shaping a two-acre sculpture; TWA Terminal Building, Idlewild Airport; Architect: Eero Saarinen" (*Architectural Forum*, August 1960), in *Eero Saarinen*, hg. v. Jayne Merkel (London: Phaidon, 2005), 210.

34 Frederick Kiesler, "Notes on Architecture: The Space House", in *Hound & Horn* 2 (1934), 296.

35 Frederick Kiesler, "Notes on Architecture as Sculpture", in *Inside the Endless House*, ed. Dieter Bogner (Vienna: Böhlau, 1998), 140.

36 Frederick Kiesler, "Short Statements about the Endless House, Pertaining to the Questions Usually Asked", in *Friedrich Kiesler: Endless House 1947– 1961* (Ostfildern: Hatje Cantz, 2003), exhibition catalog, 93.

37 See Lesák, "Die Theaterbiographie des Frederick J. Kiesler", from page 19. (Translated from German)

38 Cf. Lebbeus Woods, "Frederick J. Kiesler: Out of Time", in *Frederick J. Kiesler. Endless Space* (Ostfildern: Hatje Cantz, 2001), exhibition catalog, 63–66.

39 "Shaping a two-acre sculpture; TWA Terminal Building, Idlewild Airport; Architect: Eero Saarinen" (*Architectural Forum*, Aug. 1960),

in *Eero Saarinen*, ed. Jayne Merkel (London: Phaidon, 2005), 210.

40 Slavoj Žižek, *Was ist ein Ereignis?* (Frankfurt am Main: S. Fischer Verlag, 2014), 16.

41 See The Museum of Modern Art, Press Release for *Visionary Architecture*.

42 Ludwig Mies van der Rohe, "Arbeitsthesen", in *Programme und Manifeste zur Architektur des 20. Jahrhunderts*, ed. Ulrich Conrad (Basel: Birkhäuser, 1981), 70. (Translated from German)

40 Slavoj Žižek, „Was ist ein Ereignis?" (Frankfurt am Main: S. Fischer Verlag, 2014), 16.

41 Siehe The Museum of Modern Art, Presseaussendung für *Visionary Architecture*.

42 Ludwig Mies van der Rohe, „Arbeitsthesen", in *Programme und Manifeste zur Architektur des 20. Jahrhunderts*, hg. v. Ulrich Conrad (Basel: Birkhäuser, 1981), 70.

Correalist Vision

Sanford Kwinter

Correalistische Vision

In the late 1970s, the famed perceptual psychologist J. J. Gibson repudiated
decades of discipline-shaping research on visual perception that he
himself had largely pioneered, by declaring that "Space is a myth, a ghost, a
fiction for geometers."[1] He thereby renounced the very footing upon which
thinking about perception (vision in particular) had been based, as well as the
fundamental idea of an independent "space" in which acts of perception
and the objects they perceive allegedly live.

In lieu of space, Gibson offered the multiplex concept of "environment"
and in place of a theory of vision based on the capture and assembly of a fixed
retinal image, he proposed a plastic, flowing "ambient optical array"[2] that
continuously samples the perceiver's surroundings for points of active entry
(the famous, and famously abused, theory of affordances).

"Natural vision," he claimed, is inseparable from movement and the
concrete flow of the world: it "depends on the eyes, in [a] head, on a body, supported by the ground."[3] The animal's psychic and perceptual universe
(these together form a single thing) is in fact a dynamic and nested complex of
actions and relational contexts that modify one another continuously and
on the fly. The universe that offers itself to perception is endless because it is
"endlessly actively related." Indeed, it is endlessly engendered by the

In den späten 1970er-Jahren distanzierte sich der berühmte Wahrnehmungs-
psychologe J. J. Gibson von jahrzehntelanger Forschungsarbeit auf dem
Gebiet der visuellen Wahrnehmung, für die er selbst Bahnbrechendes geleistet
hat, mit der Erklärung: „Raum als solcher ist ein Mythos, ein Gespenst,
eine Fiktion, gut für Geometer."[1] Auf diese Weise brach er mit dem eigentlichen
Fundament des Denkens über die Wahrnehmung (insbesondere über
das Sehen) wie auch mit der grundlegenden Idee, dass es einen unabhängigen
„Raum" gibt, in dem Wahrnehmungsakte und die von ihr erfassten Gegenstände vermeintlich angesiedelt sind.

Raum ersetzte Gibson durch eine multiplexe Vorstellung von *Umwelt* und
die Theorie des Sehens, die auf der Erfassung und der Erstellung eines
fixen Netzhautbildes gründete, wich einer plastischen, *fließenden* umgebenden
optischen Anordnung,[2] die ständig die Umgebung des Wahrnehmenden
abtastet, um Punkte des aktiven Eingangs zu finden (hier also die berühmte
und auf so berühmte Weise missbrauchte Theorie des Angebotscharakters).

„Das natürliche Sehen", wie Gibson behauptet, kann nicht von der
Bewegung und dem konkreten Fluss der Welt getrennt werden: Es hängt „von
den Augen in einem Kopf [ab], der auf einem Körper sitzt und von einem Untergrund getragen wird".[3] Das psychische Universum, die Wahrnehmungswelt

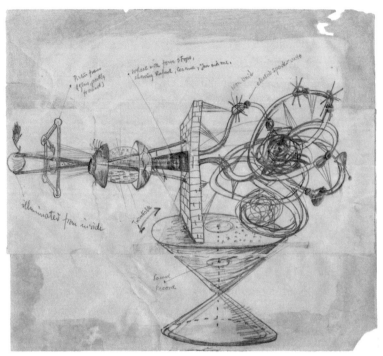

Frederick Kiesler, Study for *Vision Machine*, New York 1938–41

des Tieres (beides zusammen bildet ein einziges Objekt) ist in Wirklichkeit ein dynamischer, verschachtelter Komplex von Handlungen und Beziehungs-kontexten, die sich gegenseitig ständig und auch zeitgleich verändern. Das Universum, das sich der Wahrnehmung anbietet, ist endlos, da es *endlos aktiv in Beziehung* steht. Tatsächlich erzeugt es sich endlos durch die ständige Verschiebung dieser Beziehungen, während sich das wahrnehmende Indi-viduum im Raum bewegt.

Gibson gelang es, den empirischen Nachweis für diese Ideen zu liefern – im Laborkontext und mit Hilfe von Instrumenten, Vorführungen, Diagrammen, usw. – und dabei hat er sozusagen eine der Urszenen der Forschung endlos neu untersucht und neu formuliert, die von seiner lebenslangen Beschäftigung mit der Wahrnehmung überhaupt angetrieben wurde: die moderne Fluglandebahn und eine Reihe damit zusammenhängender Fragen wie Höhensteuerung, Orientierung, Fortbewegung und der optische Fluss bei Flugzeuglandungen während des Zweiten Weltkrieges und danach.[4] Als er als Junge vom hinteren Teil eines Zuges oder aus dem Rückfenster eines Autos blickte, staunte er oft, wie sich das Bild der Welt im Zentrum nach und nach zusammenzog, während es an den Rändern immer breiter wurde. Gibsons zentrale Einsicht

perpetual shifting of these relations while the perceiver moves in space.

Gibson was able to demonstrate these ideas empirically—in laboratory settings, with instruments, demonstrations, diagrams, etc.—and, in so doing, he might be said to have endlessly revisited and reformulated one of the primal scenes of inquiry that compelled his lifelong study of perception in the first place: the modern airplane runway and the panoply of problems associated with control of altitude, orientation, locomotion and optical flow in airplane landings during and after the World War 2.[4] As a boy, he often marveled at the way the image of the world steadily contracted at its center yet expanded at its periphery as he peered rearward from the back deck of a train or through an automobile's back window. Gibson's central insight was to have grasped that the world does not have edges so long as the eye is not artificially confined in an apparatus, indeed that vision is neither "optical" nor mathematical but, rather, "ecological" in the sense that it is always connected to the multiple contingencies and shifting contexts embedded within its environment. The eye is a matrix, not a receiver, and a moving one at that.[5]

The work of Frederick Kiesler may be said in certain ways to have provided a precocious precognition of Gibson's game-changing conceptions of the relations of perception, sense organs, and the sensed objects and events that

war, dass die Welt keine Ränder hat, solange das Auge nicht künstlich in einem Gerät eingeschlossen ist. Demnach erweist sich das Sehen als weder *optisch* noch mathematisch, sondern vielmehr als „ökologisch" in dem Sinne, dass es stets mit vielfachen Begebenheiten und sich verändernden Kontexten in Verbindung steht, die innerhalb seiner Umgebung eingebettet sind. Das Auge ist eine Matrix, kein Empfänger, und noch dazu eine, die sich bewegt.[5]

Man könnte also sagen, dass man im Werk Friedrich Kieslers eine frühe Vorwegnahme von Gibsons wegweisenden Vorstellungen findet: Es geht um das Zusammenspiel von Wahrnehmung, Sinnesorganen und erfassten Objekten und Ereignissen, die zusammen und übereinstimmend die von uns bewohnte(n) Umgebung(en) schaffen. Kieslers Vorstellung von der *Endlosigkeit* war im Grunde Ausdruck der Kontinuität eines jeden Punktes und Objekts in der Welt in Bezug auf alles, was sowohl in der Nähe als auch in der Entfernung wirksam ist. Kiesler und Gibson brachen systematisch mit jeder Vorstellung eines Rahmens als etwas die Erfahrung Ab- und Eingrenzendes. Erfahrung für beide besteht – *setzt sich* „zusammen" – aus Ausdehnungen und Relationen von Gegenständen in provisorischen, sich ständig modifizierenden Anordnungen. Letztere sind weder eingeschlossen, noch lassen sie sich einschließen in einen fixen Rahmen; vielmehr sind

together, and in concert, comprise the environment(s) in which we live. Kiesler's concept of "endlessness" was in essence an expression of the continuity of every point and object in the world with what operates beyond it, in fields both proximate and remote. Both Kiesler and Gibson systematically dispensed with any and all concept of frame as a delineating feature of experience. Experience is made up of, is "composed by" extensions and relations of things in provisional, continuously modifying arrangements with one another. They are neither encased, nor enclosable in any enduring framework. Rather, they are "fugitive" (centrifugal), perpetually linking with an outside that redefines their field of play. The eye became an organ of speculation and connection, an experiment in action.

Both Kiesler and Gibson spent their lives in sustained engagement with, and reflection on, "vision devices" and "vision machines"[6] that lay the foundations for a new way of connecting body and space. Kiesler's concept of *Correalism*, central to his philosophical project, served first and foremost to affirm—or ontologically establish, even—the continuity, conductivity, and connectedness of subject and object, meaning and object, building and nature, social actor and historical milieu, object and space, but also floor, wall and ceiling, inside and out. The doctrine of Correalism projects a seamless

sie „flüchtig" (zentrifugal) und verbinden sich stets über die Wahrnehmung mit einem Außenraum, der ihren Wirkungsbereich neu definiert. Das Auge wurde hier zu einem Organ der Spekulation und der Verbindung, zu einem aktiv stattfindenden Experiment.

Sowohl Kiesler als auch Gibson haben sich zeitlebens eingehend mit „Sehvorrichtungen" und „Sehmaschinen"[6] auseinandergesetzt, welche die Grundlage für eine neue Form der Verbindung von Körper und Raum bilden. Das für das philosophische Projekt Kieslers so zentrale Konzept des *Correalismus* diente in erster Linie dazu, die Kontinuität, die Konduktivität und die Zusammengehörigkeit von Subjekt und Objekt, Bedeutung und Gegenstand, Bau und Natur, Sozialakteur und historischem Milieu, Objekt und Raum, aber auch Boden, Wand und Decke, Innen und Außen zu behaupten, ja sogar ontologisch zu begründen. Die Lehre des Correalismus postuliert das Bild eines unmittelbaren Verwirbelns der Umwelten, das jede Trennung zwischen weltlichen Objekten, ihrem strukturellen Einsatz oder Motiven, Gewohnheiten und Wünschen, die sie ins Leben gerufen haben, aufhebt.

Kiesler gelangte sicherlich zu dieser Formulierung über eine illokutive Vorstellung künstlerischer Praxis,[7] die auf seiner lebenslangen Beschäftigung mit der Welt der bedeutungsstiftenden Verfahren – Theater, Aktionen,

ecological vortex that permits no essential division between worldly
objects, their structural deployments, or the motives, habits and desires that
brought them to be.

Kiesler undoubtedly came to this formulation through an illocutionary conception of art practice,[7] rooted in his lifelong commitment to the world of
meaning procedures—theater, actions, events, and the ambient assemblies
or "stage sets" with and against which they are made to unfold. All of this
constitutes a kind of "beyond architecture," meaning that Kiesler should really
be seen as a "new environmentalist."

Both Kiesler's and Gibson's projects represent efforts of a long unheralded
kind that emerged in the 20th century as forerunners of a new type of
thought and practice determined to release itself from the tyranny of what
Alfred North Whitehead called the doctrine of *simple location*.[8] It was
Whitehead's essential argument that things may well be conceivable within our
modern cultural tradition as separated in time and space, but that these
actually exist more as "prehensions" (events) whose ceaseless connective
action is the more essential and authentic stuff of our world. Our task, as
Kiesler sought to show, is to bring these realities into ever greater consonance
with our perceptions.

Ereignisse und Rauminstallationen oder „Bühnenbilder" – basierte, mit deren
Hilfe bzw. vor deren Hintergrund sie sich entfalten sollten. All dies bildet
eine Art von *grenzüberschreitender Architektur*, sodass Kiesler seither wirklich
als neuer *Environmentalist* zu verstehen ist.

Sowohl Kieslers als auch Gibsons Projekte zeugen von lange
unentdeckt gebliebenen Bemühungen, die im 20. Jahrhundert als Vorläufer
einer neuen Form des Denkens und der Praxis entstanden und von einer
Entschlossenheit getragen waren, sich von der Tyrannei dessen zu befreien,
was von Alfred North Whitehead als Doktrin der einfachen Lokalisierung[8]
bezeichnet wurde. Es war Whiteheads Grundgedanke, dass Gegenstände in
der modernen Tradition unserer Kultur durchaus als in Raum und Zeit getrennt
gedacht werden können, aber dass diese in Wirklichkeit gemeinsam in Raum
und Zeit existieren. Tatsächlich sind sie endlos in improvisiertem „Erfassen"
gesammelt, als Ereignisse, deren unablässig verbindende Wirkung den wahren
Grundstoff unserer Welt ausmacht. Unsere Aufgabe ist es, diese Realitäten
mit unseren Wahrnehmungen in Einklang zu bringen, wie dies schon Kiesler zu
veranschaulichen versuchte.

1   See J. J. Gibson, "Motion picture testing and research", *Aviation Psychology Research Report no. 7*. Washington, D.C.: U.S. Government Printing Office, 1947; J. J. Gibson, P. Olum, and F. Rosenblatt, "Parallax and Perspective during aircraft landings", *American Journal of Psychology*, no. 68, 1955, 372–385 and J. J. Gibson and J. Beck "The relation of apparent shape to apparent slant in the perception of objects", *Journal of Experimental Psychology*, no. 50, 1955, pp.125–33.

2   J. J. Gibson, *The Ecological Approach to Visual Perception*, Houghton Mifflin, Boston, 1979.

3   See particularly Lebbeus Woods' web page https://lebbeuswoods. wordpress.com/2009/12/22/ kieslers-double-vision/ and Gibson's introduction to *The Ecological Approach to Visual Perception*.

4   English philosopher John Austin coined the term illocutionary to denote the worldly actions and intentions executed by and within a normal locutionary or speech act. For a development of this idea in relation to art practice, see Sanford Kwinter, "The Acts We Call Home", in *Krzysztof Wodiczko* (London: Black Dog Press, 2011).

5   Alfred North Whitehead, *Science in the Modern World*, MacMillan, New York, 1925. For a summary of Whitehead's concept of space in relation to architecture, see Sanford Kwinter, "The Doctrine of Misplaced Concreteness and the 'Avant Garde' in America", in *Autonomy and Ideology: Positioning an Architectural Avantgarde in North America, 1923–1949*, ed. Robert Somol (New York, Monacelli Press, 1957).

1   J. J. Gibson, Wahrnehmung und Umwelt. Der ökologische Ansatz in der visuellen Wahrnehmung, München 1982, 4.

2   Vgl. ebenda, 54.

3   Ebenda, 1.

4   Siehe J. J. Gibson, „Motion picture testing and research", *Aviation Psychology Research Report*, Nr. 7, Washington, D.C.: U.S. Government Printing Office, 1947, ; J. J. Gibson, P. Olum und F. Rosenblatt, „Parallax and Perspective during aircraft landings", *American Journal of Psychology*, Nr. 68, 1955, 372–385 und J. J. Gibson und J. Beck, „The relation of apparent shape to apparent slant in the perception of objects", *Journal of Experimental Psychology*, Nr. 50, 1955, 125–33.

5   J. J. Gibson, „The Ecological Approach to Visual Perception", 1979.

6   Siehe insbesondere die Homepage von Lebbeus Woods […] und Gibsons Einleitung von Wahrnehmung und Umwelt.

7   Der englische Philosoph John Austin prägte den Begriff „illokutiv" um weltliche Handlungen und Absichten zu bezeichnen, die mit Hilfe von bzw. innerhalb eines normalen lokutiven Aktes oder Sprechaktes vollzogen werden. Für eine Ausarbeitung dieser Idee im Zusammenhang mit der Kunstpraxis siehe Sanford Kwinter, „The Acts We Call Home", in Krzysztof Wodiczko (London: Black Dog Press, 2011).

8   Alfred North Whitehead, „Science in the Modern World", MacMillan, New York, 1925. (deutsch: Wissenschaft und die moderne Welt, Suhrkamp: Frankfurt 1988). Für eine übersichtliche Darstellung seiner Gedanken in Bezug auf die Architektur siehe Sanford Kwinter, „The Fallacy of Misplaced Concreteness and the ‚Avant Garde' in America" in „Autonomy and Ideology: Positioning an Architectural Avantgarde in North America, 1923–1949", hg. v. Robert Somol (New York: Monacelli Press, 1997).

Open-Ended Matter

Pedro Gadanho

Die endlos offene Materie

There is no doubt that Frederick Kiesler today exerts a mesmeric fascination
on a large number of actors in the expanded field of culture, either if
we are speaking of practicing artists and architects, or scholars and curators.

As I write, a new symposium on one of many aspects of his oeuvre is
starting at Princeton University—not far from New York, where the Austrian
Cultural Forum asked an array of contemporary artists to "examine strategies
of representation and display" inspired by this architect's inheritance.[1]
Similarly, PhD investigations on Kiesler's work and ideas are popping up in
different contexts, and the 50th anniversary of his death is prompting new
major exhibitions exploring his influence on art and architecture in Stockholm,
Vienna, and New York.[2]

It is remarkable that an architect who left behind so little built work
enjoys this kind of attraction. One potential explanation is that his thinking and
proposals have a repercussion that is comparable to that of unrealized
utopias. Because they have not translated into concrete results—and potential failure—certain architectural utopias retain the allure of a yet possible
fulfillment. A moment could come, for instance, in which the urban visions of
the 60s and 70s architectural counterculture make sense again, not only as a
critical and political take on societal issues, but also as increasingly feasible

Es besteht kein Zweifel, dass Friederich Kiesler heute eine geradezu hypno-
tisierende Faszination auf eine Vielzahl von Akteuren im Kulturbereich
ausübt, ob es sich nun um praktizierende Künstler und Architekten oder um
Gelehrte und Kuratoren handelt.

Während ich jetzt gerade diesen Text schreibe, wird das jüngste Symposium
über einen der vielen Aspekte seines Werkes an der Princeton University
eröffnet – nicht weit von New York City, wo das Austrian Cultural Forum eine
Reihe von zeitgenössischen KünstlerInnen gebeten hat „die Strategien der
Repräsentation und Präsentation", die vom Erbe dieses Architekten inspiriert
wurden, zu untersuchen.[1] Gleichzeitig entstehen an verschiedenen Orten
Dissertationen zu Kieslers Werk und Ideen, während der 50. Jahrestag seines
Todes Anlass zu neuen großen Ausstellungen in Stockholm, Wien und New
York gibt, die seinem Einfluss in der Kunst und der Architektur gewidmet sind.[2]

Bemerkenswert ist es auf jeden Fall, dass ein Architekt, der so wenig
gebaute Werke hinterlassen hat, so viel Aufmerksamkeit auf sich zieht. Eine
mögliche Erklärung dafür wäre, dass sein Denken und seine Anregungen
eine Auswirkung haben, die mit nicht realisierten Utopien vergleichbar wäre.
Da sie nicht in konkrete Ergebnisse – bzw. mögliches Scheitern – umgesetzt
wurden, bleibt so manchen architektonischen Utopien die Allüre von noch

technological feats—a sense which, comparably, leads to a renewed interest in the likes of Archigram, Archizoom or Superstudio. (Fig. 1)

As much as Kiesler's writings preserve a complexity—and at times an esoteric obscurity—that makes them the ideal prey for rich and inventive theoretical appropriations, his spatial proposals offer the distinct promise of a yet unfulfilled vision. Nonetheless, one important difference between the germinations to be extracted from his manuscripts and the inspiration to be derived from his architectural investigations is that his idiosyncratic notions of an organic, biologically inspired spatial continuum are now at the distance of a CAD-CAM machine—as it has been amply demonstrated by the very first recipient of the Frederick Kiesler Prize for Architecture and the Arts, Frank O. Gehry.

With kudos for Kiesler's intuition and inquisitive intelligence, and as another potential reason for his present appeal, it is to be emphasized that he seems to have been quite conscious of the significance of keeping his ideas ambiguous and unconcluded. As Beatriz Colomina posits, in spite of his attempts to get his projects built, Kiesler may have been the first to "boycott" their realization.[3] When it came to the possibility of finally accomplishing his long-cherished *Endless House* project, Kiesler has perhaps

möglicher Erfüllung behaftet. Der Moment könnte also kommen, in dem die urbanen Visionen der architektonischen Gegenkultur der Sechziger und Siebziger wieder sinnvoll erscheinen und angesichts der technologischen Errungenschaften auch für zunehmend realisierbar gehalten werden – ein Eindruck, der ebenso zu einem erneuten Interesse an Projekten wie Archigram, Archizoom oder Superstudio führen mag. (Abb. 1)

So sehr die Schriften Kieslers eine Komplexität – und mitunter auch etwas esoterisch Obskures – zeigen, wodurch sie sich für reichhaltige und erfinderische theoretische Interpretationen anbieten, so sind gerade seine raumbezogenen Modelle von besonderem Versprechen einer noch unerfüllten Vision getragen. Nichtsdestotrotz gibt es einen bedeutenden Unterschied zwischen den intellektuellen Ansätzen, die sich aus seinen Manuskripten herleiten lassen, und der Inspiration, die man aus seinen architektonischen Studien holen kann: Die mögliche Realisierung seiner Vorstellungen eines organischen, biologisch inspirierten räumlichen Kontinuums lassen sich nun mit Hilfe eines CAD-CAM Gerät visualisieren – wie von Frank O. Gehry, dem allerersten Preisträger des Friederich Kiesler Preises für Architektur und Künste durchaus unter Beweis gestellt wurde. Auch mit Berücksichtigung von Kieslers Intuition und neugieriger Intelligenz sei als weitere mögliche Erklärung

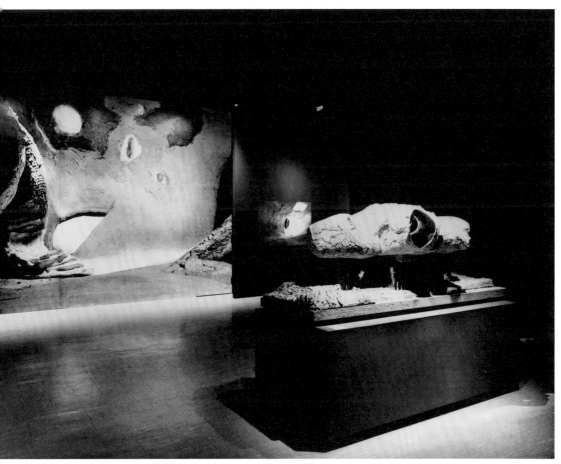

1—Frederick Kiesler, *Visionary Architecture*, Museum of Modern Art, New York 1960

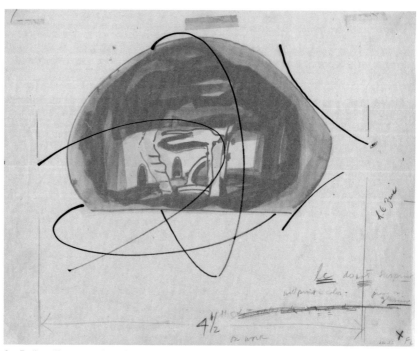

2—*Endless House*, section, New York 1950

für seine gegenwärtige Anziehungskraft betont, dass ihm die Bedeutung dessen bewusst gewesen sein muss, Mehrdeutigkeit und Unvollständigkeit im Denken zuzulassen. Wie Beatriz Colomina es auf den Punkt bringt, mag Kiesler trotz seiner Versuche, seine Projekte verwirklicht zu bekommen, der erste gewesen sein, der ihre Realisierung „boykottiert" hat.[3] Als es um die Möglichkeit ging, sein lang hochgehaltenes *Endless House* Projekt endlich vollendet zu sehen, hat Kiesler vielleicht gespürt, dass seine Ideen durch ungeahnte praktische und technologische Entwicklungen in den Schatten gestellt werden würden[4] – ähnlich wie die parallel dazu stattfindende Realisierung von Mies van der Rohes *Farnsworth House*, welches das Endergebnis eines Prozesses war, in dem sich der Idealismus dieses Architekten trotz geradezu unwürdiger Gerichtsverhandlungen und Verurteilungen vonseiten der Bevölkerung durchsetzen musste.[5]

Während also andere frühe Vertreter der Moderne sich von entschieden formulierten Manifesten und klaren Vorschlägen leiten ließen, so hat Kieslers Vorliebe für nie-enden-wollende Neuformulierungen und Pseudoannahmen[6] ihn nicht nur die kämpferische Aura der Avantgarde[7] beibehalten lassen, sie ließ ihn schließlich Partei nehmen für subtilere zeitgenössische Visionen einer unvollständigen, alternativen Moderne.[8]

sensed that pragmatic and technological contingencies could dwarf his ideas[4]—much as the parallel realization of Mies van der Rohe's *Farnsworth House* had the end-result of dragging this architect's idealism through the muddy, inferior dramas of court actions and popular condemnation.[5]

In the same vein, while other early modernists easily fell for definitive manifestos and clear-cut postulations, Kiesler's preference for never-ending reformulations and pseudo assumptions[6] has not only allowed him to retain the rebellious aura of the avant-garde,[7] but also made him eventually align with more nuanced contemporary visions of an incomplete, alternate modernity.[8]

These are certainly some of the reasons why, as a curator, I was interested in the work of Kiesler, and, in particular, in his relentless pursuit of one fundamental architectural idea[9]—or, in other words, his visceral incarnation of the endlessness nature of the design task. Being partial to Umberto Eco's views on the open work of art,[10] the idea of a multifaceted, evolving spatial and theoretical concept that is ceaselessly being explored, tested and revisited—until, in Kiesler, it finds an open-ended culmination in the *Endless House*—eventually led me to also want to *build* on Kiesler's legacy.

In this sense, however, when driven to consider the *Endless House* as a

Dies sind sicher einige der Gründe warum ich mich als Kurator für das Werk Kieslers interessiert habe und insbesondere für seine unermüdliche Beschäftigung mit einer Grundidee der Architektur[9] – oder um es anders auszudrücken: für seine sinnliche Auffassung von der Unendlichkeit der Aufgabe von Design. Meine Sympathie für Umberto Ecos Gedanken zum offenen Kunstwerk,[10] die Idee eines vielfältigen, einer im Entstehen begriffenen räumlichen und theorctischen Vorstellung, die einer ständigen Untersuchung, Prüfung und nochmaligen Betrachtung unterzogen wird – bis sie bei Kiesler eine nicht abgeschlossene Kulminierung im *Endless House* findet, führte mich schließlich dazu, auch auf Kieslers Erbe auf*bauen* zu wollen.

Als ich aber dazu angehalten wurde, das *Endless House* als Ausgangspunkt für ein Projekt einer kuratierten Ausstellung und für eine breitere theoretische Reflexion zu wählen, interessierte mich die Vorstellung des *räumlichen Kontinuums*[11] nicht so sehr – eine Idee, die an sich, *per analogem*, unterschiedliche Ausdrucksformen in der bisherigen Entwicklung der Architektur nahelegen könnte – sei es mehr in organischer oder mehr in minimalistischer Form. Mich selbst inspirierte mehr die Möglichkeit eines konzeptuellen Kontinuums, das in Kieslers Vision einer Wiedervereinigung von Architektur und bildender Kunst in der räumlichen, archetypischen menschlichen

starting point for a curatorial project and a broader theoretical reflection, I was not so interested in the notion of a *spatial continuum*,[11] an idea which *per se*, or *per analogy*, could suggest different architectural expressions— be it in more organic or more minimalist fashions. Rather, I was compelled by the possibility of a *conceptual continuum* that, in Kiesler's dream, could be seen re-uniting architecture and visual arts around the ultimate spatial and archetypal unit of human dwelling, the very basic single-family house.[12] (Fig. 2)

Endless House, Intersections of Art and Architecture, an exhibition held at the Museum of Modern Art of New York between June 27, 2015 and March 6, 2016, thus became a very special sort of homage to Kiesler. While offering a vast audience an opportunity to revisit a substantial part of MoMA's holdings on the *Endless House* project, the show ultimately proposed to observe the single-family house as both a continued site for architects' relentless disciplinary quests and a theme to which artists recurrently return in their effort to convey universal concerns. As such, echoing Kiesler's own comparison of dwelling and human biology,[13] the house cell was again and again revealed as open-ended matter on which diverse creative endeavors converge to mirror the endless character of our pursuits and designs.

Wohneinheit schlechthin darstellt, die als das grundlegende Einfamilienhaus par excellence betrachtet werden könnte.[12] (Abb. 2)

Die Ausstellung *Endless House, Intersections of Art and Architecture*, die zwischen 27. Juni 2015 und 6. März 2016 am Museum of Modern Art in New York stattfindet, ist daher zu einer ganz besonderen Hommage an Kiesler geworden. Während einem breiten Publikum die Möglichkeit geboten wird, einen bedeutenden Anteil von Materialien zum *Endless House*-Projekt aus MoMAs Beständen wieder zu besichtigen, hat sich die Ausstellung auch vorgenommen, das Einfamilienhaus als Symbol für das unermüdliche Suchen des Architekten zwischen den Disziplinen zu definieren, also als Ort zu sehen, zu dem Künstler in ihrem Bemühen immer wieder zurückkehren, um universelle Themen aufzugreifen und zu vermitteln.[13] Die Wohnzelle erwies sich damit immer wieder als Materie, deren Möglichkeiten noch offen sind, wo verschiedene kreative Unternehmungen zusammenlaufen können, und wodurch der unendliche Charakter unserer Interessen und Designformen erkennbar wird.

1 The conference and workshop *Frederick Kiesler's Magic Architecture* was held at Princeton University School of Architecture on Friday April 24, 2015. The exhibition *Display of the Centuries. Frederick Kiesler and Contemporary Art* was held at the Austrian Cultural Forum of New York from April 1 to July 27, 2015.

2 The exhibition *Frederick Kiesler: Visions at Work Annotated by Céline Condorelli and Six Student Groups* was held at the Tensta Konsthall, Stockholm, Feb. 2 – March 5, 2015. *Function Follows Vision, Vision Follows Reality* was held at the Kunsthalle Wien, Vienna, from May 27 – Aug. 8, 2015.

3 Colomina bases her proposition on Philip Johnson's comment that "Kiesler could not bear endings." As she points out, "the Endless House could remain endless only by never being finished." See Beatriz Colomina, "Space House, The Psyche of Building", in *Intersections: Architectural Histories and Critical Theories*, Iain Borden, Jane Rendell (eds.) (London: Routledge, 2000), 66.

4 As suggested by Colomina, Kiesler may ultimately have been averse to the commercial appropriation of his media-amplified ideas, which would make him again a pioneer without following—or the precise reverse of the contemporary situation in which architects' careers are based on the fact that clients want to bank on the cultural capital of celebrity architects. See Beatriz Colomina, idem, 66.

5 See Peter Blake, Mies van der Rohe, *Architecture and Structure*, (Baltimore: Penguin Books, 1964), 85.

6 It is relevant that Kiesler preferred to speak of "pseudo-functionalism" and twists the usual Modernist credo to say "form does not follow function, function follows vision, vision follows reality." See "Pseudo-Functionalism in Modern Architecture", *Partisan Review* 16, July 1949, reprinted in Yehuda Safran, ed., Frederick Kiesler 1890–1965 (London: Architectural Association, 1989), 57.

7 It is again Colomina who advances this proposition, stating that Kiesler is "perhaps the only avant-garde figure in architecture that one can speak of in the United States." See Colomina, idem, 58.

8 It should be noted that, by writing of a pseudo-functionalism, Kiesler precisely escapes the most vehement criticisms of the Modernist orthodoxy, and opens the way for the emergence and re-appreciation of an alternative, organic, Surrealist-influenced Modernism. In this sense, I would call attention to my previous reflections in "Pancho Guedes, Echoes of an Alternative Modernity", in Pedro Gadanho, *Pancho Guedes, an Alternative Modernist*, Basel:

1 Die Konferenz und der Workshop *Frederick Kiesler's Magic Architecture* fanden am Freitag dem 24. April 2015 an der Princeton University School of Architecture statt. Die Ausstellung *Display of the Centuries. Frederick Kiesler and Contemporary Art* fand vom 1. April bis 27. Juli 2015 am Austrian Cultural Forum of New York statt.

2 Die Ausstellung *Frederick Kiesler: Visions at Work Annotated by Céline Condorelli and Six Students Groups* findet vom 27. Mai bis 8. August 2015 statt.

3 Colomina gründete ihre Argumentation auf Philip Johnsons Bemerkung („Kiesler could not bear endings" – Kiesler hielt keine Ende aus.) Wie sie behauptet: „das *Endless House* konnte nur endlos bleiben, da es nie vollendet wurde." Siehe Beatriz Colomina, "Space House, The Psyche of Building", in *Intersections: Architectural Histories and Critical Theories*, hg. v. Iain Borden, Jane Rendell (London: Routledge, 2000) 66.

4 Wie Colomina anmerkt, mag Kiesler nie etwas gegen die kommerzielle Verwertung seiner durch die Medien amplifizierten Gedanken gehabt haben, wodurch er wieder zu einem Pionier ohne Gefolgschaft gemacht werden würde – oder es trifft bei ihm genau das Gegenteil der heutigen Situation zu, in der die Karrieren von Architekten darauf beruhen, dass Auftraggeber: vom kulturellen Kapital berühmter Architekten profitieren wollen. Siehe Beatriz Colomina, ebenda, 66.

5 Siehe Peter Blake, Mies van der Rohe, „Architecture and Structure"(Baltimore: Penguin Books, 1964), 85.

6 Es ist bedeutend, dass Kiesler lieber vom „Pseudo-Funktionalismus" sprach und das gewöhnliche Credo der Moderne so verdrehte, sodass es nun hieß: „Form folgt nicht Funktion, Funktion folgt Vision, Vision folgt Realität".

Siehe „Pseudo-Functionalism in Modern Architecture" *Partisan Review*, 16. Juli 1949, Wiederabdruck in, *Frederick Kiesler 1890–1965*, hg. v. Yehuda Safran (London: Architectural Association, 1989), 57.

7 Es ist wieder Colomina, die diese Behauptung vorlegt, dass Kiesler „vielleicht die einzige Figur in der Avantgarde der Architektur [sei], von der man in den Vereinigten Staaten sprechen kann." Siehe Colomina, ibid., 58.

8 Es sei angemerkt, dass Kiesler, indem er von einem Pseudo-Funktionalismus schreibt, genau den schärfsten Kritiken der modernistischen Orthodoxie entkommt und den Weg für das Hervortreten und die Wiederbeachtung einer alternativen, organischen, vom Surrealismus beeinflussten Moderne bahnt. In diesem Zusammenhang weise ich den Leser auf meine früheren Überlegungen hin: „Pancho Guedes, Echoes of an Alternative

Swiss Architecture Museum, 2007.

9 See T.H. Creighton, "Kiesler's Pursuit of an Idea", *Progressive Architecture* (July 1961), 110. As Kiesler is quoted as saying around the time he was presenting the *Endless House*, "I'm still looking, as I was 40 years ago, for a chance to build [those ideas]."

10 See Umberto Eco, *The Open Work*, (Cambridge: Harvard University Press, 1989).

11 Dieter Bogner speaks of "a continuum which reflects the demand for maximum flexibility in the layout of the interior space." He also suggests that "the coordination of heterogeneous elements/forces/tensions in an 'endless' spatial continuum" was "the central idea which conditioned [Kiesler's] entire artistic life." See Dieter Bogner, Frederick Kiesler 1890–1965, *Inside the Endless House* (Vienna: Bohlau Verlag, 1997), 22.

12 As Bogner points out, "a preoccupation with the concept of space", which in Kiesler means a broad juxtaposition of art media, as well as experiences in theater and display, translates in the *Endless House* into "a single space unit ('one space unit') in which the possibilities for development starting from a minimal basic layout are exploited to the full." The single-family house is seen by Kiesler as a laboratory for "an elastic spatial concept which must be capable, even in a small house, of providing an optimum response to the very varied social concerns of its inhabitants." See Dieter Bogner, idem, 22. On the other hand, as suggested in the press release of one of Kiesler's later exhibitions, the *Endless House* "was to synthesize painting, sculpture, architecture, and the environment to establish a space without a sense of boundaries." See Frederick Kiesler: *Endless*,

Jason McCoy Gallery. New York: 2008.

13 As Kiesler states in his memoirs aptly named *Inside the Endless House*, "there is no beginning and no end to [the house], like the human body." Curiously, he also compared the *Endless House* to a sensuous woman's body, rather than "sharp-angled male architecture"—thus again locating himself in a very specific and alternative understanding of Modernity. See Kiesler, Frederick, *Inside the Endless House*, New York: 1966, 566.

Modernity", in *Pedro Gadanho, Pancho Guedes, an Alternative Modernist*, (Basel: Swiss Architecture Museum, 2007).

9 Siehe T.H. Creighton, „Kiesler's Pursuit of an Idea", *Progressive Architecture* (Juli 1961), 110. Wie Kiesler um die Zeit seiner Vorstellung des *Endless Houses* zitiert wurde: „Ich suche immer noch, wie ich es vor vierzig Jahren tat, nach einer Möglichkeit, [jene Ideen] zu errichten."

10 Siehe „Umberto Eco", *The Open Work* (Cambridge: Harvard University Press, 1989)

11 Dieter Bogner spricht von „einem Kontinuum, das die Forderung nach maximaler Flexibilität im Grundriss des Innenraums wiedergibt." Er merkt auch an, dass „die Koordinierung von heterogenen Elementen/Kräften/Spannungen in einem ‚endlosen' räumlichen Kontinuum der zentrale Gedanke war, der (Kieslers) gesamtes künstlerisches Leben bestimmte." Siehe „Dieter Bogner, Fredrich

Kiesler 1890–1965, Inside the Endless House"(Vienna: Böhlau Verlag, 1997), 22.

12 Wie Bogner bemerkte, ist im *Endless House* „die Auseinandersetzung mit der Vorstellung von Raum", die für Kiesler eine breite Gegenüberstellung von Kunstmedien sowie Erfahrungen in Theater und in Ausstellungen bedeutet, übersetzt in „eine einzelne Raumeinheit („eine Raumeinheit") in der die Entwicklungsmöglichkeiten ausgehend von einem minimalen Grundriss voll ausgeschöpft werden." Das Einfamilienhaus sieht Kiesler als ein Labor für „einen elastischen räumlichen Begriff, der sogar in einem kleinen Haus imstande sein muss, eine optimale Reaktion auf die sehr unterschiedlichen gesellschaftlichen Anliegen seiner Bewohner zu bieten." Siehe Dieter Bogner, ebenda, 22. Andererseits sollte das *Endless House*, so wie im Pressebericht einer der letzten Ausstellungen Kieslers angemerkt

wurde, „eine Synthese von Malerei, Skulptur, Architektur und der Umwelt schaffen […], um einen Raum ohne Grenzen zu bilden." Siehe *Frederick Kiesler: Endless*, Jason McCoy Gallery, New York: 2008.

13 Wie Kiesler in seinen Erinnerungen (mit dem passenden Titel „Inside the Endless House") richtig feststellt, „gibt es keinen Anfang und kein Ende [zum Haus], wie zum menschlichen Körper." Seltsamerweise vergleicht er das *Endless House* auch mit dem sinnlichen Körper einer Frau anstatt der „scharfkantigen männlichen Architektur" – wodurch er sich wieder in einem ganz bestimmten Alternativverständnis der Moderne verortet. Siehe Frederick Kiesler, *Inside the Endless House*, New York 1966, 566.

Frederick Kiesler,
The Endless House

CBS "Camera Three" (March 20, 1960)[1]

Frederick Kiesler [tape]   The first idea comes to you simply like it is often said a dream, or an inspiration, or a vision. And then you are able to observe your life, the life of your co-human beings, and draw your conclusions. Living in boxes, no matter how many boxes you have—in a poor, in a richer, in the most luxurious house—they are still boxes and you feel encompassed by them, you feel hampered. You want to liberate yourself.

> **James MacAndrew**   What we've seen is the *Endless House*. What
> we've heard is the voice of its designer, architect and sculptor,
> Frederick Kiesler—in the words of Philip Johnson, the "greatest non-
> building architect of our time." Although Mr. Kiesler's ideas are new
> to the general public, they have existed in plans and models since the
> early twenties, and his influence on other designers (again to quote
> Philip Johnson) "has been enormous." The more radical of his ideas
> are now beginning to find public acceptance. The Ford Foundation
> has announced a grant to Kiesler to create an ideal American theater.
> The Museum of Modern Art in New York has plans to construct the
> *Endless House* in the Museum garden. A private citizen is having the
> house built in Connecticut this summer.
>   Now, the first concept of the *Endless House* was formulated and
> exhibited in Mr. Kiesler's native Vienna in 1924. A second model, this
> one backed by Picasso's *Quadriga*, was shown in New York in 1926—
> the year Mr. Kiesler became a United States citizen. In 1934, there is
> a full-sized model of an adaptation of the *Endless House* called the
> *Space House*. In 1950, a one-family model of the *Endless House*,
> exhibited in New York's Kootz Gallery.
>   Mr. Kiesler, why is the house called the *Endless House*?

FK   Well, let me make you a very simple sign—you know, the sign of infinity. Do you know that sign?

> **JM**   Yes, indeed.

FK   Now see how it could be a two room *Endless House*, a two space *Endless House* or there is a continuity in a three room, three area unit—one, two, three. You see, we are now living in boxes, no matter how many boxes we are, we have or how many boxes, they are constructed to make one apartment or one house, they are still very tight enclosures which cannot be moved, which cannot be opened up to our desires. The *Endless House*

principle is a continuous flow of areas, of spaces. These areas, you see, are not of the same height or width as they are now, more or less, in houses which are one roof and floor above the other. They are exactly schemed to take care of our individual desires being they to be absolutely alone, being together with somebody else, or finally opening up if we receive guests. Now this is the man's natural, entire other concept of housing. It means the end of the column and beam which is direct angle and which closes you in.

JM   It begins with a new concept of space, doesn't it?

FK   Yes, with a new concept of space, and a new concept of space begins simply with a new feeling for life, a greater liberation of your personality, of your individuality, a greater independence and that the house should respond to your individual needs of the moment.

JM   Now, we have here some simple models or elementary models, Mr. Kiesler, of the *Endless House*. Could you show them to us?

FK   Yes, I would gladly do so. Now this was the first stadium which led finally to the *Endless House*. You see, here you see the main shell and then you see division within the main shell. Here I tried reinforced concrete to divide a larger area into a smaller area, but that was not satisfactory because I know the wall is curved and tried to relate the floor and the ceiling and the wall in a different way like we usually see it—it still is a wall and is a division— a hard division. In another model, which was made right afterwards, I could have the main shell, certain sections as you see are taken off so we can look better in. You see, take the two areas, which are called individual areas, are also a shell construction—one around the vertical axis and one around the horizontal axis. Can you see it? The house is also elevated from the floor, one floor up, that means that the cars drive underneath through. The one support is the staircase which leads up and you come into the middle of the living room out, which is a double height room and which gives you all the width, which is necessary for a big expanse.

JM   Would these foundation units be a typical feature of the *Endless House*?

FK   I personally prefer it, but it can just as well be on the ground or could

be floating on the water or on sand. It is reinforced concrete and it is tight, airtight, and can do almost anything and is independent of deep foundations.

> **JM**   Now I see clearly how you have converted that simple idea of the geometric sign of infinity into three dimensions. I think I detect here also Kiesler the sculptor as well as Kiesler the architect.

FK   Well, in the history of architecture if you look at buildings which are architecture, you will find that is always the case. If you look at architecture which are only shelters, as for instance, our skyscrapers are, then you don't need to have the aspect, that super aspect, that concludes the very functional with the super-functional, with what is usually called aesthetics. That is a very poor word for that. It is the expression of enclosed space on a high level, almost a symbolic level.

> **JM**   I know very well that sculpture in your life has not just been supplementary. I understand that included among the owners of Kiesler pieces are such people as Governor Rockefeller of New York and many others.
>
> There was an editorial just recently that we came across in *Art News* which emphasizes the point, the relationship between a sculptor and architecture. I found this very interesting and I think you will. This editorial says in part, "Creative artists have, as long ago as the 1930s, moved from the classicism of geometric space to the organic surges of free form. A few important new buildings of the last decade have begun to show reflections of that transformation. Wright's Guggenheim Museum and Dallas Theater, Le Corbusier's chapel at Ronchamp and his Philips Electric Pavilion at the 1958 Brussels Fair, Saarinen's TWA Terminal now being constructed at Idlewild Airport— each of these illustrating new possibilities of enclosed space bound to no corner or square. A culmination," *Art News* goes on to say, "so far is Frederick Kiesler's concrete *Endless House*, building curled-up room enclosures together into a huge honeycomb."
>
> Mr. Kiesler, can you tell us briefly how this has all evolved?

FK   You ask really a lot because you know, it is about ten centuries, but let's try to put it in five minutes, in a set of ideas. Now you know the main building materials are stone and wood and later on we get into steel and we later on go into plastics. But let's start with the tree. Now a tree with all

his branches, you see, and his roots and here is the earth. You cut that off and you have a beam, a vertical beam, you take the same thing and try to put it horizontal to form a roof, but naturally you have to tie it here together so it is a problem of joints. You also have to support the other end, otherwise it is falling down, you know. Then you have to put it into foundation because it is insecure. So, there you have two main aspects which have remained field today and we will now try to convert the wood into steel beam. Now here you have a steel beam and you have the same thing here as you had it in wood. If you want a higher building, you simply add another steel beam above—I do it here below—but you also very often go into basement and sub-basement, and then you have a terrific foundation for the whole thing to hold it up and in place. The security depends on that, too. Now what you really get is a square of a grate, as you see it on our skyscrapers and on our houses. But then you have the problem of filling the holes out, the holes vertically, the holes horizontally and so you have about six or seven main contractors which range from concrete, to steel, to brick, to stone, to glass and so forth, to plaster, and so forth, and so forth. We try to do it the other way and simplify the matter. We have a cave which man first saw for shelter which is flat on the ground and where he crawls in for protection. Later on we see he developed the igloo, which is a pre-manufactured dome with the exception that the parts, the individual parts, are frozen together and are frozen to the ground. Now, in the *Endless House*, you see, there all these handicaps of building in parts which have to be fitted together, are eliminated. As a matter of fact, the *Endless House* has not a single joint no matter how big it is. It is a continuous tension construction, different from what you see and from post and lintel as you know it. Now it is rather simple, the whole concept really is nothing very inventive, and nothing extraordinary. But you start, you see, you have domes before as you know with brick constructions. In order to hold the whole thing together but then you have to put it on the colonnade all around and then you have to put the colonnade into the ground again. Otherwise, the whole thing might shake and collapse. So it is still the old-fashioned way of doing the thing but in that period that was the best one can do. Today we can do it differently. We have reinforced concrete. We don't need any columns; we don't need any beams. We just continue the shell from the floor up into the wall, into the ceiling, and back into the wall. That doesn't mean that the house has to look like an egg—it can have any shape and form as long as the floor, sides, ceilings are superordinated, that they form an integrated unit which is independent of digging it into the ground to just make up—as in architecture today is normal—a launching pad for it. That's all. Now the structure is then

here heavy on the floor, goes thinner on the ceiling—should be here eleven inches and goes here to three and a half inches. That is the main structure of the *Endless House.*

> **JM**   Is it true, Mr. Kiesler, that in the case of the *Endless House* that you created the model before drawing the plans?

FK   Yes, that is true. There was simply no other way how to do it. Because, you see, I don't usually reverse process. To me, you see, it is very unusual to hear that strange people, so-called architects, are doing prints for houses for other people to live in. Why, in primitive times, or our Indians, they have a tradition within the tribes and families how to do houses. They don't build by blueprints. Perhaps, I'm very primitive and tribal in that respect. I have to feel the space when I am modeling it, when I conceive with a purpose which I had in mind and so I first had to make the different studies—two of which you have seen there. For other ones, I had also, which is very important thing, all materials are reduced to one single material which is reinforced concrete. I had to develop an enormous variety of textures outside and particularly inside.

> **JM**   Wouldn't this concept of continuous tension, with its elimination completely of all support—the columns, everything that the builder is used to—didn't that cause a problem when you were putting this into terms of plans?

FK   Of course, not a problem for me it didn't impose and later on a problem for the builder, who is the president of the Euclid Corporation, who built the Guggenheim Museum. He got it right away and he is probably the man who is going to build it. This matter is rather simple. You see, the plans had to be developed after the model had been done.

> **JM**   Now most of us have had a look, whether we've understood it or not, of architect's plans. Now we have one of two plans of the *Endless House* here. Would you let us have a look at them?

FK   Gladly. Now this is the South view of the *Endless House* with the master's unit right in front and you see a horizontal opening which is very large which you normally would call a window, which we call, you see, a fusion light unit, and then a vertical one on the left side, you see an exit stair. That is the center

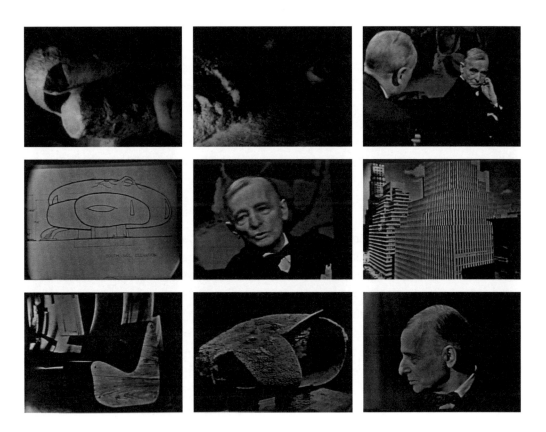

aspect—the view of the total thing. And that, of course, is the view of the North side with what is called the dining and kitchen area. The big stretch in the middle is the living room area including the children's quarters to the left.

> **JM**   Mr. Kiesler, can we see some views of later models in terms of what we regard as traditional architectural style.

FK   That will be very interesting to me, too. [tape] After the Victorian Age, where everything was over-stuffed, over-grown, over-crowded, and over-decorated, one had simply—like some human being who eats too much—to put the whole architecture on a strict diet. So everything was cleaned away—the walls became flat, white, straight, unadorned. Now that period of hunger and dieting when architecture had to loose weight, waste, and fat, is over. Now we still go on doing that, as you can see it in many new buildings, because we went on into industrializing the idea. Pre-manufacturing —that is where we are now. It is necessary to counteract that.

This *Endless House* cannot at the moment be built by industry; it must be built by hand. Very often, people would say, "Well, this is like living in a cave." No, it isn't at all, because the house had so many different areas of spaces, of so many different heights and widths, that you never feel that you are in one very distinct area all the time. Of course, it is impossible to have everything, and we have learned unfortunately to have a prosperity of desires and wishes. It is evident we have to make up our minds as inhabitants of a house—if we want it all gadgets, or if we want to live a basically happy life in it. And it is clear that we have to sacrifice certain things for it. We cannot have everything. So the difference between the *Endless House* and the so-called modern houses is that it is striving for an expression of fundamental need—not of primitive needs, but of needs which are fundamental to our well-being. But everything is departmentalized in our houses. We are regimented, and we have learned to conform to that. Now many people revolt, but they simply can't get out of the strait jacket of functional architecture. So I am here to help them a little bit.

> **JM**   I'd like to underline that with an interesting comment we found in Mr. Kiesler's writings: "Just as the scientists of the Middle Ages thought that horses produced wasps; asses, hornets; and cheese, mice, so modern men think that it is industry which produces the technological environment. In reality, the technological environment

is produced by human needs. Investigation of this crucial point
cannot be based upon the study of architecture but must be based
upon the study of the life processes of man."

Now, Mr. Kiesler, it seems to me that in the *Endless House* that we
would need a redesigning, a reconstruction of almost everything in the
interior.

FK   That is absolutely correct. After all, we live in the interior and we live
with these objects and they have to help us.

   JM   Beginning with the furniture.

FK   That is correct. But we cannot take our cues, you see, from furniture
from what they are now—being old-fashioned or modern. We have to go back,
as you read, to life processes. We must do that with all functions in which
we have to perform in the house and we have to have the house adapt itself to
us in every piece. The time is rather short to go into all that. But let me
perhaps digress a little bit and show one object that I designed in 1942, which
explains this approach to design very well. It was the Peggy Guggenheim
Gallery in New York and the key, the fundamental problem was how to relate
the visitor to the paintings which they exhibited on the walls. Now, as you
know, in museums or galleries today, they are straight long walls and the
paintings are hung like linens on a line and you just walk along, you pick one
or another one and you have a glance, and you go on, and you're through.
I tried to make it more comfortable for the visitor to get into contact with the
world of the artist. Now, to just put chairs or benches as you find sometimes
in museums is not correct because you can't have them right there where the
painting is. So here you see an object which is a rocker and this rocker had
in that exhibition of Miss Guggenheim's 18 different uses. I think in this room,
you will see four uses of the same object illustrated, each to give greater
comfort to the visitor, for no other reason. Now here it is upside down and it
carries a sculpture by Giacometti on top of it. It is just the right height for
observation, observing the sculpture. Here you see in the same way, there is
an arm in it and displaying an etching to look down. Here you see it flat on
the side so that two people can sit together and look at the paintings which
are displayed on arms and can be tilted by the visitors to their desires so
that they really make a direct, even physical, contact with the work. And this
here is the rocker in its natural position as a rocker. That was necessary

to rock forward and back because at some time you like to go a little bit back and a little bit closer in order to observe better.

> **JM** Isn't that system of hanging the pictures, didn't it pre-date what is happening in the Rockefeller Museum today?

FK You mean the Guggenheim.

> **JM** The Guggenheim, I'm sorry.

FK Well, that has been adapted before. It is one of the main issues that will be modified and further developed in most exhibitions that come about.

> **JM** How about some of the very ordinary areas in the average 20th century home, something like the bathroom, for instance?

FK Well, that is a very complicated situation. It is composed, you know, as a repetition of the same bowls in wood, then in enamel, in tin and now it might be in plastics, illuminated from below. But, you see, it is not the matter to enjoy the bathing because it gets cold, the heat cannot be regulated, etc., etc. That can be very easily be taken care of.

> **JM** This calls for the same sort of fresh, breaking through of thinking as you've done before.

FK Observation of the life processes and nothing else. But one of the main questions is, naturally, which I'm always asked, are the expenses of the thing. Now, I would like to say that a present estimate, which have been very exact according to plans, the *Endless House* is between 25 percent and 30 percent less expensive than even the same cubic content in brick.

> **JM** Is this because of the material?

FK Because of the amount of subcontractors, you see different types of subcontractors have been reduced to one single one, which is reinforced concrete. Now, it also gives you fireproofing, waterproofing, easier maintenance, and houses which would equal two rooms could, from that unit on up to five or six, can be built from almost 35 000 dollars or 40 000 dollars up to 150 000 dollars, which is really for our time a price which is inexpensive.

JM To what extent will the *Endless House* have individuality or will they all tend to sort of look alike?

FK Not at all. You know, when I first started and you saw the first model, everybody thought that the *Endless House* will have to look like an egg, a squared-off egg. But as you have seen it, it isn't at all. The possibilities are endless, the design and form of the house are absolutely endless in themselves, too. It depends on the location, it depends on desire, on the size of the family, on the amount of money available and it should not be difficult for any imaginative designer to adopt that with an infinite variety.

JM Mr. Kiesler, I'd like to thank you for being with us on behalf of *Camera Three* and on behalf of our viewers and I'd like to close by repeating very briefly something that Mr. Kiesler said. He said, "Technological environment is produced by human needs. Investigation of this crucial point cannot be based upon the study of architecture but must be based upon the study of the life processes of man." Now, if you have found [interesting] this discussion of the *Endless House* which was, by the way, the very first appearance of Mr. Kiesler's creation on television, why don't you send us your comments—just address them to *Camera Three*.

1 This is a complete transcript of a television interview that was screened by CBS on March 20, 1960. Earlier transcripts from the archive of the Austrian Frederick and Lillian Kiesler Foundation (ÖFLKS, TXT 625/0, TXT 625/1, TXT 7005/0) were revised and supplemented.

The *Endless House*: A Man-Built Cosmos

Frederick Kiesler

The *Endless House* is called the *Endless* because all ends meet, and meet continuously.

It is endless like the human body—there is no beginning and no end to it. The *Endless* is rather sensuous, more like the female body in contrast to sharp-angled male architecture.

All ends meet in the *Endless* as they meet in life. Life's rhythms are cyclical. All ends of living meet during twenty-four hours, during a week, a lifetime. They touch one another with the kiss of time. They shake hands, stay, say good-bye, return through the same or other doors, come and go through multi-links, secretive or obvious, or through the whims of memory.

The events of life are your house guests. You must play the best possible of hosts; otherwise the hosts of events will become ghosts. They will. Yes, they can, but not in the *Endless House*. There, events are reality, because you receive them with open arms, and they become you. You are fused with them and thus reinforced in your power of self-reliance. You are indeed a rich man, wealthy with happenings of no end.

Machine-age houses are split-ups of cubicles,

one box next to another,

one box below another,

one box above another,

until they grew into tumors of skyscrapers.

Space in the *Endless House* is continuous. All living areas can be unified into a single continuum.

But do not fear that one cannot find seclusion in the *Endless*.

Each and every one of the space-nuclei can be separated from the totality of the dwelling, secluded. At will, you can reunify to meet various needs: the congregation of the family, of visitors from the outer world, neighbors, friends, strollers. Or again, you'll womb yourself into happy solitude. The *Endless* cannot be only a home for the family, but must definitely make room and comfort for those *visitors* from your own inner world. Communion with yourself. The ritual of meditation inspired. Truthfully, the inhabitants of your inner space are steady companions, although invisible to the naked eye, but very much felt by the psyche. These invisible guests are the secret-service men and honor guard of your being. We cannot treat them as burglars. We must make them feel comfortable. They represent diligently the echoes of your past life and the projection of a promised or hoped-for realm of time-to-come.

It is self-evident that congregations of real people as well as those of the imagination will live together peacefully in an endless house. Neither must be restricted by prejudice of any kind. Welcome travelers. Common rest.

The *Endless House* is not amorphous, not a free-for-all form. On the contrary, its construction has strict boundaries according to the scale of your living. Its shape and form are determined by inherent life processes, not by building-code standards or the vagaries of décor fads.

Nature creates bodies, but art creates life. Thus living in the *Endless House* means to live an exuberant life, not only the life of a digesting body, of routine social duties, or the wind-up of functions of the four seasons, the automatism of day and night, of high noon and the midnight moon. The *Endless House* is much more than that and much less than the average dwelling of the rich or pseudo rich. It is less because it reverts to fundamental needs of the human in his relationship to man, to industry, to nature (that is, to eating, sleeping and sex).

The *Endless House* is not subservient to the mechanics of life activities or to techniques of manufacture; it employs them wherever profitable but it is not a slave to industrial dictatorship.

In the *Endless House* nothing can be taken for granted, either of the house itself, the floor, walls, ceiling, the coming of people or of light, the air with its warmth or coolness. Every mechanical device must remain an event and constitute the inspiration for a specific ritual. Not even the faucet that brings water into your glass, into the teakettle, through your shower and into the bath—that turn of a handle and then the water flowing forth as from the rock touched by Moses in the desert, that sparkling event, released through the magic invention of man's mind, must always remain the surprise, the unprecedented, an event of pride and comfort. There are many flowers in the garden of industry that have the enchantment of happy happenings, but not all of them have an inspiring color or scent. They must be weeded out, to prevent their overgrowth absorbing the sap of life. Ours is the decision to select, to dismiss, to elect, to reinforce.

Obviously the flow of life activities cannot be squeezed into an array of room-boxes, no matter what sizes, be they of wood, paper, steel or glass. The house, that is, the walls, floors and ceilings, must not meet one another at sharp angles and be fused together artificially, but should flow into one another uninterrupted by columns and beams. The *Endless House* solves this problem of construction through a continuity of lighter and heavier shells. The column is dead. Having created reinforced concrete, we are now in a position to achieve buildings in unending spatial formations, lateral, vertical, in any direction of an expanse we wish to achieve. But concrete must not be considered the only material in which a continuous plasticity can be achieved. With a bit of imagination and knowledge of one's craft, the spatial planning

that gives you a feeling of freedom can be expressed in practically any material, from wood to canvas, from stone to paper. The concept is the thing, not the execution. Automotive tools can be very welcome, but the architect as a craftsman can build with any material and express the ritual of life within a dwelling even with such primitive means as earth solidified in the manner of the American Indians in their adobe houses. The architect-technician will not think in terms of material as such. He will evoke from any one of them strength, closeness and depth, an abundant scale of textures.

While it is being built, the *Endless House* will grow its colors, in vast areas or condensed into compositions (fresco-like or paintings), into high or low reliefs, into the plasticity of full sculptures. Like vegetation, it grows its form and color at the same time. And so let us avoid the museum term *art* in connection with architecture, because, as we understand it today, architecture has been degraded to old-fashioned or modern-fashioned make-up and décor. Art as a ritual cannot be an afterthought. It must again become the usual link between the known and the unknown.

The *Endless House* is indeed a very practical house if one defines practicality in not too narrow a sense, and if one considers the poetry of life an integral part of everyday happenings.

The coming of the *Endless House* is inevitable in a world coming to an end. It is the last refuge for man as man.

1   ÖFLKS, TXT 2980/0. The text was published for the first time in Frederick Kiesler, *Inside The Endless House. Art, People and Architecture: A Journal* (New York: Simon and Schuster, 1966), 566 569.

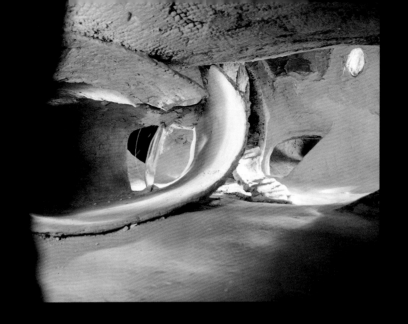

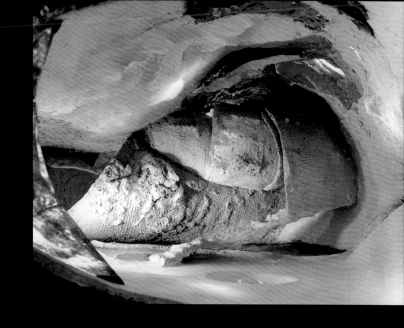

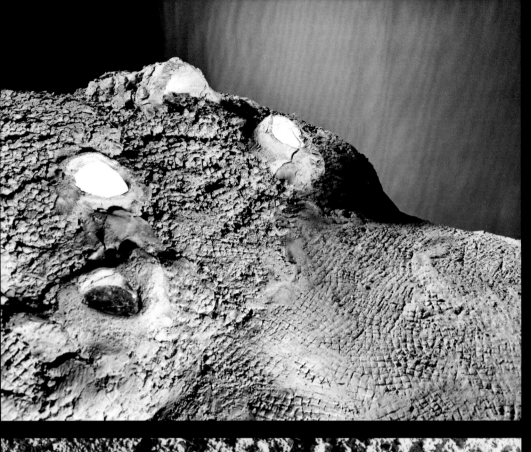

Vision and the Art of Engineering

Florian Medicus and Gerd Zillner

Vision und Ingenieurskunst

"What we need in our professions are musicians!"
—Fred Severud, May 1959

For the realization of the construction plans for the *Endless House* in the Museum of Modern Art's sculpture garden, Frederick Kiesler had to recruit an innovative office of structural engineers for support. To this end, he turned to Severud-Elstadt-Krueger Associates, a company he had already contacted in connection with the construction of the dome for the *Shrine of the Book* in Jerusalem.[1] On May 13, 1959, Kiesler invited Fred Severud (1899–1990) and his partner Hannskarl Bandel (1925–93) to his studio to discuss a possible collaboration. A hand-written copy of the minutes of the meeting with the title *Structural Analysis for the Endless House* gives some details about this consultation.[2] For the realization of his life project, Kiesler consulted the most prominent and most innovative structural engineer working at that time on the American East Coast. The list of all the projects that Severud-Elstad-Krueger Associates collaborated on in the 1950s and 1960s reads like a line-up of prominent and progressive architecture of the United States: Severud-Elstad-Krueger had worked on the construction of the J.S. Dorton Arena in Raleigh (1953), an arch system for cable nets with opposite curvature, the Mies'

„Was wir in unserer Profession brauchen, sind Musiker!"
—Fred Severud, Mai 1959

Friedrich Kiesler benötigte für die Ausführung der Konstruktionspläne des *Endless House* im Skulpturengarten des Museum of Modern Art die Unterstützung eines innovativen Statikbüros. Hierfür griff er auf Severud-Elstadt-Krueger Associates zurück, die er schon für die Konstruktion der Kuppel des *Shrine of the Book* in Jerusalem konsultiert hatte.[1] Am 13. Mai 1959 lud Kiesler Fred Severud und dessen Partner Hannskarl Bandel in sein Atelier, um die Möglichkeiten einer Zusammenarbeit zu erläutern. Ein handschriftliches Besprechungsprotokoll mit dem Titel: *Structural Analysis for the Endless House* gibt über dieses Zusammentreffen Auskunft.[2] Für die Realisierung seines Lebensprojekts wandte sich Kiesler also an den zu dieser Zeit wohl prominentesten und innovativsten Bauingenieur der amerikanischen Ostküste. Die Auflistung realisierter Projekte, an denen Severud-Elstad-Krueger-Associates in den 1950er und 60er-Jahren mitwirkten, liest sich wie eine Zusammenfassung prominenter wie progressiver Architektur der Vereinigten Staaten: J.S. Dorton Arena in Raleigh (1953); Stützbogensystem für gegensinnig gekrümmte Seilnetze! Mies' Seagram Building (1958),

Seagram Building (1958), the Saarinens Hockey Rink in Yale (1959) and the
St. Louis Gateway Arch (1965), as well as the Place Ville Marie with I.M.
Pei (1962), the Toronto City Hall (1965) and the Berlin *Congress Hall* by Hugh
Stubbins (1957).

In the minutes cited above, Fred Severud showed great interest, even if he
and his office lacked the time to deal with the *Endless House* in greater
detail. Kiesler flattered Severud by saying that he saw him as the only structural engineer with a young and creative mind, indeed, as the only one
with sufficient imagination. Severud initially declined and recommended the
following engineers for the *Endless House*: Wolfgang Zerna, Germany;
Felix Candela, Mexico; as well as Mario George Savaldor and Hans Heinrich
Bleich from Columbia University and Eduardo Torroja, Spain. In this list of
world-class innovators, the only name missing was Pier Luigi Nervi, Italy.
However, it can be gleaned from the minutes that Kiesler was not positively
disposed of the persons named—for whatever reasons. For his *Endless
House*, he wanted to enlist the services of Severud and no other! And in spite
of initial rejection, he was ultimately able to win him over.

The work on the structural plans for the *Endless House* can be
reconstructed from two letters and a plan which have been stored in the

Saarinens Hockey Rink in Yale (1959) oder der St. Louis Gateway Arch (1965).
Und auch den Place Ville Marie mit I. M. Pei (1962), die Toronto City
Hall (1965) und die Berliner *Kongresshalle* von Hugh Stubbins (1957) hatten
Severud-Elstad-Krueger konstruktiv bearbeitet.

Im oben angeführten Protokoll zeigte sich Fred Severud sehr interessiert,
wenngleich ihm und seinem Büro aber die Zeit fehlte, sich mit dem *Endless
House* eingehender zu befassen. Kiesler schmeichelte Severud und sagte,
dass er ihn für den einzigen Bauingenieur mit einem jungen und kreativen
Verstand, ja, für den einzigen mit entsprechender Phantasie hielte. Severud
lehnte vorerst ab und empfahl dem *Endless House* nachstehende Ingenieure:
Wolfgang Zerna, Deutschland; Felix Candela, Mexiko; sowie Mario George
Salvadori und Hans Heinrich Bleich von der Columbia University und Eduardo
Torroja, Spanien. In dieser Aufzählung an Innovations-Weltmeistern fehlt
eigentlich nur Pier Luigi Nervi, Italien. Dem Protokoll lässt sich aber ent-
nehmen, dass Kiesler den genannten Personen gegenüber negativ eingestellt
war – aus welchen Gründen auch immer. Für sein *Endless House* wollte er
Severud, und keinen anderen! Und trotz anfänglicher Ablehnung sollte er
dessen Mitwirken letztendlich auch bekommen.

Die Arbeit an den Ingenieursplänen für das *Endless House* lässt sich

archives of the Frederick Kiesler Foundation. On May 21, 1959 Kiesler sent a
blueprint and on July 8, 1959 three *prints* of the *Endless House* to Severud.[3]
The plans he sent formed the basis for a plan dated September 14, 1959
from the Severud-Elstad-Krueger office. (Fig. 1) This decidedly precise plan contains both specifications for the construction and reinforcement of the
shell structure and detailed information on the execution in shotcrete.[4] Foundation, access and pool basin are depicted in a quite pragmatic way.
This is also true of the bottom side of the shell construction, conceived as a
slab on to which the actual shell was supposed to have been *mounted* (Fig. 2).

The present plan becomes all the more interesting since here a
corrugated shell was suggested on the inside, that is, something that can be
found again, formally, in the *Shrine of the Book*, but in this regularity it
would have given the *Endless House* a very special and, above all, *completely
different* surface character (Fig. 3). These ribs in turn would have had to
have been negatively formed and thus reinforced accordingly. Given the already
very ambitious geometry, this would have resulted in excessive expense
and effort. However, there could have also been constructive reasons for the
horizontal tensile reinforcement depicted in the plan being regarded as
necessary and only possible in this form.

anhand zweier Briefe und eines Plans rekonstruieren, welche sich im Archiv
der Friedrich Kiesler Stiftung erhalten haben. Am 21. Mai 1959 schickte
Kiesler einen *Blueprint* und am 8. Juli 1959 drei *Prints* des *Endless House* an
Severud.[3] Die übermittelten Pläne bildeten die Grundlage für einen
mit 14. September 1959 datierten Plan aus dem Büro Severud-Elstad-Krueger.
(Abb. 1) Dieser ausgesprochen präzise Plan enthält sowohl Angaben
zu Schalung und Bewehrung als auch detaillierte Hinweise zur Ausführung in
Spritzbeton.[4] Fundierung, Zugang und Poolbecken sind recht pragmatisch
dargestellt; ebenso die als Platte gedachte Schalenunterseite, auf die die
eigentliche Schale dann hätte „aufgesetzt" werden sollen. (Abb. 2) Dabei wird
der vorliegende Plan umso interessanter, als hier eine auf der Innenseite
„corrugated", also gewellte oder gerippte Schale vorgeschlagen wird; also
etwas, das sich formal beim *Shrine of the Book* wiederfindet, aber in dieser
Regelmäßigkeit dem Innenraum des *Endless House* doch eine ganz eigene
und vor allem *ganz andere* Oberflächencharakteristik gegeben hätte. (Abb. 3)
Diese Rippen hätten wiederum negativ geschalt und entsprechend bewehrt
werden müssen, was hinsichtlich der ohnehin sehr ambitionierten Geometrie
wohl einem unverhältnismäßig hohen Aufwand gleichgekommen wäre.
Es könnte aber auch konstruktive Gründe gehabt haben, dass man die im Plan

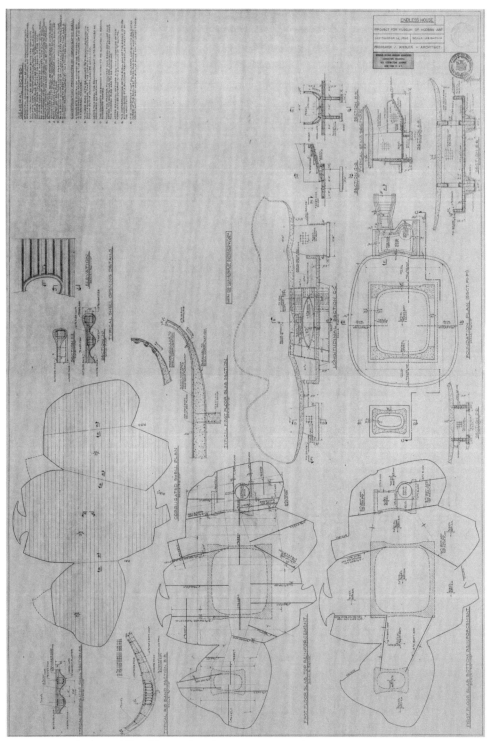

1—Severud-Elstad-Krueger Associates, execution plan for the *Endless House*, Sept. 1959

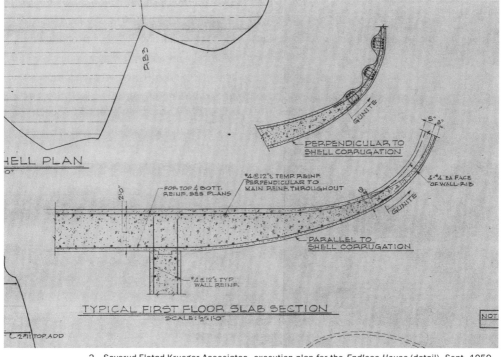

2—Severud-Elstad-Krueger Associates, execution plan for the *Endless House* (detail), Sept. 1959

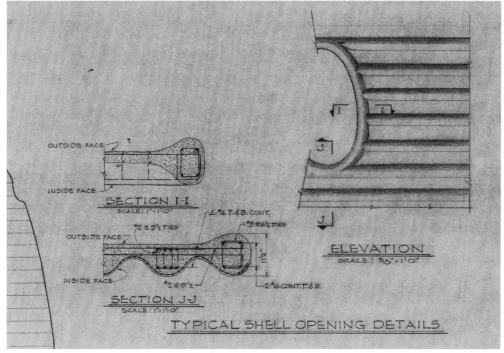

3—Severud-Elstad-Krueger Associates, execution plan for the *Endless House* (detail), Sept. 1959

Also informative here is the description of the *Construction procedure of corrugated shell*: on the bottom side of the shell, a form-giving wooden scaffold was supposed to have fixated the rib furring so that the undulating contour and reinforcement would have been implemented as described. This would have been followed by several rounds of shotcrete ('Gunite (wet-mix)' being applied as the successor of the 'Shotcrete (dry-mix)') procedure. After hardening and striking, a coat was to be applied to cover the inside. In short: the renowned office of Fred Severud saw Kiesler's vision as feasible in terms of construction and structural engineering!

As we know, Frederick Kiesler's *Endless House* was not implemented for the Museum of Modern Art in New York. Nevertheless, Severud-Elstadt-Krueger Associates identified with the project. In April 1963, Hannskarl Bandel used a photograph of the *Endless House* model as an illustration for an article entitled "The shell as backbone", which he had published in *Architectural & Engineering News*[5]—we do not know whether he was sad or relieved that it was never realized.

dargestellte horizontale Zugbewehrung für notwendig erachtete und nur in dieser Form für machbar hielt.

Aufschlussreich ist zudem die Beschreibung der „Construction procedure of corrugated shell": Über der Schalenunterseite hätte ein formgebendes Holzgerüst die Rippenlattung in der Art fixieren sollen, dass die gewellte Kontur und Bewehrung wie dargestellt umgesetzt werden könnte. Dem wären mehrere Beton-Spritzdurchgänge gefolgt (*Gunite* (*wet-mix*) schon als Nachfolger des *Shotcrete* (*dry-mix*)-Verfahrens). Nach dem Aushärten und Ausschalen sollte dann noch eine innere Deckschicht folgen. Kurz: Das renommierte Büro um Fred Severud hielt Kieslers Vision für konstruktiv und verfahrenstechnisch machbar!

Friedrich Kieslers *Endless House* für das Museum of Modern Art in New York wurde bekanntlich nicht umgesetzt. Trotzdem identifizierte man sich bei Severud-Elstadt-Krueger-Associates mit dem Projekt. So verwendet Hannskarl Bandel im April 1963 eine Aufnahme des *Endless House*-Modells zur Illustration eines Artikels mit dem Titel „The Shell as Backbone", den er in den *Architectural & Engineering News* publizierte[5] – ob wegen der Nichtrealisierung wehmütig oder erleichtert, ist uns jedoch nicht überliefert.

1   ÖFLKS, LET 5211/0, letter from
Kiesler & Bartos to Fred Severud
(Severud, Elstad & Krueger,
Engineers) of Feb. 1958; ÖFLKS,
LET 5212/0, Kiesler & Bartos
to Paul Rongved (Strobel &
Rongved, Engineers) of Feb. 7,
1958. On "Shrine of the Book" cf.
Jill Meißner, "Kiesler and Bartos.
The Shrine of the Book", in ed.
Peter Bogner, Kiesler and Bartos,
The Shrine of the Book, Vienna
2015, 6–34.

2   ÖFLKS, TXT 3815/0. The introductory quote was taken from the
minutes: "Mr. Kiesler & Mr.
Severud spoke of the difficulty of
finding engineers with creative
spirit. (")They're all cast from the
same standard mold to turn out
standard projects.(") (")What we
need in our profession("), said
Mr. Severud, (")are musicians!(")
(")On this project, (") continued
Mr. Severud, (")The man has to
live with it!(").

3   ÖFLKS, LET 503/0, letter from
Kiesler to Fred Severud from May
21, 1959; ÖFLKS, LET 3164/0,
letter from Kiesler to Fred
Severud from July 8, 1959.

4   ÖFLKS, PLN 302/0.

5   Hannscarl Bandel, "The shell as
backbone", in *Architectural &
Engineering NEWS*, April 1963;
reprint from the archives of
Severud Associates: "By carrying
this principle (elliptic and
parabolical shells) to its logical
and interested finale, we come to
the endless house of Frederick
Kiesler." (non-paginated) Other
than this clipping, the archives of
Severud Associates, the successor firm that still exists today,
contains no material on Kiesler's
Endless House project. Information from Brian A. Falconer,
Principal Severud Associates
Consulting Engineers, PC, March
and April 2015.

1   ÖFLKS, LET 5211/0, Brief von
Kiesler und Bartos an Fred
Severud (Severud, Elstad &
Krueger, Engineers) vom
4. Februar 1958; ÖFLKS, LET
5212/0, Kiesler & Bartos an Paul
Rongved (Strobel & Rongved,
Engeineers) vom 7. Februar 1958.
Zum „Shrine of The Book" vgl.:
Jill Meißner, „Kiesler and Bartos.
The Shrine of The Book", in
*Kiesler and Bartos, The Shrine of
the Book*, hg. v. Peter Bogner,
Wien 2015, 6–34.

2   ÖFLKS, TXT 3815/0. Dem
Protokoll ist das einleitende
Zitat entnommen: „Mr. Kiesler &
Mr. Severud spoke of the
difficulty of finding engineers
with creative spirit. ["]They're all
cast from the same standard
mold to turn out standard
projects.["] ["]What we need in
our profession["], said
Mr. Severud, ["]are musicians!["]
["]On this project,["] continued
Mr. Severud, ["]The man has to
live with it!["].

3   ÖFLKS, LET 503/0, Brief von
Kiesler an Fred Severud vom
21. Mai 1959; ÖFLKS, LET
3164/0, Brief von Kiesler an Fred
Severud vom 8. Juli 1959.

4   ÖFLKS, PLN 302/0.

5   Hannscarl Bandel, „The shell as
backbone", in *Architectural &
Engineering NEWS*, April 1963;
Reprint aus dem Archiv Severud
Associates; „By carrying this
principal [elliptic parabolical
shells] to its logical and inter-
rested finale, we come to the
endless house of Frederick
Kiesler". [o.S.]. Bis auf dieses
Clipping haben sich im Archiv von
Severud Associates, der heute
noch existierenden Nachfolge-
firma, keine Materialien zu
Kieslers *Endless House* Projekt
erhalten. Auskunft von Brian A.
Falconer, Principal Severud
Associates Consulting Engine ers,
PC, März und April 2015.

Endless Variants and Kiesler's *Endless House*

Arne Hofmann and Clemens Preisinger

Unendliche Varianten und Kieslers *Endless House*

In 2009, when Florian Medicus invited us for the first time to participate in a seminar on the subject of the *Endless House*, we happily accepted. At this time, the research project *Algorithmic Generation of Complex Beam Frame Constructions* had reached a critical stage. The computer-based tools that had been developed in the course of the research project worked for the most part, but what was missing was a practical trial. Putting them to the test as part of a course offered a welcome opportunity.

Under the guidance of Klaus Bollinger, we had been studying the implementation of a computer-based design setting for beam constructions consisting of line-like elements since 2008. The goal of the project was to come up with alternatives to the regular and often monotonous forms that prevailed in the design of timber-frame constructions. These novel geometries were, however, not to be arbitrary and based purely on artistic intuition, but, rather, should take into account the demands of external physical givens. We were able to achieve this by combining the parametric generation of geometries, static computation programs and effective optimization procedures in a super-ordinate chain of digital processes.

The basic idea underlying the parametric generation of geometries is that it allows for the essence of an architectural form to be captured by the way the

Im Jahr 2009, als Florian Medicus uns zum ersten Mal fragte, ob wir Interesse hätten, an einem Seminar zum Thema *Endless House* mitzuwirken, willigten wir freudig ein. Das Forschungsprojekt *Algorithmische Generierung Komplexer Stabtragwerke* war zu diesem Zeitpunkt in einem entscheidenden Stadium angelangt: Die im Zuge des Forschungsvorhabens entstandenen, computer-basierten Werkzeuge funktionierten großteils – was fehlte war ihre Erprobung im Praxistest. Der Einsatz im Rahmen einer Lehrveranstaltung stellte dafür eine willkommene Gelegenheit dar.

Unter der Leitung von Klaus Bollinger hatten wir seit 2008 an der Umsetzung einer computerbasierten Entwurfsumgebung für Tragwerke aus linienhaften Elementen geforscht. Das Ziel des Projekts bestand darin, Alternativen zu den beim Entwurf von Fachwerkstrukturen vorherrschenden, regulären und oftmals monotonen Formen aufzuzeigen. Diese neuartigen Geometrien sollten allerdings nicht willkürlich sein und rein auf künstlerischer Intuition basieren, sondern Anforderungen aus äußeren physikalischen Gegebenheiten berücksichtigen. Dies wurde durch die Verbindung parametrischer Geometrieerzeugung, statischer Berechnungsprogramme und leistungsfähiger Optimierungsverfahren in einer übergeordneten digitalen Prozesskette erreicht.

algorithm is formulated. A certain geometry thus becomes the final result of a sequence of computer commands which are controlled by an arbitrary number of input values—the parameters. The creative activity is no longer the creation of a concrete artifact but the formulation of a general instruction for generation.

In contrast to the direct, manual definition of geometry in conventional computer-aided graphic systems (CAD), an automatic procedure offers the possibility to create variants of a design quickly and without great effort. This enables the study of alternatives and backs decision-making at the early stage of design. As part of the research project, the geometry parametrization takes place by means of a user-defined series of connected, predefined program units.

The algorithmic definition of geometry allows for the application of optimization algorithms. The input values of a geometry parametrization can be interpreted as coordinates in an abstract design space. On the basis of user-defined evaluation criteria—which are often seen as target functions—such a space can be searched for optimum solutions. In this specific research project, the load-bearing properties of the structure are used as an evaluation parameter. This can be determined quickly, simply and reliably. For the

Die grundlegende Idee hinter parametrischer Geometriegenerierung liegt darin, dass sich die Essenz einer architektonischen Form durch die Formulierung eines Algorithmus fassen lässt. Eine bestimmte Geometrie wird so zum Endresultat einer Abfolge von Computerbefehlen, welche durch eine beliebige Anzahl von Eingabewerten – den Parametern – kontrolliert wird. Die schöpferische Tätigkeit liegt demnach nicht mehr in der Erstellung eines konkreten Artefakts, sondern in der Formulierung einer allgemeinen Generierungsanleitung.

Im Gegensatz zur direkten, manuellen Definition von Geometrie in herkömmlichen computerunterstützten Grafiksystemen (CAD), bietet eine automatisierte Vorgehensweise die Möglichkeit, schnell und ohne großen Aufwand Varianten eines Entwurfs zu erzeugen. Dies erleichtert das Studium von Alternativen und unterstützt die Entscheidungsfindung im frühen Entwurfsstadium. Im Rahmen des Forschungsprojekts erfolgte die Geometrieparametrisierung durch das benutzerdefinierte Hintereinander-schalten vorgefertigter Programmeinheiten.

Mit der algorithmischen Definition von Geometrie wird diese zugänglich für die Anwendung von Optimierungsalgorithmen. Die Eingabewerte einer Geometrieparametrisierung lassen sich als Koordinaten in einen abstrakten

computer-aided computation of the response of constructions, the finite
element method now exists, a tested procedure that makes it possible to treat
any complex structure. This method is based on the conceptual break-down
of a beam frame construction into small sections that can be easily calculated.
The response of the entire structure under external influences is finally
obtained from the total of the contributions of the individual parts that were
observed before. The greatest deformation or material wear under given
strain can serve as the evaluation criterion for the response of a structure in
comparison to others.

Genetic algorithms proved to be effective in the search for optimal parameter values for tasks related to optimizing structure. They copy the process
of natural evolution in a simplified way and were developed while conducting
research on artificial intelligence.[1] A pre-defined program library containing
various variants of genetic algorithms was used in the research project.

Figure 1 illustrates the functional units of the digital process chain developed in the research project for the static optimization of parametric
defined structures. This combines techniques from the realms of architecture
and engineering and therefore represents a multi-disciplinary approach
to the generation of forms.

Entwurfsraum interpretieren. Auf der Basis von benutzerdefinierten Bewer-
tungskriterien – diese werden auch oft als Zielfunktionen bezeichnet –
kann ein solcher Raum nach optimalen Lösungen durchsucht werden. Im
gegenständlichen Forschungsprojekt wurde das Tragverhalten der
Struktur als Bewertungsmerkmal verwendet. Dieses lässt sich schnell, einfach und zuverlässig bestimmen: Für die computerunterstützte Berechnung
des Verhaltens von Bauwerken steht mit der Finite Elemente Methode
ein erprobtes Verfahren zur Verfügung, welches die Behandlung beliebig komplexer Strukturen ermöglicht. Die Grundlage dieser Methode bildet die
gedankliche Zerteilung eines Tragwerks in kleine, einfach zu berechnende
Abschnitte. Das Verhalten der Gesamtstruktur unter äußeren Einflüssen
erhält man anschließend aus den aufsummierten Beiträgen der zuvor betrach-
teten Einzelteile. Als Bewertungskriterium für das Verhalten einer Struktur
im Vergleich zu einer anderen kann etwa die größte Verformung oder Material-
beanspruchung unter gegebenen Lasten dienen.

Bei der Suche nach optimalen Parameterwerten für Strukturoptimierungs-
aufgaben haben sich genetische Algorithmen als effektiv erwiesen. Diese
bilden den Prozess der natürlichen Evolution in vereinfachter Form nach und
wurden im Kontext der Erforschung künstlicher Intelligenz entwickelt.[1] Im

Figure 2 shows an example of a computer-generated load-bearing structure. It is a study that was made for an architectural competition.[2] The task was to generate an irregular support geometry under an observation deck. Dimensions and location of the deck, as well as areas on the ground where the foundation was to be placed, were specified in advance. The support geometry was created in two steps: Pairs of input parameters first defined the endpoints of the supports in the deck area and on ground level. In the second step, structural parts that fell below the predefined smallest, reciprocal distance were united in the central point of the shortest connecting line. As figure 2 shows, this simple rule of generation, when applied repeatedly to the already connected parts, resulted in a sponge-like, cellular structure. The greatest deformation under load capacity and dead load served as criterion for assessing static efficiency. The search for an optimal load-bearing geometry comprised the static calculation of several ten thousands of variants of geometry and produced the result depicted in figure 2. The structure is not a pure load-bearing construction, it also creates free spaces and levels that give the user possibilities to enter the space. In the generating process, a compromise was made between the load-bearing structure, the spaces that open up between the structure, and the

Rahmen des Forschungsprojekts kam eine vorgefertigte Programmbibliothek, die unterschiedliche Varianten genetischer Algorithmen beinhaltete, zum Einsatz.

Abbildung 1 veranschaulicht die Funktionseinheiten der im Forschungsprojekt entwickelten, digitalen Prozesskette zur statischen Optimierung parametrisch definierter Strukturen. Diese verbindet Techniken aus den Bereichen Architektur und Ingenieurwesen und stellt somit einen multidisziplinären Ansatz zur Formgenerierung dar.

Ein Beispiel für eine computergenerierte Tragstruktur zeigt Abbildung 2. Es handelt sich dabei um eine Studie für einen Architekturwettbewerb.[2] Die Aufgabe bestand darin, eine irreguläre Stützengeometrie unter einer Aussichtsplattform zu generieren. Abmessungen und Lage der Plattform sowie Bereiche am Boden, wo Fundamente platziert werden durften, waren vordefiniert. Die Erzeugung der Stützengeometrie erfolgte in zwei Schritten: Paare von Eingabeparametern legten zunächst die Endpunkte der Stützen im Bereich der Plattform und auf Bodenniveau fest. Im zweiten Schritt wurden Strukturteile, die einen vordefinierten kleinsten, gegenseitigen Abstand unterschritten, im Mittelpunkt der kürzesten Verbindungslinie vereint. Wie Abbildung 2 zeigt, führte diese einfache Erzeugungsregel bei wiederholter

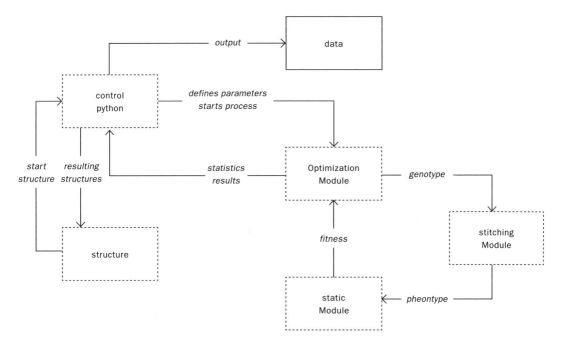

1—Digital process chain for static optimization of parametrically defined structures.

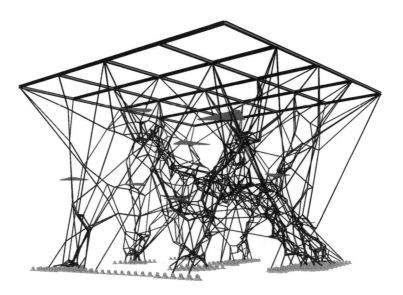

2—Irregular, computer-generated, computer-generated load-bearing structure for an
   observation deck.

functional marginal parameters below the information pavilion. The final result is not a clear answer to a clear question but, rather, one that allows for many different interpretations and perceptions.

As part of the seminar "Advanced Structural Design B", the participants of the course that was held at the University of Applied Arts in the 2010 summer semester focused on Kiesler's *Endless House*. The goal was to prove the technical feasibility of Kiesler's ideas. Moreover, a modern re-interpretation of his *Endless House* was supposed to be obtained with the help of modern digital design tools.

Using Kiesler's models and plans, the students first created a three-dimensional surface model. As figure 3 shows, two strategies were compared while breaking up the planar structure into beams. Partial image (a) shows the surfaces broken down into a relatively regular network consisting of triangles. This type of rod generation fails to take into account external givens such as loads and support point. The division of surface is solely based on its intrinsic properties: a finer division into shorter rod elements takes place where smaller curvature radiuses appear on the surface so as to keep the deviation between initial geometry and network small.

The second variant of beam frame generation was based on the combination

Anwendung auf die schon verbundenen Teile zu einer schwammartigen, zellenhaften Struktur. Als Bewertungskriterium der statischen Effizienz diente die größte Verformung der Plattform unter Nutzlast und Eigengewicht.
Die Suche nach einer optimalen Tragwerksgeometrie umfasste die statische Berechnung mehrerer zehntausend Geometrievarianten und führte zu dem dargestellten Resultat. Die Struktur ist nicht reines Tragwerk, sondern erzeugt gleichzeitig Freiräume und Ebenen, die dem Nutzer Möglichkeiten eröffnen, den Raum zu begehen. Im Generierungsprozess findet eine Verhandlung zwischen der Struktur als Tragwerk, zwischen den Räumen, die sich zwischen der Struktur ergeben und den funktionalen Randparametern unterhalb des Infopavillons statt. Das Ergebnis ist nicht die eindeutige Antwort auf eine eindeutige Frage, sondern lässt viele verschiedene Interpretationen und Wahrnehmungen zu.

Im Rahmen des Seminars *Tragkonstruktionen 3* widmeten sich an der Universität für angewandte Kunst im Sommersemester 2010 die Teilnehmer und Teilnehmerinnen dem Studium von Kieslers *Endless House*. Das Ziel bestand darin, die technische Machbarkeit der kieslerschen Ideen nachzuweisen. Darüber hinaus sollte mit modernen, digitalen Entwurfswerkzeugen eine Neuinterpretation seines *Endless House* erreicht werden.

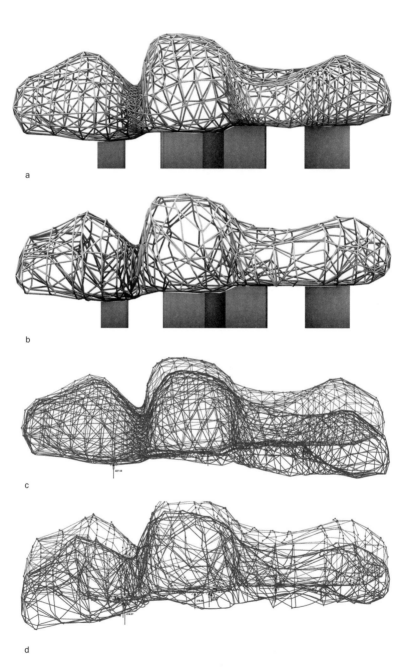

a

b

c

d

3—Variants of reinterpreting Kiesler's *Endless House* as a beam structure: a) regular
geometry; b) irregular load-bearing structure; the details in images c) and d) show
the distorted load-bearing structures under their own weight and load capacity for the
structures depicted in the details a) and b). To visualize these deformations these
structures were enlarged about 300 times.[3]

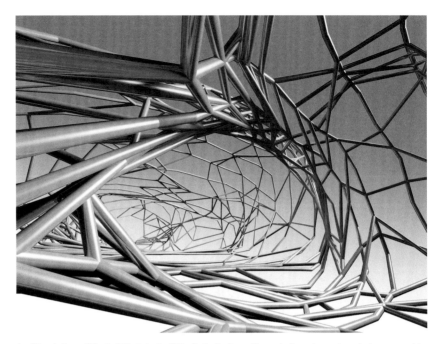

4—Dissolution of the building shell of Kiesler's *Endless House* in line elements using a parametric
definition of geometry together with static optimization.

Unter Zuhilfenahme von Kieslers Modellen und Plänen erstellten die
Studierenden zunächst ein dreidimensionales Flächenmodell. Wie Abbildung 3
zeigt, wurden bei der Auflösung der flächenhaften Struktur in Stäbe zwei
Strategien verglichen. Teilbild (a) zeigt die Zerlegung der Flächen in ein relativ
regelmäßiges, aus Dreiecken aufgebautes Netz. Diese Art der Stab-
generierung berücksichtigt die äußeren Gegebenheiten wie Lasten und
Auflagerpunkt nicht. Die Aufteilung der Fläche orientiert sich ausschließlich an
deren intrinsischen Eigenschaften: Eine feinere Teilung in kürzere Stabele-
mente erfolgt dort, wo in der Fläche kleine Krümmungsradien auftreten, um
dadurch die Abweichung zwischen Ausgangsgeometrie und Netz klein zu halten.
    Die zweite Variante der Stabwerkserzeugung basierte auf der Verbindung
parametrisierter Geometrie und statischer Optimierung. Da seitens der
Studierenden schon erhebliches Vorwissen über digitales, parametrisches
Entwerfen vorhanden war, bereitete ihnen die Benutzung der von uns
bereitgestellten Generierungswerkzeuge keine großen Schwierigkeiten. Die als
Flächenmodell vorliegende Grundform teilten sie in Querrichtung durch
annähernd parallele Ebenen. Die dabei entstehenden, ringförmigen Schnitte
dienten als Grundlage der Geometrieparametrisierung. Jeweils ein Parameter
definierte eine Position auf einem der vordefinierten Ringe. Somit ergab sich

of parametric geometry and static optimization. Since the students
already had considerable preliminary knowledge of digital, parametric
design, they did not find it very difficult to use the generation tools that we
provided them with. The basic form serving as a surface model was
divided in transversal movement by means of almost parallel levels. The
resulting ring-shaped cuts served as the basis for geometric parametrization. One parameter in each case defined a position on one of the
predefined rings. This resulted in a beam running longitudinally
from a list of parameters. Its length corresponded to the number of cuts.
The structure depicted in figure 3, partial image (b) resulted from
about 300 freely selectable input parameters. External influences were taken
into account by defining significant loads and bearing conditions. The
latter were derived from the building bases arranged by Kiesler. Given the
large number of free parameters, it was difficult but, ultimately, possible to optimize the load-bearing structure. Partial images (b) and (d) in
figure 3 depict the resulting geometry as well as the related deformation
image. The optimized beam frame structure, with a lower construction
weight, shows an almost equally great deformation as the structure created
by means of surface triangulation.

ein in Längsrichtung verlaufender Stabzug aus einer Liste von Parametern,
deren Länge der Anzahl der Schnitte entsprach. Die in Abbildung 3, Teilbild (b)
dargestellte Struktur resultierte aus etwa 300 frei wählbaren Eingangs-
parametern. Die Berücksichtigung äußerer Einflüsse erfolgte durch die Definition der maßgebenden Lasten und Lagerungsbedingungen. Letztere
ergaben sich aus den von Kiesler angeordneten Gebäudesockeln. Aufgrund
der großen Anzahl von freien Parametern gestaltete sich die Optimierung des Tragwerks langwierig aber bewältigbar. Die Teilbilder (b) und (d) in
Abbildung 3 veranschaulichen die resultierende Geometrie sowie das
zugehörige Verformungsbild. Das optimierte Stabtragwerk weist bei geringerem
Konstruktionsgewicht eine etwa gleich große, maximale Verformung auf,
wie die mittels Flächentriangulierung erzeugte Struktur.

Abbildung 4 zeigt eine Innenansicht des optimierten Tragwerks. Eine
Konzentration von Linienelementen ergibt sich dort, wo diese auf
Grund äußerer Gegebenheiten ihre größte Wirksamkeit entfalten. Wegen der
Vielzahl möglicher Varianten stellt die erzeugte Struktur mit großer
Wahrscheinlichkeit nicht das in statischer Hinsicht absolute Optimum dar. Es
zeigt sich allerdings, dass die Kombination parametrisierter Geometrie-
erzeugung und moderner Optimierungsalgorithmen neue Wege im Bereich des

Figure 4 shows an inner view of the optimized load-bearing structure. There is a concentration of linear elements where these are able to deploy greatest efficiency as a result of outer factors. Given the many possible variants, the generated structure is in all likelihood not the absolute optimal one in static terms. However, it became clear that the combination of parametric geometry generation and modern optimization algorithms open up new vistas in architectural design. At the same time, this procedure allowed for parallels to be drawn with the theories that Kiesler formulated in his Correalist Manifesto. Kiesler did not see buildings as something static but, rather, as a process that mediates between various general conditions: "each building and designed artifact […] in the correalist design process [is] integrated in a network of actors, functions and translations."[3]

According to Kiesler, a designed object engages in an exchange with the forces of its surroundings. As a result of the described methodology, this interaction between object and outside world becomes possible in the design process. We would like to assume that this deductive approach of letting structures grow virtually would have been entirely in keeping with Kiesler's intentions.

architektonischen Entwurfs eröffnet. Gleichzeitig können in dieser Vorgehensweise Parallelen zu den von Kiesler in seinem *Correalistischen Manifest* formulierten Theorien gezogen werden. Kiesler hat Gebäude nicht statisch betrachtet, sondern immer als Prozess, der zwischen verschiedenen Rahmenbedingungen vermittelt, gesehen: „Jedes Bauwerk und entworfene Artefakt […] im correalistischen Entwurfsprozess [ist] eingewoben in ein Netz von Akteuren, Funktionen und Übersetzungen."[3]

Nach Kiesler steht ein Entwurfsobjekt im Austausch mit den Kräften seiner Umwelt. Durch die beschriebene Methodik wird diese Interaktion zwischen Objekt und Außenwelt im Entwurfsprozess möglich. Wir möchten gerne davon ausgehen, dass diese deduktive Vorgehensweise, Strukturen virtuell wachsen zu lassen, ganz in Kieslers Sinn gewesen wäre.

1   D. E. Goldberg, Genetic Algo-
    rithms in Search, Optimization
    and Machine Learning, Recent
    trends, 1st edition (Boston, MA,
    USA: Addison-Wesley Longman
    Publishing Co., Inc., 1989).
2   Michael Wallraff Vertikaler
    öffentlicher Raum / Vertical
    Public Space MAK—
    Österreichisches Museum für
    angewandte Kunst /
    Gegenwartskunst, Vienna.
3   Österreichische Friedrich und
    Lilian Kiesler-Privatstiftung, *From
    Chicken Wire to Wire Frame
    Kiesler's Endless House*, catalog
    for the exhibition June 11 –
    Sept. 17, 2010, curated by Dieter
    Bogner, 2010.

1   D. E. Goldberg, „Optimization
    and Machine Learning, Recent
    trends", 1st edition (Boston, MA,
    USA: Addison-Wesley Longman
    Publishing Co., Inc., 1989).
2   *Michael Wallraff Vertical Public
    Space*, MAK – Österreichisches
    Museum für angewandte Kunst /
    Gegenwartskunst, Wien.
3   Österreichische Friedrich und
    Lilian Kiesler-Privatstiftung, *From
    Chicken Wire to Wire Frame
    Kiesler's Endless House*, Katalog
    zur Ausstellung 11. Juni – 17.
    September 2010, kuratiert von
    Dieter Bogner, 2010.

IoA Student Works
on the *Endless House* (2010)
and the *Sisler House* (2014)

Florian Medicus

IoA Studentenarbeiten
zum *Endless House* (2010)
und *Sisler House* (2014)

"Kiesler could not bear endings."
—Helen Borsick, *Fame Is Endless*[1]

One of the central questions regarding the *Endless House* is: did Kiesler really want to build the house? We know that around 1959 he was serious about it— so serious that he had detail and engineering plans drawn up (see, for instance, Fig. 1 on page 262). But after so many years of such intense work, did he really want to know it in such detail or would he have already then preferred to have endlessly "continued digging in the inside of this cave?" [*creuser à l'interieur de cette caverne*], as Beatriz Colomina surmised[2]. In a sense, each solid building represents a compromise, the fruition of an intention and perhaps even a small death of dreams. And especially with respect to the *Endless House*, it must unfortunately remain undecided whether realization would have meant triumph or failure—while the triumph of its non-realization is certainly undisputed today!

However, in Nietzsche's *Gay Science*, I did find a sentence on "knowing to find the end," which reads as follows: "Masters of the first rank are recognized by the fact that in matters great and small they know how to find an end perfectly, be it the end of a melody or a thought; of a tragedy's fifth act or an

„Kiesler could not bear endings."
—Helen Borsick, *Fame Is Endless*[1]

Eine der zentralen Fragen im Bezug auf das *Endless House* lautet wohl: Wollte Kiesler das Haus wirklich bauen? Wir wissen, dass er es um 1959 ernst damit meinte; so ernst, dass er Detail- und Ingenieurpläne anfertigen ließ (siehe etwa Abb. 1 auf Seite 262). Aber wollte er es nach den vielen Jahren *endloser* Beschäftigung wirklich so genau wissen oder wäre es ihm schon damals lieber gewesen, „im Inneren dieser Höhle weiterzugraben" [creuser à l'interieur de cette caverne], wie Beatriz Colomina vermutete.[2] Jeder Bau stellt in gewisser Weise eine Vollendung der Absicht dar; und im Bezug auf das *Endless House* müssen wir leider unentschieden bleiben in der Frage, ob die Realisierung Triumph oder Versagen bedeutet hätte, wohingegen der Triumph seiner Nicht-Realisierung heute unbestritten ist!

In Nietzsches „Fröhlicher Wissenschaft" fand ich allerdings einen Absatz über „das Ende zu finden wissen", in dem es heißt: „Die Meister des ersten Ranges geben sich dadurch zu erkennen, dass sie, im Großen wie im Kleinen, auf eine vollkommene Weise das Ende zu finden wissen, sei es das Ende einer Melodie oder eines Gedankens, sei es der fünfte Akt einer Tragödie oder

act of state."[3] Here the material evidence, even a sophisticated implementation would have only been a possible end. But such an end would also be the premature end of a myth that has been well cultivated to this day. So why bring to an end something that was perhaps not meant to end? At the same time, I am convinced (unlike Philip Johnson, by the way!) that Kiesler would have been more than delighted to see and walk through his *Endless House*! And it is not just for this reason that, in the seminars described here, we focused less on the difficult question of the architect's intentions and more on the following one: how could we keep as much as possible of Kiesler and at the same time plan, calculate and ultimately build in the most contemporary way possible?

The seminar series "Unbuildable?!" (as part of the course "Advanced Structural Design") at the Institute for Architecture of the University of Applied Arts in Vienna is asking itself questions from the perspective of implementation, based on the visionary, unbuilt projects of the 20th century: could it have been built differently at that time? And how could it be planned, calculated, optimized and realized efficiently today with the technologies at our disposal? Following Tatlin, Melnikov, Lissitzky, Mies, Wachsmann, Domenig/ Huth and Isozaki, Frederick Kiesler was addressed twice: the *Endless*

Staats-Aktion."[3] Und das Ende selbst eines *endlosen* Architekturprojekts führt im Idealfall in dessen Realisierung und den materiellen Nachweis aller nur möglichen Obsessionen! Und obwohl Architekten auch die Angst vor der räumlichen Prüfung gut kennen, bin ich mir (anders als Philip Johnson übrigens) sicher, Kiesler hätte sein *Endless House* nur allzu gern gesehen und selbst durchschritten!

Die Seminar-Reihe *Unbuildable?!* (Teil des Kurses „Advanced Structural Design") am Institut für Architektur der Universität für angewandte Kunst in Wien stellt sich anhand von visionären, ungebauten Projekten des 20. Jahrhunderts aus Sicht der Umsetzung die Fragen: Hätte es damals gebaut werden können? Und könnte es heute, mit den uns zur Verfügung stehenden Technologien, effizient geplant, berechnet und realisiert werden? Nach Tatlin, Melnikov, Lissitzky, Mies, Wachsmann, Domenig/Huth und Isozaki wurde Friedrich Kiesler gleich zweimal behandelt: 2010 das *Endless House* und 2014 die spätere Fassung, das *House for Mary Sisler (Sisler House)*.

Diese Seminare starten mit einer Research-Phase, in der der Architekt, das Projekt selbst, die zeitlichen (materiellen bzw. konstruktiven) Umstände der Zeit, gegebenenfalls auch vergleichbare Strömungen und Ansätze

House in 2010, and in the later version, the House for Mary Sisler (*Sisler House*) in 2014.

These seminars kick off with an extensive research phase in which the architect, the project itself and the given (intellectual as well as material and/or constructive) circumstances of its evolution are studied, along with comparable movements and approaches where relevant. Following this, the group elaborate precise 3D models that are then geometrically built and optimized in terms of construction. Here *Karamba* (see text by Hofmann & Preisinger, pp. 268), a software developed together with our institute, has proved to be very flexible and powerful. Given the many exciting results we obtained, we would also like to continue using it to familiarize our students with the knowledge of significant projects and the decisive role of the interplay of architects and engineers while acquainting them with the most recent possibilities and methods of realization.

1   Helen Borsick, *Fame Is Endless*, Plain Dealer, Cleveland, Ohio, Feb. 5 1967. (Übersetzt aus dem Englischen.)

2   Beatriz Colomina, "La Space House et la psyché de la con-struction", in *Frederick Kiesler. Artiste-Architecte* (Centre Georges Pompidou: 1996), 71.

3   Friedrich Nietzsche, "The Gay Science", in *Cambridge Texts in The History of Philosophy* (Cambridge: 2001), 160.

untersucht werden. Im Anschluss daran erarbeiten Gruppen präzise 3D-Modelle, die dann geometrisch aufgebaut und konstruktiv optimiert werden. Hierbei hat sich die an unserem Institut mitentwickelte Software *Karamba* (siehe Text von Hofmann & Preisinger, S. 268 ff) als sehr flexibel und leistungs-stark erwiesen. Ganz generell wollen wir aufgrund der vielen spannenden Ergebnisse weiterhin davon ausgehen, dass wir so den Studierenden zum einen die Kenntnis signifikanter Projekte und zum anderen die aktuellsten Mög-lichkeiten und Methoden der Realisierung näherbringen können.

1   Helen Borsick, „Fame Is Endless", *Plain Dealer*, Cleveland, Ohio, Feb. 5, 1967.

2   Beatriz Colomina, „La Space House et la psyché de la construction", in *Frederick Kiesler. Artiste-Architecte* (Centre Georges Pompidou, 1996), 71.

3   Friedrich Nietzsche, „Die fröhliche Wissenschaft" (Frankfurt am Main und Leipzig: Insel Verlag, 2000), 175.

Advanced Structural Design B (2010),

Institute of Architecture, University of Applied Arts Vienna

Endless House

Students
Thomas Milly
Martin Kleindienst
Yi-Chen Lu
Martina Lesjak
Anna Kokowska
Dominik Strzelec
Sille Pihlak
Christoph Pehnelt
Oliver Lößer
Florian Fend
Josip Bajcer
Anutorn Polphong
Daniela Kröhnert
Galo Moncayo
Matthew Tam
Dena Saffarian

Tutors
Klaus Bollinger
Wilfried Braumüller
Florian Medicus
Clemens Preisinger

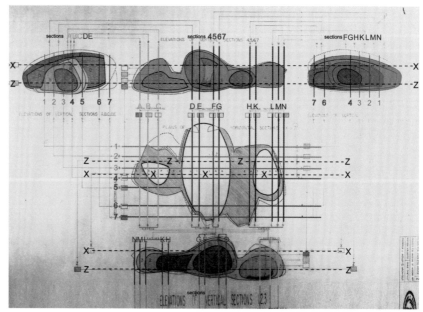

1—Geometric reconstruction based on original plans

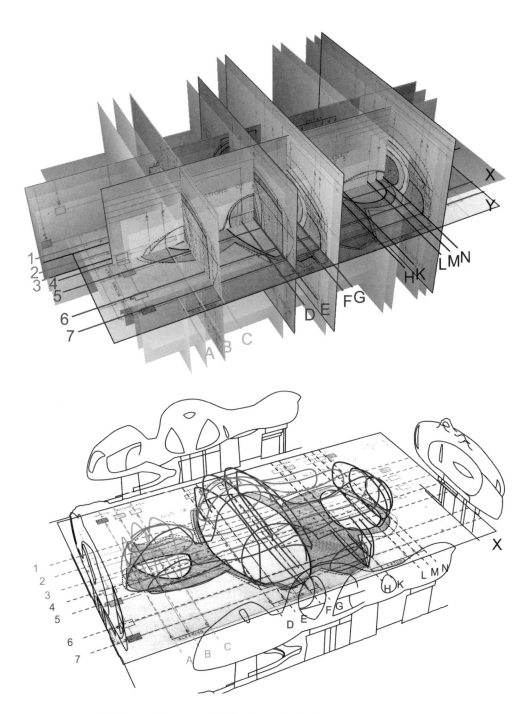

2/3—Geometric reconstruction (sections, elevations)

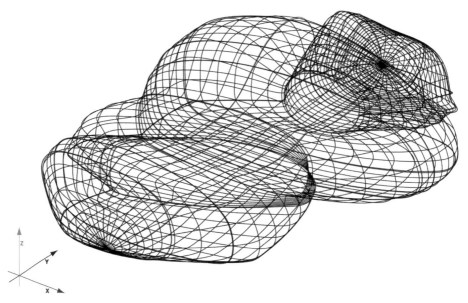

4—Geometric reconstruction, final surface-model

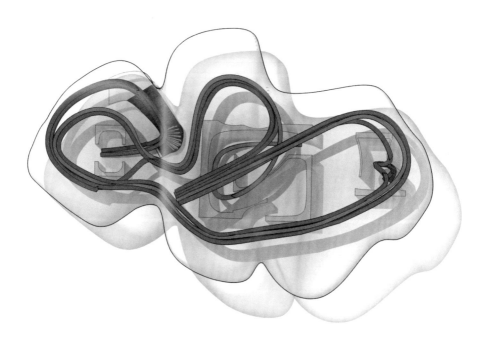

5—Circulation diagram

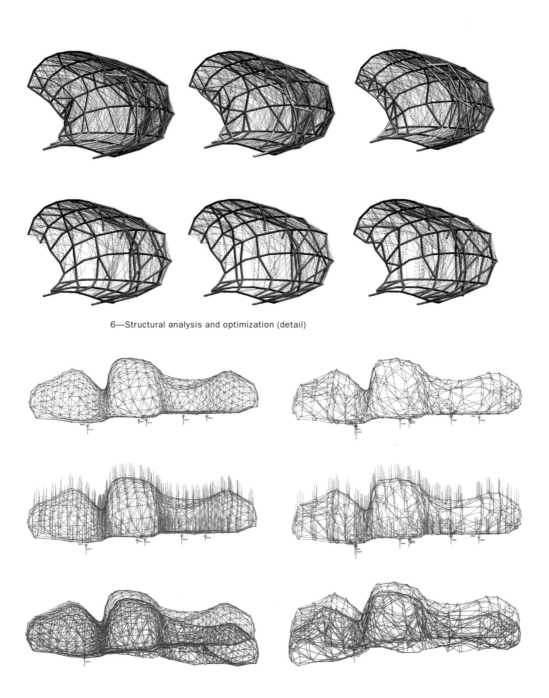

6—Structural analysis and optimization (detail)

7—Analysis of regular and irregular load-bearing structure

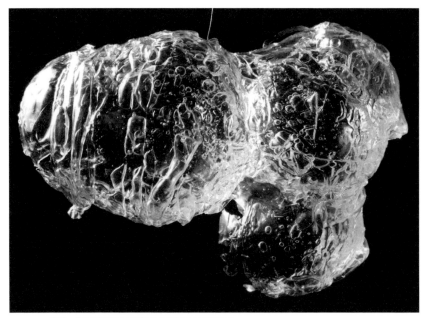

8/9—Translucent surface models (gelatine)

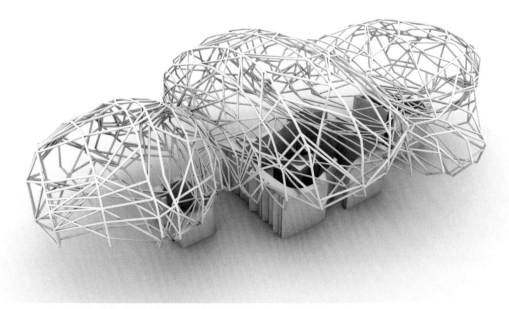

10—Optimized load-bearing structure

11—Final rendering (translucent surface)

Advanced Structural Design B (2014), Institute of Architecture, University of Applied Arts Vienna

Sisler House

Students
Atanas Zheelev
Mariya Korolova
Banafsheh Fahimipour
Ceren Yonetim
Feng Lei
Aryan Shahabian
Miro Straka
Herwig Scherabon
Yulia Karnaukhiva
Jughwho Park
Aiste Dzikaraite
Anna Sergeva
Sophie Gierlinger
Martino Hutz
Bernd Seidl
Mark Margeta
Carina Zabini
Sophia Keivanlo
Mathias Bank Stigsen
Andreas Körner
Eva Busakova
Nasim Nabavi Tafreshi
Saba Nabavi Tafreshi
Melanie Kotz

Tutors
Klaus Bollinger
Andrei Gheorghe
Florian Medicus
Clemens Preisinger

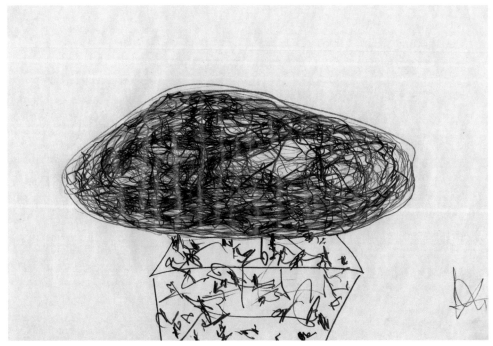

1—Frederick Kiesler, Study for *Endless House*, New York 1960

2/3—Geometric reconstruction based on original plans

4/5—Surface studies

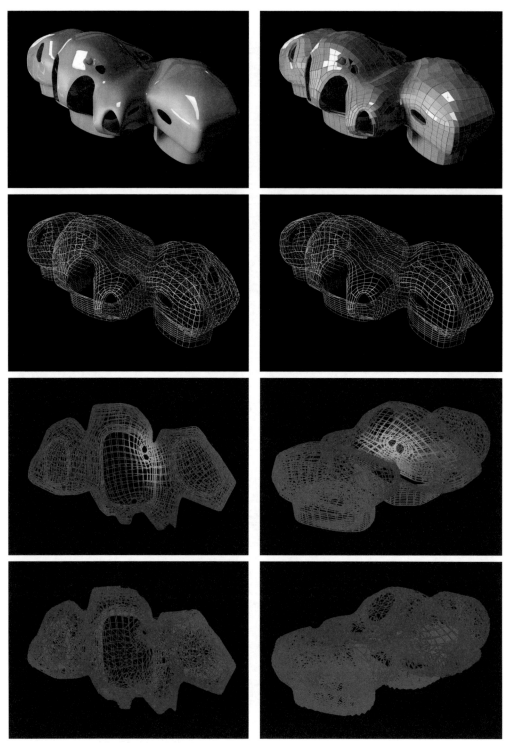

6–13—Structural analysis and optimization

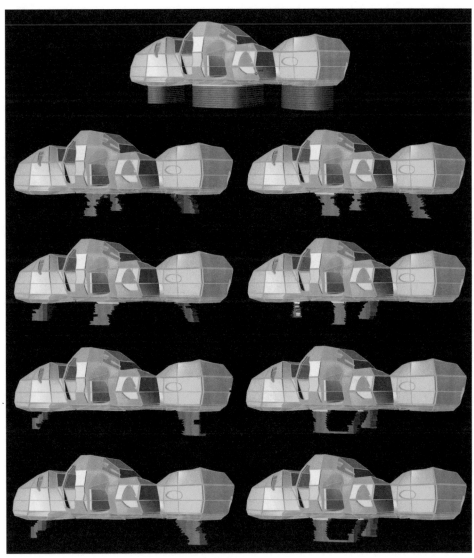

14—Structural analysis of cores (Inspire software)

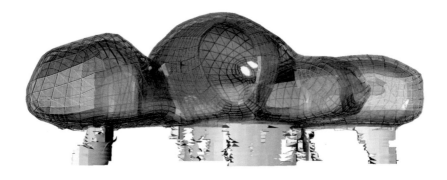

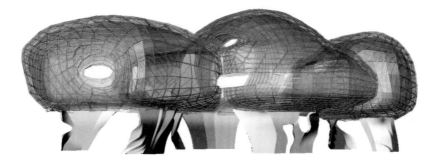

15/16—Structural analysis of cores (Inspire software)

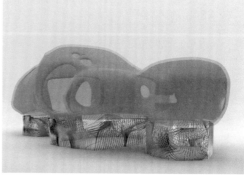

17/18—Final core-structure (Inspire and Karamba software)

19—Frederick Kiesler, drawing of *Endless House* (detail)

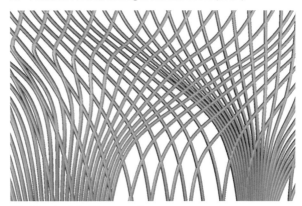

20—Structural design proposal

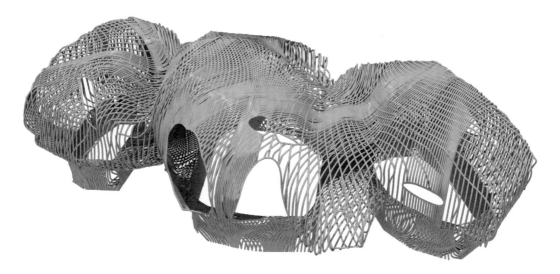

21—Final "endless" mesh-structure (Karamba software)

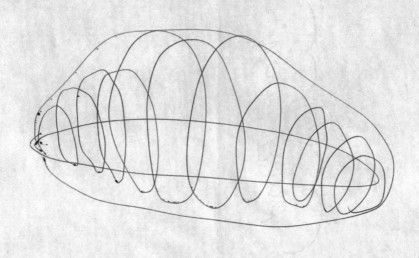

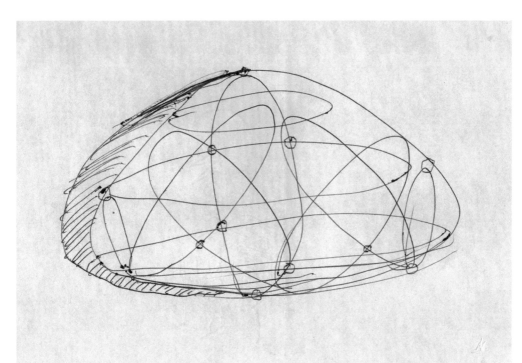

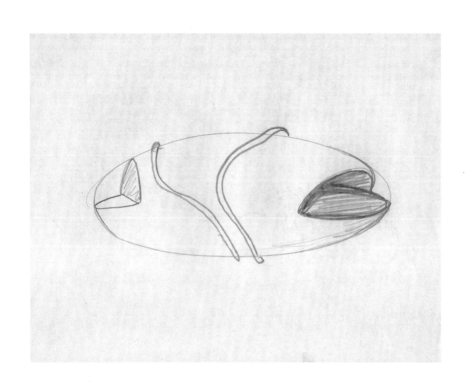

Wir Architekten müssen mit der Reinigung unseres
eigenen Stalles beginnen. Wir müssen den Eigen-
dünkel aufgeben, Spezialisten aller Bausachen zu sein.
Und die Ingenieure, die Fabrikanten der Baumaterialien,
die Landwirte, die Bauherren, die Decorateure, die
Künstler; die die
Geschichtshistoriker und
Modeaesteten — sie alle – wir
alle, müssen Teilnehmer
des Exodus ~~werden~~
aus dem Labyrinth unseres heutigen
Sozietät werden, ~~dass wir~~ Distanz zu unserem eigenen Handeln
gewinnen, um mit gereinigtem Gewissen zur Arbeit zurückkehren.

Erwachen im Paradies des Selbstbetrugs.

Eine innere Stimme gewarnt:

„Treibt jene . . . .

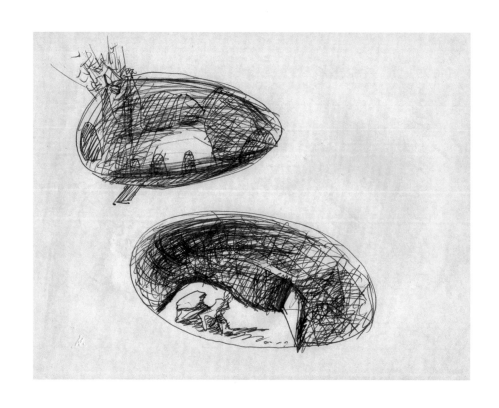

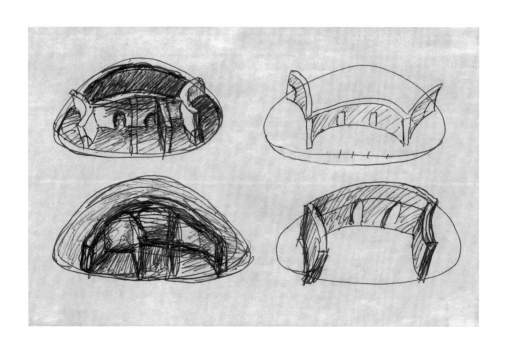

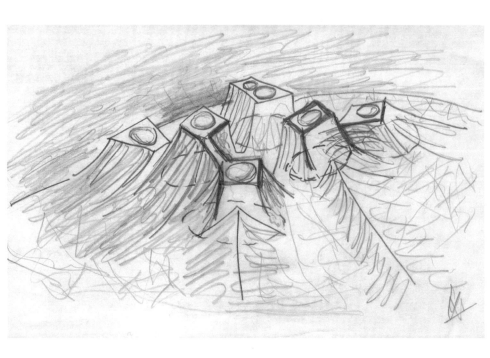

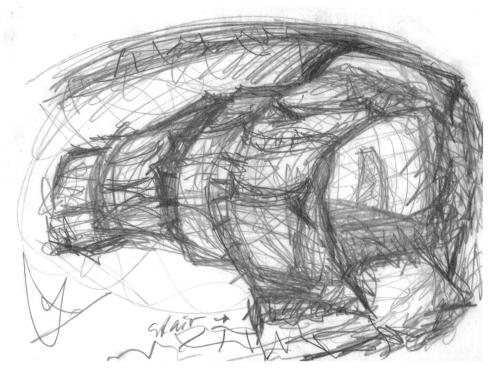

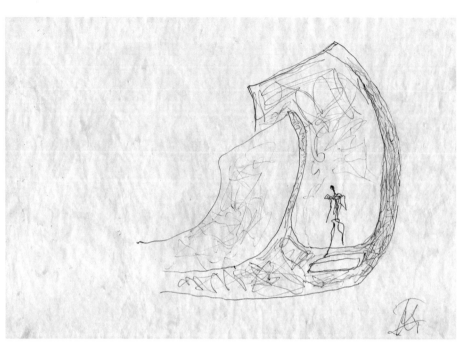

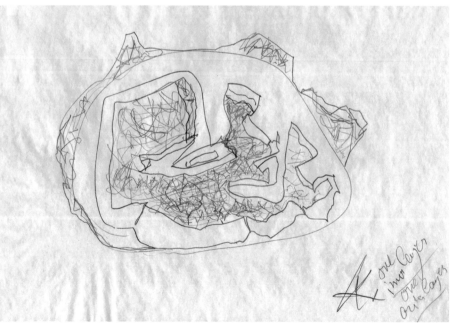

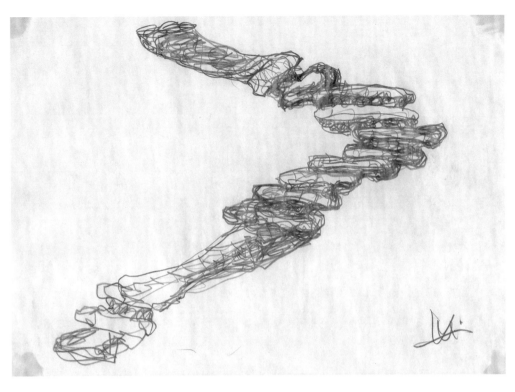

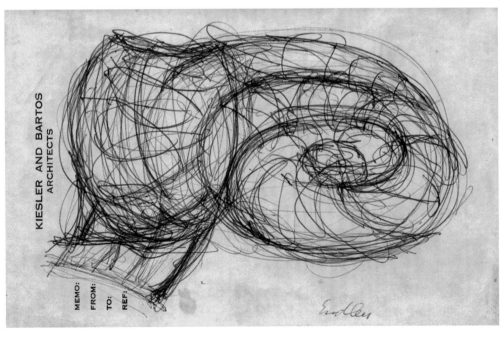

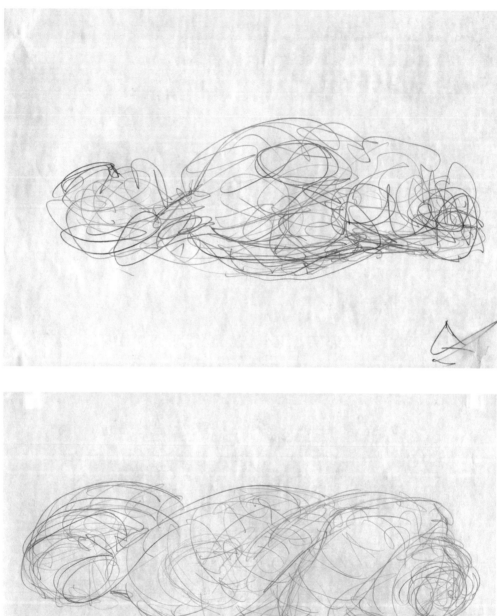

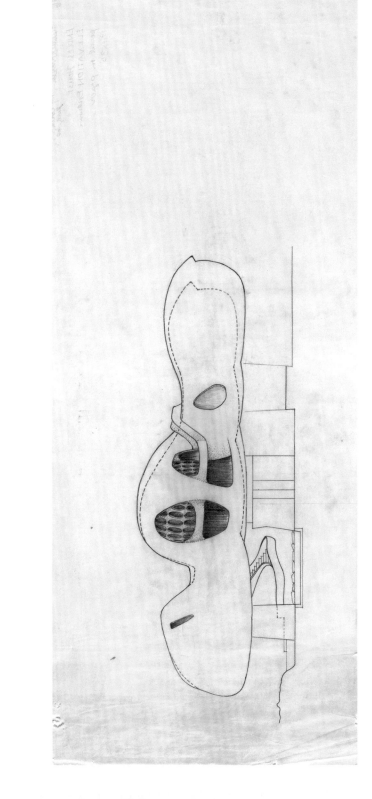

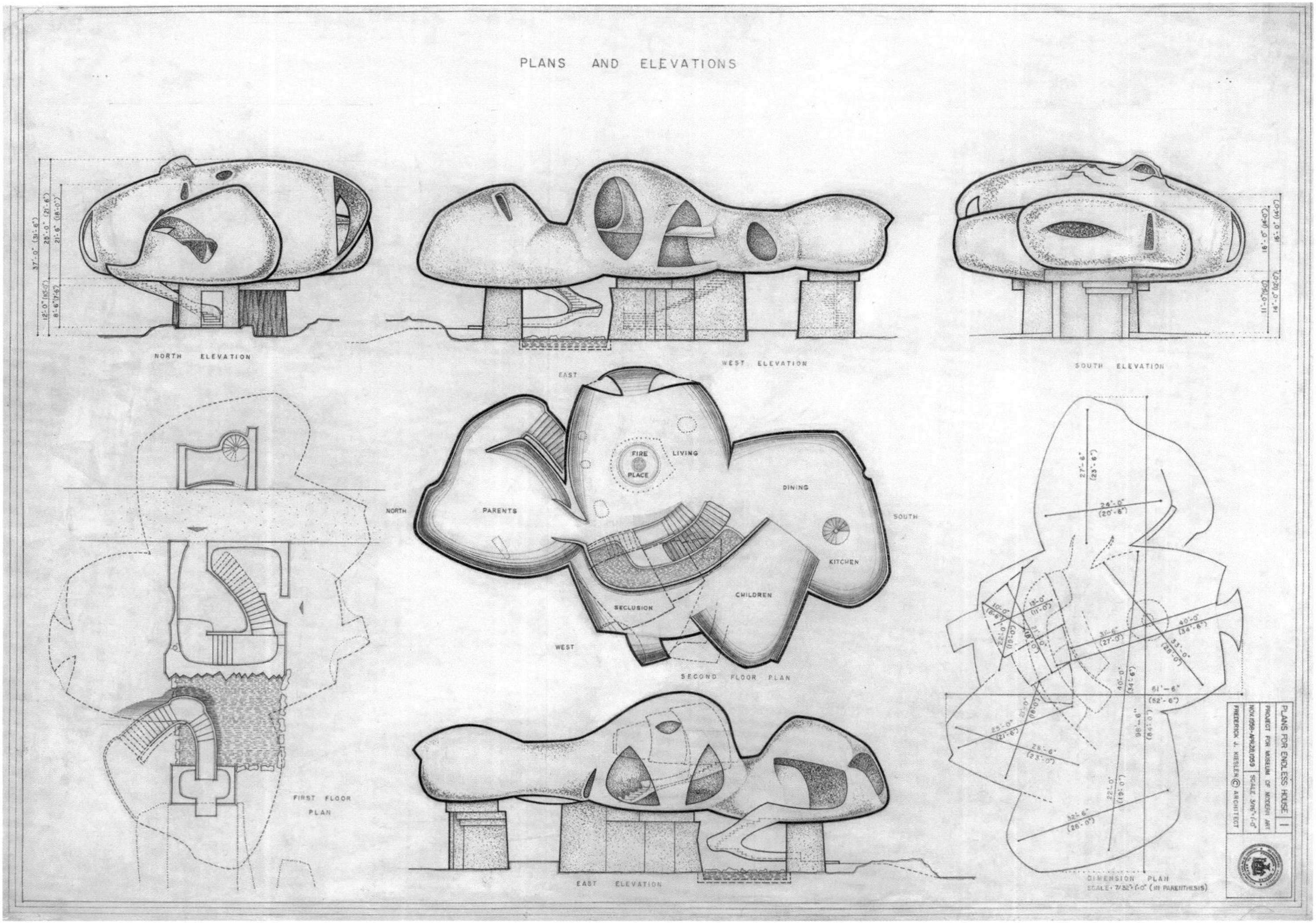

PLANS AND ELEVATIONS

SOUTH ELEVATION

WEST ELEVATION

EAST

SOUTH

KITCHEN

DINING

CHILDREN

LIVING

FIRE PLACE

SECLUSION

WEST

NORTH

PARENTS

SECOND FLOOR PLAN

EAST ELEVATION

NORTH ELEVATION

FIRST FLOOR PLAN

PLANS FOR ENDLESS HOUSE 1
PROJECT FOR MUSEUM OF MODERN ART
NOV.1958 - APR.28,1959   SCALE 3/16"=1'-0"
FREDERICK J. KIESLER © ARCHITECT

DIMENSION PLAN
SCALE 3/16"=1'-0" (IN PARENTHESES)

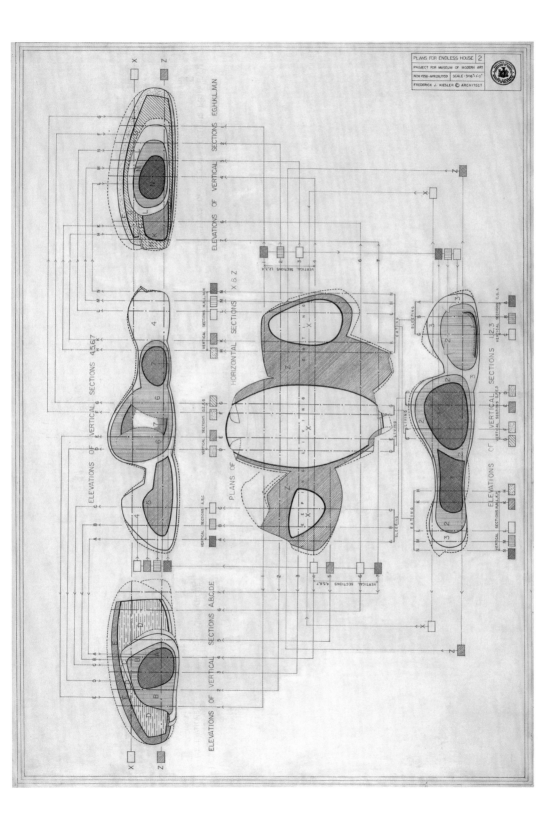

PLANS FOR ENDLESS HOUSE 2
PROJECT FOR MUSEUM OF MODERN ART
NOV. 1958 - APR 28, 1959   SCALE 3/16"=1'-0"
FREDERICK J. KIESLER © ARCHITECT

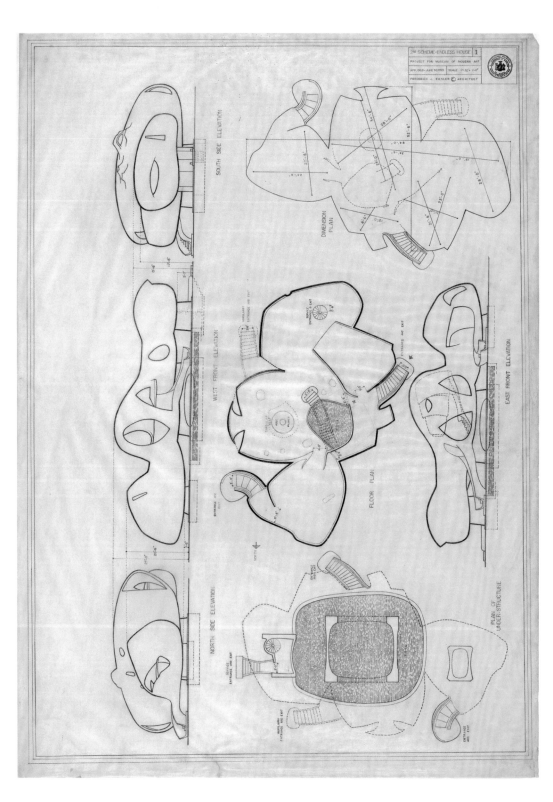

Around, Amid, Among,
Above, Ayont . .
The *Endless House…*

Brian Hatton

Darin, darauf, darunter,
dazwischen, darüber hinaus . .
das *Endless House…*

"Ayont" is a Scottish word for the preposition '"beyond". Prepositions like "before", "behind", "beneath", "across", "athwart", and "about" relate things in space or time. But movement or metamorphosis involves both space *and* time, where changing relations imply altering prepositions—"around", "behind", "above", "beyond". . Imagine continuous variation, wandering into a world of prepositions unruled by definite terms or subjects. A world that also has erotic aspects—Think of John Donne's *To His Mistress Going To Bed*:

"License my roving hands and let them go Before, behind, between, above, below."

I have often thought of Kiesler's *Endless House* as such a whirl of prepositions, wherein ("whereabouts", "wherethrough" . .) floor, walls, and ceilings merge in a single topologic plane, and the space they guide becomes, as in a Klein bottle or Möbius belt, a single fairway of outside curving inside curving outside . . and so on—"around", "about", "ayont".

What would be the "topic" of such a *topo*logy? Or, as a topic is but a predicate of a subject's engagement, what or who would be the agent or subject of such a winding, wending house? A subject initiates and undergoes events, whose motives engender "motifs" of form, rather as a sonata develops "1st & 2nd subjects." In a story, a subject is one around whom events

Präpositionen wie „über", „unter", „um", „durch" oder Adverbien wie „innen", „außen", „hinauf", „herab" setzen Dinge in einen örtlichen oder zeitlichen Zusammenhang. Doch Bewegung oder Meta-Morphose passiert in Raum *und* Zeit, wo sich die Zusammenhänge – und folglich auch ihre Beschreibungen – ändern können: „dahinter", „daneben", „darüber hinaus "… Wo alles permanent im Wandel ist, betreten wir eine Welt der Präpositionen, in der Begriffe und Subjekte nie endgültig sind. Eine Welt mit durchaus erotischen Seiten – man denke an John Donnes *Auf das Zubettgehen seiner Dame*:

„Lass meine Hände schweifen, sag nicht nein, hinauf, hinab, hinüber, zwischendrein …"[1]

Ich habe mir Kieslers *Endless House* oft als ein solches Getümmel der Präpositionen vorgestellt, worin („worüber", „wodurch") Boden, Wände und Decken zu einer einzigen topologischen Ebene verschmelzen und der Raum, den sie umfassen, wie in einer Klein'schen Flasche oder einem Möbiusband zu einer einzigen Fläche wird, wo außen sich nach innen krümmt sich nach außen krümmt sich nach innen … und so weiter: „herum", „herein", „heraus".

Was wäre der *Topos*, das Thema, einer solchen *Topo*logie? Oder, nachdem ein Thema im Grunde nur eine Aussage über die Teilhabe eines Subjekts ist: Wer oder was wäre Akteur oder Subjekt in einem solchen Haus der Windungen

occur. A hero makes them happen, an antihero endures them through pathos
or comedy—as a prisoner is subject to a prison. Or, like Kafka's K in *The
Trial*, where the only agency is an unfathomable law of an unknown authority.

Might buildings, like stories, have subjects who are the keys to entering
their motives? If so, they are not just functions. The subject of a prison cell is
not just the prisoner but also the guard, who is bound to keep watch. Nor
could we define the subject of Schütte-Lihotzky's Frankfurt Kitchen within her
busy-bee-lines; for their ultimate purpose was to release their subject to
freedoms beyond their functions. For "function," as Kiesler wrote, is "not a
finite fact or standard, but a process of continuous transmutation."[1]

"Beyond"—a sublime threshold where functions morph into spatial continuity. What best symbolized that modernist vision, where all prepositions
would abound without bound? Remarkably, functionalism's zenith in the
1920s also saw, in Mies' *Barcelona Pavilion*, a paradigm of that most unfunc-
tional ideal: the *open plan*—and, in Kiesler's *Raumstadt*, the open section:
"No walls, no foundations. . A system of spans (tension) in free space."[2]
A utopian realm, "open plan" was where F. L. Wright declared, "space may
go out or come in where life is being lived."[3] So instead of walls going around
a subject, subjects would move around walls—like Barcelona's onyx wall,

und Wendungen? Ein Subjekt initiiert und durchlebt Ereignisse, deren
Motivationen formale Leitmotive hervorbringen, so wie eine Sonate ein erstes
und ein zweites Thema entwickelt. Subjekt einer Erzählung ist, wer im
Zentrum der Ereignisse steht. Ein Held löst diese selber aus, ein Antiheld
erleidet sie oder erträgt sie mit Humor – so wie ein Häftling als ein dem
Gefängnis unterworfenes Subjekt (und somit also auch Objekt); oder wie Josef
K. in Kafkas *Der Prozess*, wo die einzige aktive Kraft das unergründliche
Gesetz einer unbekannten Behörde ist.

Könnten Gebäude, ähnlich wie Erzählungen, Subjekte haben, durch die
sich ihre Motivationen erschließen lassen? Wenn ja, dann sind sie nicht bloß
Funktionen. Das Subjekt einer Gefängniszelle ist nicht nur der Häftling,
sondern auch der Wärter, der ihn beaufsichtigen muss. Ebenso lässt sich das
Subjekt von Margarete Schütte-Lihotzkys Frankfurter Küche nicht anhand
ihrer kurzen Wege definieren: Denn deren Zweck war es letztlich ja, ihr Subjekt
in eine über ihre Funktion hinausgehende Freiheit zu entlassen. „Funktion" ist, wie Kiesler schrieb, „kein unveränderlicher Umstand oder Standard,
sondern ein Prozess permanenter Umwandlung".[2]

„Darüber hinaus": eine erhabene Schwelle, an der Funktionen in räumliche Kontinuität übergehen. Was symbolisierte diese moderne Vision voll

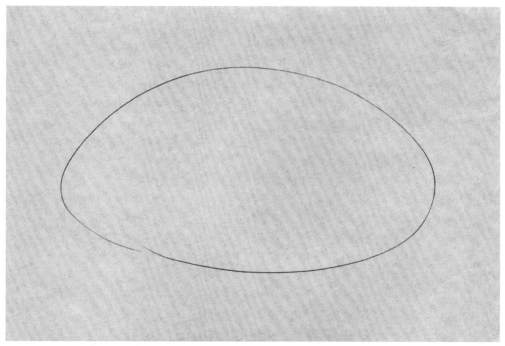

Frederick Kiesler, Study for *Endless House*, New York 1950

grenzenloser Präpositionen am besten? Interessanterweise trat am Höhepunkt des Funktionalismus in den 1920er-Jahren in Mies van der Rohes *Barcelona-Pavillon* auch ein Paradigma des unfunktionellsten aller Ideale zutage: der *offene Grundriss* – und in Kieslers *Raumstadt* war es der *offene Querschnitt*: „Keine Mauern, keine Fundamente […] ein System von Spannungen (tension) im freien Raume."[3] Der „offene Raum" war ein utopischer Bereich, wo – wie Frank Lloyd Wright anmerkte – „der Raum dort herausgehen oder hereinkommen kann, wo das Leben gelebt wird".[4] Anstelle von Wänden, die das Subjekt umgeben, sollten sich die Subjekte um die Wände herumbewegen – wie bei der Onyx-Wand in Barcelona, um die herum der Besucher in einer subjektiven Topologie einer Endlosschleife des „fließenden Raumes" folgt.

Wer war dieses unbegrenzte Subjekt, das sich frei „in", „neben", „zwischen" dem Kontinuum des offenen Raumes aufhielt? Für mich ist es die romantische Figur des Wandernden, wie man ihn als „einsamer Wanderer" bei Rousseau findet, in Goethes *Wanderers Nachtlied*, in Wordsworths „Ich wandert' einsam wie die Wolke"[5], in Blakes entfremdetem „London": „Ich wand're durch verkaufte Gassen"[6], in Caspar David Friedrichs „Wanderer über dem Nebelmeer" und in Nietzsches mythischem „Zarathustra".

wherearound an occupant traces, in subjective topology, an endless loop of "flowing space."

Who was that boundless subject who dwelled free "amid", "among", "around" the continuum of the open plan? That imagined denizen, I think, was the romantic figure of a wanderer: in Rousseau's *Reveries of a Solitary Walker*, Goethe's *Wandrers Nachtlied*, Wordsworth's *I Wandered Lonely as a Cloud*. Or in Blake's alienated "London": "I wandered through each chartered street," or in Caspar David Friedrich's *Wanderer über dem Nebelmeer* and Nietzsche's mythic *Zarathustra*.

Myths, Roberto Calasso observed,[4] "are made up of actions that include their opposites within themselves"—such as the reversals of subject relations in Kiesler's *Endless Theater*, whose helical stages spiraled around each other in exchanging roles of actors and audience—hardly a workable auditorium, but a mythic image of theater itself. The *Endless House*, too, was a *coniuncto oppisotorum*—a topologic conflation of cave and cloud. As cave, it was a continuous fold, like that of which Hamlet declared "I could be bounded in a nutshell and count myself the king of infinite space." Yet, raised and floating (beyond those "bad dreams" that haunted Hamlet), continuously mutable and permeable, it was also a cloud, like that remarked by

Mythen, so Roberto Calasso, „bestehen aus Handlungen, die immer auch ihr Gegenteil in sich tragen"[7], ähnlich wie die Umdrehung der Subjektbeziehungen in Kieslers *Endless Theatre*, dessen spiralförmige Bühnen sich umeinander wanden, wobei die Rollen von Darstellern und Publikum permanent wechselten – ein mythisches Bild des Theaters an sich, wenngleich als (Theater-)Raum kaum bespielbar. Auch das *Endless* House war eine *Coniunctio oppositorum* – eine topologische Verschmelzung von Höhle und Wolke. Als Höhle war es eine unendliche Falte, ähnlich jener, von der Hamlet sagt: „Ich könnte in eine Nussschale eingesperrt sein und mich für einen König von unermesslichem Gebiete halten." Doch erhöht und schwebend (über jene „bösen Träume" hinaus, die Hamlet verfolgen), permanent veränderlich und durchlässig, war es auch wie eine Wolke, ähnlich jener, auf die Hamlet Polonius hinweist: „beinahe in Gestalt eines Kamels … ganz wie ein Walfisch".

László Moholy-Nagy nannte seine Betrachtung der Moderne *Sehen in Bewegung*, was auch zu Kieslers ruheloser Mythographie des Raumes passt. Mythen sind wie Wellen, meint Calasso: Sie kehren immer wieder – und in ähnlicher Form erinnert auch Kieslers Thema der Endlosigkeit an *Finnegans Wake*; dort, so Moholy-Nagy, griff James Joyce „Giambattista Vicos Vorstellung von einer zyklischen Wiederholung der Geschichte auf" und „versuchte die

Hamlet to Polonius: "much like a camel [...] very like a whale."

László Moholy-Nagy entitled his account of modernism "Vision In Motion", which also fits Kiesler's restless spatial mythography. As Calasso says, myths recur and reflux like waves. Similarly, Kiesler's *Endless* theme also brings to mind James Joyce's *Finnegan's Wake*, which, Moholy-Nagy wrote, "took up Vico's idea of cyclically recurring history" and "tried to avoid the limitation of a precise subject-rendering [...] In a trance-like atmosphere [...] no value is placed on details as such, only on their discrete relatedness [...] No up, no down, no forward, no backward, no sequence of direction, position, time, space. Only the synthesized absolute relationship of events and personalities, like an equipoised sculpture, hovers in the universe."[5]

If that sounds like Kiesler's *Raumstadt*, so too the winding cave-cloud of the *Endless House* recalls the "open finish" of *Finnegan's Wake*—the River Liffey's flow to the sea, wherefrom it sprang as rain in that "commodius vicus of recirculation" that began the "Wake": "... Whish! A gull. Gulls. Far calls. Coming, far! End here. Us then. Finn, again! Take. Bussoftlhee, mememormee! Till thousandsthee. Lps. The keys to. Given! A way a lone a last a loved a long the"

Begrenzung zu umgehen, die mit der genauen erzählerischen Beschreibung eines Sachverhalts verbunden ist [...] In der tranceähnlichen Tagtraum-stimmung [...] wird auf einzelne Details nicht als solche Wert gelegt, sondern nur insofern sich zwischen ihnen diskrete Bezüge ergeben. [...] Es gibt kein Oben und Unten, kein Vorwärts und Rückwärts, keine Folge von Richtung, Standort, Zeit, Raum. Nur die Synthese aus absoluten Beziehungen zwischen Ereignissen und Personen schwebt wie eine ausgewogene Plastik im Kosmos."[8]

Da schwingt etwas von Kieslers Raumstadt mit, und auch die gewundene Höhlen-Wolke des *Endless House* erinnert an das „offene Ende" von *Finnegans Wake*: Der Fluss Liffey fließt ins Meer, aus dem er als Regen entsprang – in jenem „commoden Rezirkulus viciosus"[9], der am Beginn des Buches steht: „Wsch! Ne Möwe. Möwen. Ferne Rufe. Komm, fern! End hier. Aus dann. Finn, necken! Nimm. Dochlaife, rinnerum! Bis tausendästsieh. Lppn. Die Schlüssel zu. Gegeben! Hin weg all ein zu letzt ab seits und lang des"[10]

1 Frederick Kiesler, "Pseudo-Functionalism In Modern Architecture", in *Partisan Review* 7 (1949), 738.

2 Frederick Kiesler, *Contemporary Art Applied in the Store and its Display* (New York: Brentano's, 1930), 48.

3 *Frank Lloyd Wright, An American Architecture*, ed. E. Kaufman (New York: Horizon Press, 1955), 76–78.

4 Roberto Calasso, *The Marriage Of Cadmus And Harmony*, Ch.XIII.

5 László Moholy-Nagy, *Vision In Motion* (Chicago: Paul Theobald, 1956), 345.

1 Übersetzt von Christa Schuenke, in John Donne, *Zwar ist auch Dichtung Sünde* (Leipzig: Verlag Philipp Reclam jun., 1982 u. 1985).

2 Frederick Kiesler, "Pseudo-Functionalism in Modern Architecture", in *Partisan Review 7* (1949): 738. (Übersetzt aus dem Englischen)

3 Kiesler, „Vitalbau – Raumstadt – Funktionelle Architektur", in *De Stijl* 10&11 (1925), 144.

4 *Frank Lloyd Wright, An American Architecture*, hg. v. E. Kaufman (New York: Horizon Press, 1955), 76–78.

5 Übersetzt von Dietrich H. Fischer: http://www.william-wordsworth.de

6 Übersetzt von Walter A. Aue: http://myweb.dal.ca/waue

7 Roberto Calasso, *The Marriage Of Cadmus And Harmony*, Kap. XIII.

8 László Moholy-Nagy, *Sehen in Bewegung*, übersetzt von Herwig Engelmann (Leipzig: Spector Books, 2014), 344–345.

9 Übersetzt von Wolfgang Schrödter, in James Joyce: *Finnegans Wake – Gesammelte Annäherungen* (Berlin: Suhrkamp, 1989).

10 Adaptierte Übersetzung, basierend auf: James Joyce, *Finnegans Wehg*, übersetzt von Dieter H. Stündel (Darmstadt: Häusser, 1993), 638.

Artistic Contributions

Asymptote Architecture, Judith Barry, Olafur Eliasson,
Heidulf Gerngross, Hans Hollein, Ian Kiaer, Jürgen Mayer H.,
Bruce Nauman, Smiljan Radić, Tomás Saraceno, Andrea Zittel,
Heimo Zobernig

Künstlerische Beiträge

Asymptote Architecture
Hani Rashid and
Lise Anne Couture

(Kiesler Prize laureates 2004)

Beukenhof Auditorium and
Crematorium (2012)

Schiedam, The Netherlands

The Beukenhof Auditorium and Crematorium provides the city of Schiedam and its neighboring areas with a much-needed new and modern architectural approach to the need for such places of worship and repose. This new building is to be inserted into the city's urban fabric and lush environs as a cultural locus, taking into consideration the abstract meanings and poetics of such a place of importance and pertinence to the people of Schiedam. The approach to the architectural design is one that celebrates the meaning of such a building for the many diverse religions and cultures that will share this place. The architecture, while addressing the unique traditions, rituals and sensibilities of the different faiths that the building will accommodate, is also presented as a fluid and sensual sculptural presence that merges the building's form with the natural and lush surroundings. The architecture is experienced while set against the elegant tree-lined canals and the serene landscape that sits alongside the building, where the building is effectively a poetic work that embraces both nature and life.

The architecture of the Beukenhof Auditorium and Crematorium is based on and influenced by a long history of ecclesiastical architecture where temples, shrines and memorials sought to perform space as an enigmatic and physical condition predicated on elegance and permanence.

Judith Barry

(Kiesler Prize laureate 2000)

For when all that was read was … so as not to be unknown (2012)

For when all that was read was … so as not to be unknown is Judith Barry's guidebook to the "Brain" section at *Documenta 13* in Kassel, Germany. Carolyn Christov-Bakargiev, artistic director of *Documenta 13*, thematized this rotunda space as the international exhibition's through-line: a curated "paradox, a space of many secrets, a space of violence, and a space of potential healing." The guidebook, which uses its unique paper architecture to remap the associative histories and labyrinthine nature of the "Brain" takes the form of a series of pages, an artist's book, and also a sculpture. Contained yet expansive, it is printed as a poster but can also be folded into a legible, three-dimensional object; exhibition materials are presented in a non-hierarchal, non-linear array, as if to suspend its contents in a recursive space.

Memory and history—their alignments, evasions, exchanges and tenuous distinctions—are persistent themes in Judith Barry's multidisciplinary art practice. Beginning with language-based performances in the late 1970s and 80s, and continuing through installations, exhibition designs, and graphic interventions, Barry has explored these issues in a variety of modes and contexts. She transformed the 1991 Carnegie International exhibition into Ars Memoriae Carnegiensis, inviting viewers to create an imaginary museum using ancient mnemonic techniques of the "memory theater." Other previous works include the fabrication of a miniature book that draws parallels between genre painting and 19th century pseudoscience, as well as the development of an interactive computer game that attempts to predict how visitors to a digital museum might produce new forms of art experiences.

For when all that was read was … so as not to be unknown derives from an extended investigation of the material text: its historical development from early seals and emblems, to the codex as a contemporary system for storing knowledge. In its sculptural, three-dimensional form, Barry's guidebook performs the function of a book. Acting as a cache of information, the folded architecture conceals poster texts within an interior space, presenting only the imagery of the "Brain": a multi-layered, modular cover.

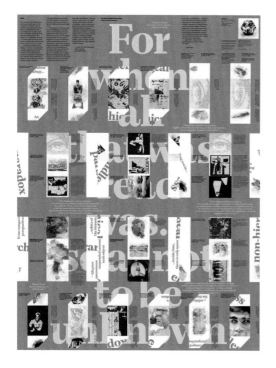

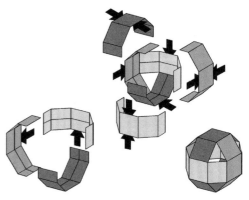

Olafur Eliasson

(Kiesler Prize laureate 2006)

La situazione antispettiva
(2003)

The idea of endlessness is often
thought of in terms of infinity, which
in fact is a linear notion and still
predictable. The potential in Kiesler's
idea of endlessness, I believe,
lies in the endless definitions of
endlessness. It is not just about
being caught in a loop, spiraling and
morphing; it is the whole question
of what determines dimensions
in general. It is also about the things
that we have not yet found out,
the things we do not know that we do
not know. Endlessness is a cele-
bration of potentiality.

Olafur Eliasson, *La situazione
antispettiva* (2003), stainless steel,
stainless steel mirrors, 5 × 5 × 15 m.
Installation view at Danish Pavilion,
50th Biennale di Venezia, Venice,
2003. Photographer: Olafur Eliasson
Collection of 21st Century Museum of
Contemporary Art, Kanazawa, Japan
© 2003 Olafur Eliasson

Heidulf Gerngross

Various projects (1964–66)

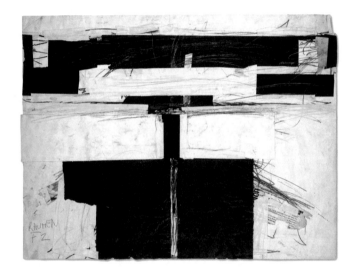

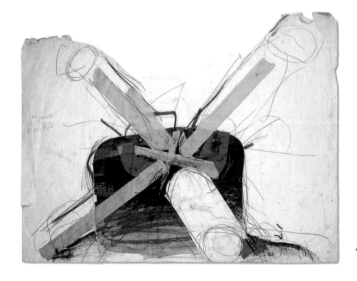

WAUNZ (1965/66), polyester model ↗

←↖ Heidulf Gerngross, *untitled*
(1964/65), collages from the series
"Raumen"

Hans Hollein

Various projects (1960)

↑ *City* (1960), drawing
↖ *"Projekt für eine Stadt"* (1960), collage
  "Schnitt durch ein Teil der Stadt" (1960) →
  (Images © Archiv Hans Hollein)

Ian Kiaer

Tooth House (2014)

It's not so easy to know quite where to place my debt to Kiesler. Naturally, there's his contribution to questions of display, design and exhibition; the attention given to relations of floor, wall and ceiling and their points of meeting, that in time move from horizontal and vertical certainty to more sensual biomorphic folds and caverns. Then there is endlessness itself, the sense of a project being ever questioned and thought, where potential is held open in a way that avoids all fear of bad infinity. How could it, with a mind that draws dwelling from a tooth and refuses to drain magic from modernity?
—Ian Kiaer (2015)

↑ Ian Kiaer, *Tooth House*, plinth (2014), polystyrene, foil, overall dimensions: 106.3 × 36 × 26.5 cm (© the artist, Courtesy Alison Jacques Gallery, London, installation view: Focal Point Gallery, Southend, photo: Michael Brzezinski)

Ian Kiaer, *Tooth House* (2014), plastic, 300 × 201 × 1260 cm (© the artist, Courtesy Alison Jacques Gallery, London, photo: Michael Brzezinski) ↗

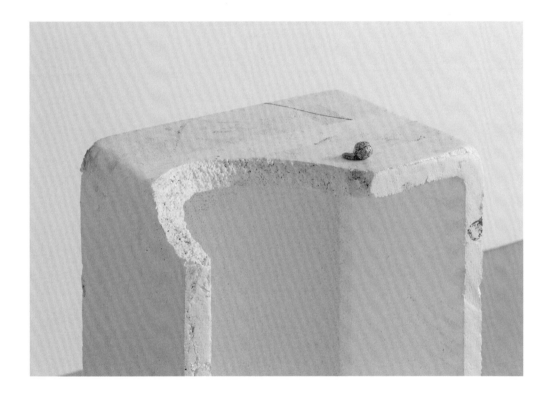

Jürgen Mayer H.

Untitled (2013)

The sheer infinite spectrum of specific data-protection patterns from letters, numbers and logos to organic, camouflage and ornamental graphics can be read as an "*Ursuppe*", a "primordial soup" of our times, all before meaning and yet a strategic field to generate an ambivalent space from, to thicken the skin of discretion and to inhabit the flatness of exposure and control.

Metropol Parasol, a mixused project in the center of Sevilla completed in spring 2011, tests this concept of an envelope for public urban life. The multiple levels of activation and programming, of retreat and performativity, of intimacy and mass experience create an urban complexity under the cover of an undulated gridded roof-scape.
—Jürgen Mayer H. (2015)

Jürgen Mayer H., *untitled* (2013), collage, 34 × 26.5 cm (original) (images © Jürgen Mayer H., 2014)

Footnote – Jürgen Mayer H.

Bruce Nauman

(Kiesler Prize laureate 2014)

Untitled (1968–72)

This piece was supposed to be built underground. So I scribbled the green pastel over it along with some green-blue ink to indicate grass. The idea was that there would be a shaft leading into this underground space. It was like a large saucer underground. The ceiling above your head would be relatively flat and in the center of the room the floor would be relatively flat, but as soon as you started moving around to define the perimeter of the room you'd be walking uphill in every direction.
—Bruce Nauman (2007)

Bruce Nauman, *Untitled* (study for model for Underground Space: Saucer) (1968–72), ground level/ underground saucer/ shaped space, graphite, chalk pastel and ink on paper (Courtesy Sperone Westwater Gallery, New York, © Bruce Nauman)

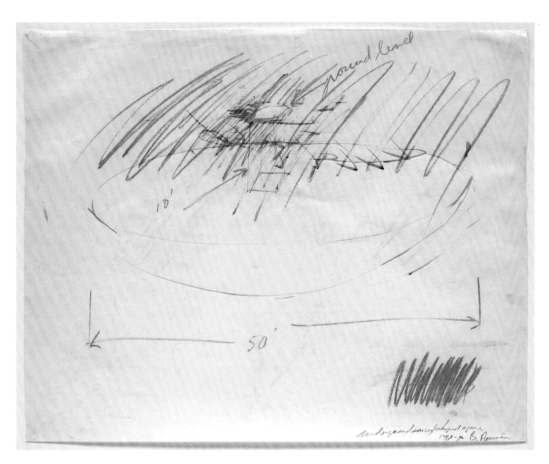

Smiljan Radić

Hands

"... the house is a machine for living.
No Sir! The house is a spatial
SHELTER to be filled with the
EXUBERANCE of the LIFE that we
have yet to INVENT... "
—Frederick Kiesler (1959)

Tomás Saraceno

Various projects (2006–13)

Tomás Saraceno, *Poetic Cosmos of* ↗
the Breath (2013, installation view),
Mobile M+: Inflation!, Hong Kong,
China (image © Studio Tomás
Saraceno Commissioned by M+ and
Arts Catalyst)

↖ Tomás Saraceno, *On Space Time*
← *Foam* (2012, installation view),
Hangar Bicocca, Milan, (Courtesy:
Tomás Saraceno; Tanya Bonakdar
Gallery, New York; Andersen's
Contemporary, Copenhagen; and
pinksummer contemporary art,
Genoa. Image © Alessandro Coco and
Studio Tomás Saraceno)

Tomás Saraceno, *The Endless Series* →
(2006). The photographs were
taken at Salar de Uyuni, Bolivia with
the support of Barbican Art
Gallery. (Courtesy Tomás Saraceno,
Tanya Bonakdar Gallery, New York;
Andersen's Contemporary,
Copenhagen; and pinksummer
contemporary art, Genoa.)

Andrea Zittel

(Kiesler Prize laureate 2012)

Various projects (2009/10)

Perhaps what inspires one most about Frederick Kiesler is how his brain worked. He was interested in things like *matter, interacting forces, human need, continuous motion* and *elastic spaces.*

He felt that every object in the universe should be considered in relation to its environment, and he described this as an exchange of interacting forces, which he called: "co-reality and the science of relationships."

A few of my other favorite quintessential Kiesler titles and phrases include:

"Biotechnique versus Architecture: Develop new functions and don't search for forms for old Functions." (This was the title of a lecture that he gave at MIT)

"Architecture Generator and de-Generator of Human Energy" (another lecture title)

And in the galleries that he created for Peggy Gugenheim's Art of this Century—Kiesler claimed that he was "promoting contacts between inanimate objects and people searching for contact"

Frederick Kiesler was so visionary in his time not because his work broke through boundaries and categories, but because he didn't even seem to recognize that boundaries existed.

—Andrea Zittel

Andrea Zittel, *A–Z Carpet Furniture:*   ↗
Cabin (2012), nylon carpet,
365.8 × 487.7 cm (Photo by Jessica Eckert, Courtesy Andrea Rosen Gallery, New York, © Andrea Zittel)

← Andrea Zittel, *A–Z Prototype for Pocket Property* (1999), concrete, steel, wood, dirt, plants, 9 × 18 m, 3 m above water level, 54 tons weight (Courtesy Andrea Rosen Gallery, New York, © Andrea Zittel)

Andrea Zittel, *A–Z Cellular Compart-*   →
ment Units (2001), stainless steel, birch plywood, glass and household objects, overall: 243.8 × 365.8 × 487.7 cm, 10 units: 121.9 × 121.9 × 243.8 cm (each). Installation view: *A–Z Cellular Compartment Units*, May 10 – June 15, 2002 at Andrea Rosen Gallery, New York (Courtesy Andrea Rosen Gallery, New York, © Andrea Zittel)

Heimo Zobernig

(Kiesler Prize laureate 2010)

Untitled (1981)

Heimo Zobernig, *untitled* (1981),
(model for a section of
endlessly curving space), steel,
9.5 × 12 × 12 cm (Photo Archiv
HZ, Gertraud and Dieter Bogner
collection, Buchberg, Austria)